WINDFALL

TIM FALCONER

WINDFALL

VIOLA MACMILLAN

AND HER

NOTORIOUS MINING SCANDAL

Published by ECW Press
665 Gerrard Street East
Toronto, Ontario, Canada M4M 1Y2
416-694-3348 / info@ecwpress.com

Editor for the Press: Michael Holmes
Copy editor: Lynn Cunningham
Cover design: Michel Vrana
Cover image: Canadian Museum of Nature

LIBRARY AND ARCHIVES CANADA CATALOGUING IN PUBLICATION

Title: Windfall : Viola MacMillan and her notorious mining scandal / Tim Falconer.

Names: Falconer, Tim, 1958- author

Description: Includes bibliographical references and index.

Identifiers: Canadiana (print) 20240498038 | Canadiana (ebook) 20240500091

ISBN 978-1-77041-995-7 (softcover)
ISBN 978-1-77852-336-6 (ePub)
ISBN 978-1-77852-337-3 (PDF)

Subjects: LCSH: MacMillan, Viola. | LCSH: Windfall Oils & Mines. | LCSH: Securities fraud—Canada—History—20th century. | LCSH: Mines and mineral resources—Ontario—History. | LCSH: Mineral industries—Ontario—History.

Classification: LCC HV6771.C32 O64 2025 | DDC 364.16/8—dc23

This book is funded in part by the Government of Canada. *Ce livre est financé en partie par le gouvernement du Canada.* We acknowledge the support of the Canada Council for the Arts. *Nous remercions le Conseil des arts du Canada de son soutien.* We would like to acknowledge the funding support of the Ontario Arts Council (OAC) and the Government of Ontario for their support. We also acknowledge the support of the Government of Ontario through the Ontario Book Publishing Tax Credit, and through Ontario Creates.

PRINTED AND BOUND IN CANADA

PRINTING: MARQUIS   5   4   3   2   1

This book is printed on FSC®-certified paper. It contains recycled materials, and other controlled sources, is processed chlorine free, and is manufactured using biogas energy.

ECW Press is a proudly independent, Canadian-owned book publisher. Find out how we make our books better at ecwpress.com/about-our-books

In memory of Elsie Falconer,
an impressive businesswoman
and even better mother

NOTE TO READERS

I've used metric measurements in most places, except when discussing diamond drilling and some other aspects of mineral exploration.

One 1964 dollar is worth $9.81 in 2024 dollars.

CONTENTS

SIGNIFICANT CHARACTERS

Viola MacMillan: prospector, mine developer, president of the Prospectors and Developers Association (PDA) and largest shareholder of Windfall Oils and Mines

George MacMillan: president of Windfall, husband of Viola

WINDFALL

Willis Ambrose: consulting geologist and geology professor
Roger Archibald: law partner of Tom Cole
T.F.C. (Tom) Cole: Windfall's lawyer and secretary and a director
Doris Drewe: former MacMillan employee, Windfall director
Marjorie Humphrey (née Oliver): advice columnist, Windfall director
Ron Mills: farmer, Windfall director
Sui Shing "Rocky" Szetu: consulting geologist and geophysicist

TEXAS GULF

Ken Darke: geological engineer and project manager
Charles Fogarty: executive vice-president
Walter Holyk: chief geologist (later, exploration manager)

Richard Mollison: vice-president, exploration

TIMMINS

John Angus: manager, Timmins branch, T.A. Richardson
Nedo (Ned) Bragagnolo: real estate broker, investor
Leo Del Villano: mayor of Timmins
John Larche: prospector
Donald (Don) McKinnon: prospector
Melvin (Mel) Rennick: fieldman, Noranda Exploration
Alfred (Fred) Rousseau: prospector
Fenton Scott: geologist

DRILLERS

Fernand Boucher: foreman of the Windfall drill crew
Edgar Bradley: partner in Bradley Brothers, based in Timmins
Wilbert Bradley: partner in Bradley Brothers, based in Noranda
Roch Grignon: Bradley Brothers, employee
Frank Spencer: partner in Bradley Brothers, based in Noranda
Walter Turney: core grabber

MINING INDUSTRY

Ralph Allerston: prospector, royal commission witness
Arthur Cockeram: first president of PDA
Ernest Doney: miner who sold his Victor Mine lease to Viola MacMillan
Patrick Heenan: geologist, Conwest Exploration
George Jamieson: prospector who sold MacMillan claims next to Kam-Kotia
Douglas Kerr-Lawson: president, Swastika Laboratories
Gilbert LaBine: prospector and mine developer
Murdock Mosher: prospector, co-founder of PDA
James Murdoch: president, Noranda Mines
Walter Segsworth: mining engineer, co-founder of PDA

Arthur White: mine financier, purchased ViolaMac
Art Wilson: prospector, mentor to Viola MacMillan
Ralph Woolverton: eastern supervisor, Noranda Mines

STOCK MARKET

Art Barnt: partner, Tom & Barnt
Strachan Bongard: stockbroker, Bongard & Company
Robert Breckenridge: partner, Breckenridge, McDonald
Harold Field: floor trader, Breckenridge, McDonald
Howard Graham: president, Toronto Stock Exchange (TSE)
George Hunter: partner, T.A. Richardson
Don Lawson: vice-president, Moss, Lawson
Cecil Lecour: floor trader, T.A. Richardson
Ted Jones: partner, Jones & Bradley
Mansell Ketchen: vice-president in charge of administration, TSE
Harry Richardson: stockbroker, Tom & Barnt
William Robertson: manager of T.A. Richardson's Noranda branch
William Somerville: executive vice-president, TSE
Marshall Stearns: chairman, TSE; senior partner, T.A. Richardson

INVESTORS

Cuthbert "Cuffy" Dixon: senior partner, Doherty, Roadhouse
Vernon (Vern) Oille: mining engineer, Noranda Exploration
Richard Edwards: geologist, Noranda Mines
Louise Campbell: wife of John Campbell

GOVERNMENT OFFICIALS

John Campbell: director, Ontario Securities Commission (OSC)
Jack Kimber: chairman, OSC
Hans Froberg: consulting geologist to OSC
Forbes McFarland: Ontario mining commissioner
John Robarts: premier of Ontario

George Wardrope: Ontario minister of mines
Arthur Wishart: Ontario attorney general

ROYAL COMMISSION

Patrick Hartt: commission counsel
Arthur Kelly: judge, commissioner of the royal commission
Joseph Sedgwick: lawyer for the MacMillans

JOURNALISTS

Graham Ackerley: reporter, *Northern Miner*
Maurice (Mort) Brown: senior assistant editor, *Northern Miner*
Alistair Dow: reporter, *Toronto Daily Star*
Greg Reynolds: reporter, Timmins *Daily Press*
James (Jim) Scott: assistant business editor, *Globe and Mail*
Claude Taylor: public relations man, correspondent for *New York Herald Tribune*

OTHERS

Elizabeth Dreany: Viola's stepsister
Harriet Huggard: Viola's mother
Joe Huggard: Viola's brother
Sadie Huggard: Viola's sister
Thomas Huggard: Viola's father
"Black Jack" MacMillan: George's uncle, prospector
Kelso Roberts: lawyer
Harriet Rodd: director of a women's hostel in Windsor
John Rodd: Windsor lawyer

TIMELINE

Warning: Contains spoilers

1903

April 21: Viola MacMillan born Violet Rita Huggard

1923

Viola MacMillan marries George MacMillan

1941

Viola MacMillan elected secretary-treasurer of the Ontario Prospectors and Developers Association; George MacMillan elected president

1944

Viola MacMillan elected president of the PDA

1961

December: Viola and George MacMillan buy control of Windfall Oils and Mines

1963

November 8: A Texas Gulf Sulphur drill hits massive zinc, copper and silver deposit near Timmins; company keeps it quiet

1964

April 16: Texas Gulf announces discovery of zinc, copper, silver deposit

April 18: Viola MacMillan goes to Timmins and buys twelve claims

April 22: Windfall directors approve the purchase of the twelve claims from MacMillan

June 15: MacMillan appears on CBS's *To Tell the Truth*

July 1: Diamond drilling begins on Windfall claims

July 3: Windfall closes at $0.56

July 5: Drilling on Windfall site stops

July 6: Windfall opens at $1.01; rises to $2; closes at $1.95

July 7: Windfall press release says officials are encouraged by the proximity of the hole to the Texas Gulf discovery

July 10: The Toronto Stock Exchange demands Windfall provide more information on the drill hole. The stock closes at $4

July 13: The TSE allows trading in Windfall to continue despite being dissatisfied with the company's information

July 14: Representatives from Windfall, the TSE and the Ontario Securities Commission meet in OSC offices

July 15: The OSC issues statement

July 18: Drilling on Windfall site resumes

July 21: Windfall reaches a high of $5.70; closes at $4.75

July 24: George MacMillan delivers samples to Swastika Laboratories

July 27: Unidentified man and woman send telegrams with false assay results from New York City

July 30: After Windfall closes at $4.15, the company issues a press release saying assay results show no commercial mineralization

July 31: Windfall opens at $0.80; closes at $1.04. Ontario Attorney General Arthur Wishart announces that two days earlier he'd ordered the OSC to investigate trading in Windfall and two other companies

August 4: Premier John Robarts announces royal commission

August 10: Justice Arthur Kelly named commissioner

August 25: Arthur Wishart suspends John Campbell

September 24: Campbell resigns as director of the OSC

1965

January 11: Viola MacMillan resigns as PDA president

March 1: Witness testimony begins at royal commission

October 7: Royal commission report released; Viola and George MacMillan charged with two counts of fraud

1967

March 10: Viola MacMillan convicted of wash trading for buying and selling 244,000 shares of Consolidated Golden Arrow

1968

January 11: After losing her appeal, Viola MacMillan goes to jail

March 15: MacMillan released after serving seven weeks of a nine-month sentence

1969

February 10: Viola and George MacMillan acquitted on fraud charges

1978

September 27: George MacMillan dies
October: Viola MacMillan receives pardon on wash trading conviction

1991

January: Viola MacMillan inducted into Canadian Mining Hall of Fame

1993

April 21: On the day she turns ninety, Viola MacMillan goes to Ottawa
to become a member of the Order of Canada
August 26: Viola MacMillan dies

PROLOGUE

"I, Viola MacMillan, am president of the Prospectors and Developers Association of Canada. I am also an active mining prospector myself. I have been engaged in every phase of the business from grubstaking and swinging a pick to organizing and bringing the mines into production," Bud Collyer announced. The host of *To Tell the Truth* was introducing MacMillan and two imposters on an episode of the popular prime-time TV game show in June 1964. "Among my more successful strikes have been the ViolaMac Mine in Porcupine, Ontario; the Lake Cinch, a uranium mine in Saskatchewan; and Windfall, a property in the Timmins area, adjacent to the recent Texas Gulf Sulphur strike. Over the years, I have discovered and developed mines which, up to now, have produced $40 million worth of ore."

To Tell the Truth, which had run on the CBS television network since 1956, featured a panel of four minor celebrities who asked three contestants questions to determine which one was real and which two were bluffing. At just five feet tall and not much more than one hundred pounds, contestant number two was smaller than the others. She also appeared to be older. And she certainly didn't look like a prospector: she was dressed in a buttoned-up tweed jacket, a skirt that went down to just below her knees, dark pumps and a single strand of pearls. She seemed more like somebody's well-heeled grandmother than someone from the bush.

When panellist Kitty Carlisle, who wore five strands of pearls, asked her about the cost of land near the massive base metal deposit that Texas Gulf had just discovered, contestant number two replied, "Some have paid as high as $100,000, and stock on top of that, for a group of twelve claims." Although the answers from the two other women tended to be much vaguer or clearly made up, the only panellist who guessed correctly was Tom Poston, a pasty-faced actor known for his bugged-out eyes and bewildered countenance. Choosing contestant number two, he said, "She looked richer than the others." For fooling three of the panellists, the prize was a three-way split of $750 and a carton of Winston cigarettes.

While MacMillan had answered questions honestly, though sometimes evasively, the show didn't quite tell the truth when introducing her. She did not have "a successful strike" on the Windfall property, though she hoped she soon would. And within a few weeks, much of the Canadian mining industry, and thousands of penny stock investors, would believe that's exactly what she had. For the sixty-one-year-old, a big new mine would be one more impressive achievement in a distinguished career.

Although she fell in love with prospecting in 1926, MacMillan had long ago discovered her real talent was on the business side of mining, including buying and selling claims, raising money for exploration projects and creating syndicates to develop properties. Toronto was the centre of mining finance in Canada, and it became her home base, though she continued to make regular trips to the bush and to her mines. By the late 1950s, she and her husband, George, owned a big brick house on the edge of Forest Hill, a prosperous Toronto neighbourhood; a 240-hectare property overlooking Holland Marsh north of the city; and a fruit ranch in British Columbia. During the winter, she liked to spend time in Miami, where she had an apartment at the chic Surf Club. But MacMillan often stayed in her Adelaide Street penthouse. It was around the corner from the art deco building on Bay Street that housed the Toronto Stock Exchange and close to the offices of many of the men she did business with—and just an elevator ride up from her own office.

On top of her mining interests, she'd served as the president of the Prospectors and Developers Association (PDA) since 1944. After overcoming resistance from some of the men, she kept getting re-elected every year. She transformed a rudderless provincial clump of prospectors into an influential national organization with a membership that also included geologists, engineers and anyone else who mattered in mineral exploration in Canada. She didn't just advocate for the industry in her speeches—"We must rise and cast off our shackles"—she successfully lobbied politicians for more favourable laws.

After suffering a heart attack in 1959, MacMillan tried to follow her doctors' orders and retire. Despite staying on as PDA president, she sold some of her companies and reduced her workload. But she couldn't shake her hunger for a big strike and would come to regret pursuing that dream. "And oh, how often I have wished through all the years that have passed since then that I had been content with this modest 'empire' and had not tried to expand beyond it," she later admitted in her autobiography, "because it was the next company I acquired that involved me, and I still insist it was through no fault of my own, in a scandal so dreadful that even a quarter of a century later I can't think about it without shuddering."

That company was Windfall Oils and Mines. And the scandal that made her shudder was one of the most notorious, and most significant, in Canadian mining history.

CHAPTER ONE

HOT GROUND

After their Trans-Canada Air Lines flight touched down in Timmins mid-morning on Saturday, Viola and George MacMillan checked into the Empire Hotel. They always stayed at the squat, four-storey red brick building when they were in town. Which was often. The first time, back in the early 1930s, the couple wondered how they would afford it, but that was no longer a problem. Even better, on April 18, 1964, the hotel was filled with even more mining people than usual. When Viola ran into some prospectors she knew in the lobby, she learned that they had claims for sale and were negotiating deals out of a third-floor suite. Acting quickly was crucial if she was going to get what she wanted, which she usually did.

For MacMillan, who never seemed to stop moving, it had been a hectic week. The annual convention of the Canadian Institute of Mining and Metallurgy had started on Monday at the Queen Elizabeth Hotel in Montreal. Most of the other women at the three-day meeting were wives of delegates, and their agenda included a fashion show at the Holt Renfrew store and high tea atop a bank building. MacMillan had a different itinerary; after all, she was a respected veteran of the industry and the long-time president of the Prospectors and Developers Association. On Tuesday, she'd hosted a reception and sat at the head table during the men's banquet. As a rare woman in mining, she always made a good story for the press, and earlier that day, the *Montreal Star* had run a piece on her. Although MacMillan was a week and a half away from turning sixty-one, she told the reporter, "Tomorrow may be the day I make my major discovery. We'll never be too old to go prospecting, even if we die on the trail."

The theme of the conference was the Canadian Arctic, though the thirty-three technical sessions covered a variety of topics. But one subject dominated in the hallways, reception rooms and bars and restaurants. The more than 1,000 delegates spent a great deal of their time talking about northern Ontario. Rumours had been swirling for weeks that Texas Gulf Sulphur Company had a base metals strike in Kidd Township just north of Timmins. At MacMillan's reception, she quietly told some guests about the assay results from the first drill hole. Although the American mining giant had not released any information—the company was still denying it had found anything—her figures would prove to be surprisingly accurate. She knew what she was talking about.

Two days later, on April 16, Texas Gulf finally confirmed the discovery of a massive deposit of copper, zinc and silver. MacMillan quickly found herself caught up in the excitement and joining the stampede of prospectors to Timmins. But she hadn't gone there to take part in the claim-staking rush that was underway, though she'd done that often enough in the past. Instead, she was looking to buy claims.

While they were checking into the Empire Hotel, the MacMillans also saw Graham Ackerley and went over to talk to him. The *Northern Miner* reporter had broken the story of the big strike after Texas Gulf had given him a tour of its drill site a week earlier. A staffer with the weekly for only eighteen months, he'd worked in the newspaper business off and on for two decades. He'd also been a full-time prospector in the late 1940s and frequently taken on exploration and fieldwork jobs in the '50s. The MacMillans, who'd known Ackerley for more than a decade, invited him up to their room for coffee. Other than Texas Gulf employees and contractors, he was the only person to have stepped foot on the company's site. Hoping his information would help them identify the best ground to pursue, the MacMillans pumped him for everything he knew about the discovery and the geology of the surrounding area. Although he told them what he'd learned during his visit at the beginning of the week, he wasn't much help with the regional geology. During the half-hour conversation, Ackerely realized that George knew as much about that as he did. Maybe more.

One of the men in town selling claims was John Larche. After going to work in a gold mine in 1943, when he was just fifteen, he became a full-time prospector in 1955. Viola had helped him get started and hired him to do exploration work on several occasions. She considered him "the most knowledgeable prospector" in the area and, despite the differences in their ages, a good friend. Like most people in the mining business, especially around Timmins, Larche had been hearing the gossip about a Texas Gulf strike for months. Earlier in April, he and Alfred Rousseau, his long-time partner, had teamed up with Donald McKinnon, a travelling foreman for a lumber company who did some prospecting on the side. Together they staked and registered forty claims. Then, armed with a generous supply of liquor, beer and cigars for themselves and their anticipated guests, they set up shop in suite 358 of the Empire Hotel and waited for the offers to come in. The suite quickly proved to be a great place to trade rumours and socialize, and so many mining people and reporters dropped by that the prospectors were soon going through almost a case of booze a day.

Offers also came in. Larche and Rousseau handled the sales, and McKinnon mostly stayed out of it because they were worried that his employer might try to take his share. By the time Viola and George showed up, a dozen properties had already sold. In February, claims in the area could be had for one hundred dollars; now they were going for thousands of dollars. As the MacMillans and Larche pored over the maps that showed what was still available, one package stood out. The jewel was a parcel of four claims in Prosser Township. Larche, Rousseau and McKinnon had been able to snag them on April 11 because of a staking error by Texas Gulf. The property was within five kilometres of that company's big find, and an airborne geophysical survey indicated the presence of an anomaly. In mining, a geophysical anomaly is a change from the norm; in this case, that meant much higher magnetic readings. But the prospectors had set a steep price for them. As Larche said later, "We knew we had a hot piece of ground."

Viola MacMillan, who wanted ground with promising geology and as close to the big find as possible, was keen. Unfortunately, by the time she arrived, Rousseau had been negotiating with Melvin Rennick, a fieldman with Noranda Exploration. The prospectors said they'd been discussing a deal that included $100,000 down and, because the company wouldn't offer shares, another $900,000 in a year if it found something on the property. But they wanted free stock more than money because it would be worth more if the claims held a mine. Still, they told Rennick they would give him right of first refusal before agreeing to any other deal.

□

Ken Darke, a Texas Gulf geological engineer, was in a plane flying to the Arctic in 1958 when it smashed into a hill. With a broken back, he couldn't crawl from the wreckage. But he survived and the crash didn't scare him off returning to the field or even going to the Far North in a small aircraft again. Although the bespectacled native of Trail, British Columbia, looked the part of a nerdy engineer, he loved his cigars and was intense, ambitious and dogged. In October 1963, he was working on Baffin Island but scheduled to finally go on vacation. After stints in Alaska, Arizona, Texas, Wyoming, North Carolina and now the Canadian Arctic, it had been two years since his last proper holiday. The twenty-nine-year-old headed to Timmins instead.

He delayed his time off for a chance to get another look at a rock outcrop in the northeast corner of Kidd Township. After examining it a couple of times while mapping the area four years earlier, he'd considered it promising enough to write a memo to his boss about it. The problem was getting the mineral rights, so the company turned its attention to other projects, including a deposit of zinc, lead and silver on the northern tip of Baffin Island.

Darke had mapped the Timmins area because Texas Gulf's chief geologist, Walter Holyk, had convinced his bosses to approve a major exploration program called the Canadian Shield Project. Another British Columbian, from Revelstoke, Holyk was a former officer in the Royal Canadian Air Force who'd completed a PhD at the Massachusetts Institute of Technology. Following the 1956 discovery of a large lead-zinc deposit near Bathurst, New Brunswick, he'd made the case that Texas Gulf's next target should be the Precambrian rock that covers much of the central eastern part of the country, including a good chunk of Ontario. The American mining giant was known for its rigorously scientific approach to looking for minerals, and he proposed using the same methods that had worked in New Brunswick. That included collecting all the existing geological research and aerial photographs, as well as doing fieldwork to determine the best places for airborne electromagnetic surveys.

The project began in 1957, and two years later, the results of a 1959 EM survey over the Timmins area, conducted by helicopter, were encouraging. But Texas Gulf, a Houston-based company with executive offices in New York, completed subsequent geophysics and geology work and sixty-five drill holes without finding anything of commercial value. The exploration team left the region during the winter of '61–'62 without following up on the spot Darke had written the memo about because it was on patented land. That meant the owner of the property also held the mineral rights, so no one could stake claims on it. Finally, in June 1963, Texas Gulf paid the landowner $500 for an option on the mineral rights. Darke returned to Timmins in mid-October.

Taciturn by nature, he kept a low profile as he completed some pre-paratory work before two geophysicists could come in to do a ground EM survey. The bedrock was well buried in the area and there were so few outcrops amid all the swamp that geophysical instruments were crucial to knowing where to drill. Darke located—or "spotted"—the first hole, designated Kidd 55-1, and diamond drillers began setting up on Thursday, November 7. They started drilling the next day and would keep going around the clock as they bore through the ground at a sixty-degree angle, extracting a continuous cylinder of rock, known as core, as they went.

On Friday night, Darke was in his room at the Bon Air Motor Hotel. Although it was eleven o'clock, he was still working. He heard a knock at the door, and when he opened it, he was surprised to see René Gervais standing there. The foreman of the drill crew held a length of core in his hands. The geologist took the sample and immediately saw that it was rich in copper. After a largely sleepless night, he left the motel before the sun was up. At the drill site, he examined more of the core with a hand lens even as new lengths continued to come out of the ground. After two feet of sand and boulders and twenty-four of clay, the drillers had hit eight feet of ore that Darke estimated was 3 percent copper. Below that was a section with only trace amounts of the metal, followed by even richer ore. At one hundred feet, the drill had hit a zone of zinc. And so it went. Two days later, the crew had finished the hole. Though it was Sunday night, Darke rushed back to Timmins, taking only forty minutes to hike through the muskeg to his jeep, a trip that usually took an hour. As soon as he made it to his motel, he phoned Holyk, which led to a chain of calls, until executive vice-president Charles Fogarty woke up the company president to tell him about the remarkable drill results.

Holyk arrived in Timmins later the next day and on Tuesday went to the site with Darke. The two men realized they needed to do everything they could to keep what they'd found a secret. After agreeing to stay at the site until Christmas in exchange for more pay, the drillers moved their rig to another spot. To help make sure no one flying overhead would think the company was drilling a second hole, they also moved their tents and set them up in the same configuration as they'd been before. They planted trees to conceal where the drill platform had been and covered the muskeg tractor's tracks with pine boughs. The following Sunday, Darke thanked the crew with two bottles of Seagram VO whisky and twenty-four bottles of beer. But just moving the rig wasn't enough. To keep the workers busy, he had them start drilling Kidd 55-2. They didn't realize Darke and Holyk had intentionally spotted the hole where it would produce nothing interesting, hoping that would dull the drillers' excitement over what they'd pulled out of Kidd 55-1.

The subterfuge was necessary. Despite the decoy hole, real ones would have to follow to ensure the first wasn't a fluke and to get a better sense of the dimensions of the ore body. But first, Texas Gulf hoped to lock up all the promising ground around the site by staking claims and optioning patented land. That was going to take time, and the job would be more difficult and more expensive if there was competition for claims and properties commanded much higher option prices because owners knew the miner was onto something. Complicating the task was all the patented land in the region because of the veterans' lots. Earlier in the century, the government had granted property, along with the mineral rights, to war veterans, including those who'd fought in the Fenian Raids, the Boer War and the First World War. (Kidd-55 was on land owned by the widow of a Boer War veteran.) The hope was that they would farm the land and help develop the Great Clay Belt, a huge swath of the Canadian Shield covered by fertile clay loam. While some vets did take advantage of the offer, all but a few soon found that the long, cold winters, heavy rains and crop-killing summer frosts made farming in the area a ludicrous pursuit. Many vets never even bothered to check out their lots. Some later accepted meagre bids for their land from lumber companies during the Depression. Years later, those who'd held on, or their descendants, were surprised when the mineral rights suddenly made the properties valuable.

Darke required a lot of maps from the mining recorder's office to know what was already staked, what was available and what was patented land. The recorder was a government administrator charged with overseeing a region's mining activity, including the registering of claims. To avoid raising suspicion, Darke arranged for other people to order and pick up some of the maps. Then he hired several prospecting teams to stake and register claims. For one thing, a mining licence entitled the bearer to stake only eighteen claims a year; for another, separate crews reduced the chance anyone would realize the company was amassing almost 250 claims.

One glitch was the Prosser Township claims that got away. Darke had given a staking team an aerial photograph and incorrectly indicated that the road ran along the boundary between the Prosser and Wark Townships. Realizing the blunder, Larche, Rousseau and McKinnon restaked four claims and asked the mining recorder to do an inspection. The ground was theirs. Darke inquired about buying the claims, but confident they could get more from someone else, the prospectors said no. Still, between all the other staking and options on patented land, Texas Gulf would lock up control of 60,000 acres by mid-April.

All that activity, even done quietly, made preventing rumours impossible. The gossip had started in December. One source was the helicopter navigator, who told people in the Empire Hotel's Fountain Court bar about all the core his chopper was transporting to the airport on its way to be assayed in Salt Lake City. Since the samples were in cardboard core boxes that were wrapped in burlap, sheathed in more cardboard and bound with wire, he had no idea what they contained, let alone how much. Another source of scuttlebutt was the drillers, who left the site for Christmas, but they'd mistaken the mineralization in the core for nickel. In February, the *Northern Miner*, the industry's Toronto-based weekly journal of record, asked Texas Gulf if it had made a discovery and received a firm denial.

Of course, one great drill hole is no guarantee of a mine. Far from it. At the end of March, with almost all the necessary land secured, it was now safe to do more drilling. The company brought in four drill rigs. Inevitably, that generated more gossip. After the *Globe and Mail* ran a story under a "Gigantic Copper Strike Rumoured" headline on Tuesday, April 9, Texas Gulf's stock rose, and speculators bid up the price of junior mining companies working in the area. On Saturday, the *New York Times* and the *New York Herald Tribune* reported the rumours, with the latter running its story on the front page. Coverage in Canadian papers was one thing, but now the American press was sniffing around. Worse, the *Herald Tribune* story in particular contained exaggerations and factual errors, including reporting the participation of PCE Explorations in the discovery. None of the New York executives had even heard of the junior miner. Realizing it needed to respond, Texas Gulf issued a carefully worded press release on Sunday morning. In it, Fogarty admitted that the company was encouraged enough to expand its drilling program and would have more to say when it "had progressed to the point where reasonable and logical conclusions can be made." That sounded optimistic, but another line stood out as an attempt to tamp down the gossip: "The work done to date has not been sufficient to reach definite conclusions and any statements to size and grade of ore would be premature and possibly misleading."

Despite a high degree of confidence it had found a mine, the company was still early in its drilling program, so the statement was technically true. Investors and industry people interpreted the phrasing in their own way, though. Some took it as a note of responsible caution, others saw it as a denial and, speaking of misleading, still others considered it a non-denial denial designed to calm the market. Dissembling or not, it did little to stop the rumours.

The next step in the attempt to control the narrative was to show the site to Ackerley. Although the *Northern Miner* was a Canadian publication, it had a circulation of about 7,000 south of the border. On Monday morning, he climbed in a helicopter and, as he later recounted, "Ten minutes against a stiff headwind. And then, down below, five rigs working on a grid pattern. From the air it looks like a 200-foot grid. That's it! They've got a big one!"

When the chopper landed, Ackerley toured the site, looked at selected sections of core from the first hole and saw some assay results. In return for this special access, the paper agreed to let Texas Gulf's manager of exploration, Richard Mollison, vet the story before publication. Mollison and Holyk flew to Montreal for the Canadian Institute of Mining and Metallurgy convention the next day. They planned to meet with George Wardrope, Ontario's minister of mines, but when they arrived, the Queen Elizabeth Hotel was so thick with gossip that they realized they couldn't show their faces at the conference. Instead, the next morning, they flew Wardrope and his deputy minister back to Toronto in the company plane, filling them in on the discovery en route.

At the airport, Mollison arranged to return his copy of Ackerley's draft. He'd made no changes, though he did encourage including a couple more names. When the *Northern Miner* hit the streets on April 16, it revealed the discovery of a ten-million-ton ore body laced with copper, zinc and silver. Knowing the report was coming out that morning, Texas Gulf had arranged a press conference where it corrected Ackerley's story: the ore body was more than twenty-five million tons.

The good news didn't end there. Rather than in some remote place such as Baffin Island, the find was conveniently located just twenty kilometres north of Timmins and not far from power lines, the railroad and a highway. The top of the ore body was so close to the surface that mining could initially begin with a less expensive open-pit operation. According to preliminary estimates the deposit would produce US$850 million worth of copper, zinc and silver and generate a profit of at least US$10 per ton of ore.

Texas Gulf didn't tell the whole truth, though. One executive spun a tale of how and when the company learned of the strike that managed to include deception, embellishment and understatement. The *New York*

Times reported that Darke "had to trek 10 miles through the snow to his jeep three or four weeks ago because weather prevented helicopters from reaching the site. After his hike, Mr. Dark (sic) raced to the nearest telephone and awakened company executives in New York about midnight with news of the first inklings of the discovery."

No one at the press conference mentioned that between the time the geological engineer really alerted his bosses in November and the time they claimed he did in March, several Texas Gulf officers and employees, and some of their family and friends, purchased shares in the company. Darke, Holyk, Mollison and Fogarty were among the buyers.

□

The Texas Gulf discovery ignited three frenzies. The first one was in Timmins. Many big mining rushes had taken place in remote locations and led to the creation of towns such as Dawson City, Cobalt and Kirkland Lake where there had previously been only bush. Initially, these were haphazard mining camps full of tents and quickly assembled buildings, before eventually achieving some sense of orderly planning. Timmins didn't exist until two years into the 1909 Porcupine gold rush and benefited from being partially planned as a community for Hollinger Mine workers. By 1964, it had matured into a bilingual city with a population of close to 30,000, though it was technically still a town because it had never applied for city status. Maybe that designation seemed too pretentious for the residents of a sprawling, rugged and unglamorous place dominated by aging buildings and suffering from declining fortunes.

The big strike came just in time. For more than half a century, workers had been pulling gold—over $1.5 billion worth of it—out of the ground. The region still had a dozen operating mines, but they were nearing the end of their productive lives and were shedding jobs. Hollinger, which employed 1,500, had announced plans to cease operations in the summer of 1965; others were not far behind. For a community built on gold, the prospects were dire, and an undercurrent of pessimism was building. The Christmas shopping season had been bleak for merchants. Real estate agents had lots of sellers and no buyers. A few people had left town and others were starting to say, "Well, it is about time to start moving; Timmins isn't going anywhere."

The pessimism vanished on April 16 as boomtown pandemonium took hold. A massive silver and base metals deposit meant new jobs, new investment and a much brighter future. Aside from miners, Texas Gulf would need a railway spur and a road from the highway and was already considering building a smelter to process the ore.

The swarm of visitors included prospectors, mining executives, engineers, promoters, brokers and the curious. They came by plane, train, bus and private car; some hitchhiked. After the hotels filled up, the roomless asked to stay in the jail. The restaurants and beer parlours did roaring business. Taxi companies reactivated retired vehicles to meet demand, especially for trips from the airport. Stores ran out of prospecting equipment, camping gear and toiletries such as toothpaste, shaving cream and razors. Three-day-old copies of the *Northern Miner* with a cover price of two bits fetched two bucks.

No wonder residents celebrated; according to one report, "work here came to a virtual halt as thousands of people thronged the streets in a Mardi Gras atmosphere." Among the jubilant was Leo Del Villano, the town's mayor, who proclaimed, "We're sitting on top of a jewelry store." A whisky salesman, he was loud and colourful and loved attention. He knew how to play to the cameras. Predicting the population would grow to 50,000, he crossed out the 29 of the 29,300 on the town's road sign and wrote 50. And he employed a bit of sleight of hand to make it look as though he was lighting Larche's cigar with a fifty-dollar bill. In fact, a piece of paper behind the money was aflame so the bill was only singed; after all, the mayor was happy, not nuts. Photos of both stunts made the papers.

The second frenzy was outside town as prospectors and mining companies, who assumed the Texas Gulf strike would be the first of many, scrambled for claims. Given the region's long winters, April was not a good time to be in the bush, but there was no time to wait for better conditions. With up to eighteen helicopters transporting prospectors willing to pay one hundred dollars an hour and lucky enough to book one, people were calling it "the whirlybird staking rush." One prospector jumped out of a chopper as it landed at the airport, marched into the terminal and announced that he'd trade a dollar for a dime. A teenager took him up on the offer. The claim-staker inserted the coin into a vending machine, took out a bottle of pop and said, "I've been waiting for this drink for three days." Those prepared to drive out to the bush found renting or buying a jeep no longer possible. With the snow still a metre and a half deep in some places, snowshoes sold out so quickly that residents who dug out their old ones could get at least forty dollars for them.

Prospectors staked just about everything within eighty kilometres and some ground beyond that. Even though much of the land in the region was patented, the mining recorder in Timmins registered more than 20,000 claims in 1964, and more than half of those were in the first four months; the total for the previous year had been 1,995. One team staked the Timmins Municipal Airport and sold the rights to the International Nickel Company of Canada, better known as Inco, but the mining recorder refused to register the claims. Texas Gulf had already nabbed all the available land it wanted, aside from the four Prosser Township claims. But Larche, McKinnon and Rousseau weren't the only ones with claims to sell and Viola MacMillan wasn't the only one looking to buy. Many small exploration companies purchased claims or exercised options in the area. Big players were also interested. Inco made a deal with the Abitibi Power and Paper Company to begin exploration on land that the latter had the timber rights to near the discovery. All the activity wasn't just the result of outsiders. Some residents bought five-dollar mining licences and headed into the bush to stake claims.

Del Villano wasn't the town's lone media celebrity. Nedo Bragagnolo, who also enjoyed the attention, had been a local hockey star, even signed an NHL contract. But because he didn't want to play for the Boston Bruins, he gave up the game. Or that was the story. Now a real estate broker, he told reporters that he began accumulating claims after noticing a Texas Gulf helicopter flying over his house every day. In February, he sold twelve to Bunker Hill Extension Mines. Later, he sold another dozen to PCE Explorations and many more to other companies. In addition, the thirty-three-year-old had mortgaged property worth $250,000 so he could buy shares in several mining stocks that rose in value after the news broke. He also earned a bottle of fifteen-year-old whisky for going up to the Empire Hotel's suite 358 to negotiate the sale of some claims for Larche and Rousseau when the prospectors found themselves up against a Bay Street financier who'd flown to Timmins in a private plane. The press crowned Bragagnolo a millionaire, and the son of a miner who'd died young from silicosis said, "It's ironic that the mines killed my father and made me a fortune."

The bit about him sensing something was up from watching the helicopters was a tall tale because the young entrepreneur was guarding a big secret of his own. He and John Angus, the manager of the Timmins branch of the T.A. Richardson & Company brokerage, were good friends. In November 1963, Bragagnolo suggested the two of them start collecting claims because he thought Texas Gulf had found something. This wasn't simply conjecture, and helicopters had little to do with it. He'd been putting together rumours and evidence that indicated a discovery. For one thing, the realtor found it suspicious when Ken Darke, whom he'd first met in 1959 and was now working out of an office next door on Pine Street, asked him to get some maps from the mining recorder. Initially, Angus didn't show much interest in the idea but reconsidered in January when his pal suggested they ask Darke to join them. The Texas Gulf geological engineer initially declined the offer.

"Whether you come in with me or not," the realtor said, "I'm going in."

"Well, since you are going in," said Darke, "I might as well go in with you all." He overcame his conflict-of-interest concerns because he hoped the deal would help prevent a staking war. The arrangement allowed him to tell Bragagnolo, who was overseeing the project, to stay away from areas his employer was interested in. The company wanted all the ground with anomalies and didn't care about the rest. Still, he refused to reveal anything about what Texas Gulf had found. Bragagnolo would ask, "Is there an ore body there?" and Darke would laugh and say, "Be patient."

The partners hired experienced stakers and eventually accumulated 241 claims. After the trio had sold some of the properties, Angus left the partnership due to brokerage industry rules. He'd made more than $180,000. Bragagnolo and Darke stayed at it and reaped $900,000 plus a bevy of shares in mining companies. None of the buyers knew they were paying for ground Texas Gulf had already deemed unworthy of staking.

The third frenzy was on the Toronto Stock Exchange, more than 550 kilometres to the southeast. The fever had started weeks before the Texas Gulf announcement, based on all the rumours buzzing around. Prices of some penny mining stocks with claims in the area had doubled or even tripled. Texas Gulf shares were the smarter investment. Back in November, they were trading at $17 on the New York Stock Exchange. On April 16, they closed at $37. (By the end of April, they'd be trading above $58 and would eventually hit $170.) That put them out of reach for most people, while the high-risk, high-reward penny stocks of junior mining companies were plentiful and affordable. For $50 and a $2 broker's fee, a speculator could buy one hundred shares of a company trading at fifty cents. On the day of the big announcement, the TSE set a record with more than sixteen million shares traded. The most active mining stocks were Bunker Hill Extension Mines and PCE Explorations, two of the companies that had bought claims from Bragagnolo. The volume increased the next day, a Friday, with almost twenty-nine million shares changing hands, crushing the North American record for one day of trading set by the New York Stock Exchange on Black Tuesday in October 1929.

Most investors were gambling far more than $50. The average transaction saw 1,700 mining shares change hands for between $700 and $750, a lot of money at the time. The spree didn't stop when the market closed on Friday as people looking to buy penny stocks phoned brokers at home on the weekend. The callers included lawyers, doctors and executives but also cab drivers, cops and widows. The regional branches of T.A. Richardson and Doherty, Roadhouse & McCuaig Brothers in Timmins were jammed with people desperate not to miss a chance to get rich; others crowded outside, hoping to get in. For many, it was their first foray into the market. Even some local high schoolers were investing. Radio station CKGB moved equipment into the Doherty, Roadhouse office and updated the stock quotes every half hour.

So many neophytes were jumping in that, despite making a killing on fees, brokers began to worry people would suffer big losses and stay away from the market for a long time. Some brokerage houses refused to put in buy orders for penny stocks unless clients paid for them in full first. TSE president Howard Graham was so alarmed he issued a warning. "New and unsophisticated investors are taking very real risks in venturing into the speculative market," he said. "Some undoubtedly will make money, but a great many more must certainly be prepared to lose their money." Not that anyone was listening.

□

After coffee with Ackerley, Viola MacMillan went downstairs and gave an impromptu press conference to half a dozen reporters. She sat with them at a table in the bar and answered their questions, switching between her roles as PDA president and a successful mining promoter, while adding asides and cracking off-the-record jokes. Since it was Saturday and no one was on deadline, the journalists eventually put away their notepads and just enjoyed a drink and a leisurely conversation with her. As the afternoon wore on, the gaggle of reporters swelled to fourteen and included journalists from the Toronto papers, CBC and a writer for the *Saturday Evening Post*, all in town to cover the Texas Gulf story. Eventually, MacMillan suggested they go for dinner.

Over dinner, she proposed a party for the out-of-towners and asked local man Greg Reynolds of the Timmins *Daily Press* to help round up a crowd. Later, about fifty guests—including journalists, mining promoters and prospectors, the mayor and other politicians and bureaucrats—gathered at the Senator Hotel. Reynolds had never met MacMillan until that day, but at one point in the evening, she confided in him, "We are on the verge of a big deal." She and George were returning to the Empire Hotel to continue the negotiations. When the reporter asked when she expected to be finished, she said, "It might take all night."

Back in suite 358, which was still busy with celebrating mining people, Rousseau handled most of the negotiating for the prospectors, but Larche and McKinnon were there. Viola was more determined to get the claims than George was, and at one point she made him leave the suite. Around one o'clock, Rousseau went into the other room, closed the door and phoned Rennick to tell him they were close to an agreement with the MacMillans. The Noranda fieldman, who needed to talk to his bosses, said, "I will call you back in twenty minutes." When he did, he said, "Take your deal. We can't match it."

Viola was in her element. Amid the industry's excitement over the Texas Gulf discovery, which she loved to see, she was hammering out a deal, which she loved to do. That the negotiations were over a coveted piece of land made it even better. "I hope I live through another experience like that night," Viola said later. "It was wonderful." Finally, at about three o'clock in the morning, the two sides reached an agreement. She would buy twelve claims, including the prized four in Prosser Township and two parcels in nearby Wark Township, for $100,000 and 250,000 of her own shares in a company she and her husband controlled called Windfall Oils & Mines.

The Windfall story began with Viola MacMillan using her smarts, instincts, connections, experience and financial acumen to obtain claims that Texas Gulf wanted and didn't get. She hoped they would yield a major discovery.

CHAPTER TWO

GLAMOUR JOBS

Every summer, wealthy visitors arrived at Windermere Wharf by lake steamer. From there, it was just a short walk to one of the largest and most luxurious resorts in the Muskoka district, an area of Ontario that had been growing increasingly popular with vacationers since the 1880s. Windermere House was an imposing white building that sat high above the shore of Lake Rosseau. The three-storey hotel had two towers and seven dormers in the wing facing the water, and a deep wooden verandah that was two floors high stretched across the front. Another three-storey wing ran along the road, giving the lodge enough spacious rooms for more than 200 guests, many of whom showed up with trunks and stayed for weeks. Often from Toronto or American cities, vacationers were attracted to the natural setting, the purity of the air and the first-class treatment. They spent their days boating and fishing, bathing at the beach and taking part in genteel activities such as tennis, lawn bowling and croquet. Although the house rules forbade "drinking parties, carousing and objectionable noise," guests enjoyed their evenings by listening to music in the concert hall and dancing in the ballroom.

Violet Rita Huggard could only fantasize about being one of those guests. The thirteenth of her father's fifteen children, she was born in 1903. The small farm next to Windermere House that she grew up on was the family's third property since her birth. Her father, Thomas Huggard, who came from Irish stock, sold his farm at nearby Dee Bank and moved to one closer to Windermere when Violet was nine days old. The family moved again when she was four, although her father kept the old property this time, and her brother Bert stayed behind to work it. The region's hilly and rocky terrain did not make for easy farming, which is why so many of the area's landowners had long ago opted to run hotels and resorts instead.

Money was always short. Violet wore hand-me-down dresses from summer visitors and her mother sewed pants for her from flour bags and petticoats from sugar bags. With so many offspring, the Huggards had access to lots of free labour, at least until the kids were old enough to leave home and find other jobs. Along with growing some crops, the family kept chickens, pigs, cattle, sheep and horses. Violet was still young when milking the cows became one of her pre-school chores. In the summer, she took the milk and cream to nearby cottagers. Thomas Huggard had the contract to deliver the mail in the area, though often his wife ended up doing the route, travelling by horse and buggy in the summer and horse-drawn sleigh in the winter. Not that Harriet Huggard didn't already have more than enough to do, what with the farm, the children and her other jobs. Though untrained, she served as the local midwife, helping to bring more than 200 babies into the world. And she had cleaning contracts at Windermere House and the one-room brick schoolhouse that opened in 1913 on an acre of land Thomas Huggard had sold for one hundred dollars.

While the new school eliminated the need for a three-kilometre walk to Dee Bank, it gave Violet additional responsibilities: lighting fires in the morning before classes started and cleaning up at the end of the day. She and her sister Sadie also helped their mother at the resort, which meant getting down on their hands and knees to scrub the pine floors. The wealthy guests were so charmed by the bright girl that they wanted to take her away and give her an education, but her parents weren't about to agree to that. Sometimes, Violet and Sadie would sneak onto the verandah and peer into the ballroom to watch the elegant men and women dance in their evening finery. The scene revealed a completely different world than her own and she was understandably enchanted.

That fancy life appeared to recede even further from her after war broke out in Europe in 1914 and three of her brothers, including Bert, enlisted. Her father had recovered from a heart attack a few years earlier and was in his early sixties. Unable to look after two farms by himself or afford to hire anyone to help him, he made Violet drop out of school. Thomas hadn't gone to school and couldn't read or write—his daughter read newspapers and wartime letters from his sons to him. And while Harriet may have had more evolved ambitions for her boys, she thought education would be wasted on her daughters because their life's path was to get married and have children, and they didn't need school for that. If they wanted a job before marriage, there were always plenty of openings for hotel maids.

Her parent's decision that she leave school was a great disappointment for the twelve-year-old. Violet wanted an education, and she dreamed of a better future. "The summer visitors had made me realize there was a great big, exciting world outside Windermere, and I wanted one day to be part of it," she later remembered in her autobiography. "Some of the lady visitors were stenographers, and that seemed to me a very glamorous thing to be."

After the war, Thomas Huggard sold the farm to some Toronto business-men who were creating the Windermere Golf and Country Club. With the proceeds, he bought Fife House, a hotel just east of Windermere House, though it was smaller, more casual and less expensive. That news came around the same time Violet learned she'd passed the high school entrance exam. Ignoring her mother's disdain for education, she'd crammed for three months. After spending the summer of 1919 scrubbing floors, waiting tables and handling reservations at Fife House, she bought a trunk with the six dollars she had saved from her tips. But the eighty-pound sixteen-year-old had only enough clothes to fill it halfway before taking the train to North Bay, where she would live with Elizabeth, a stepsister from her father's first marriage.

Moving away from home provided an opportunity to do something she'd long wanted to do: give herself a new name. Perhaps this is an overly romantic way of looking at it, but that decision seems almost inevitable for someone who would go on to invent herself. After all, in life and in literature, people often took different names before creating new, more successful existences for themselves. She'd always hated Violet, which had been a source of teasing when she was growing up. Now she would be Viola.

Although the original plan was high school, she realized that with her heart set on being a stenographer, it made more sense to start on courses at the local business college instead. But after just two months, her father no longer had the money to pay for school. She had to look for work. Opportunities in North Bay were scarce, so Elizabeth's grown son, Leonard Dreany, suggested she join him in Windsor, Ontario. The Ford Motor Company of Canada had begun operating in the area in 1904, and other car companies and parts manufacturers had followed over the years. After the war, the industry was expanding, and because cars built in Canada faced lower tariffs in other Commonwealth countries, Windsor became "The Auto Capital of the British Empire." With such a healthy economy, Dreany said his young aunt would have no trouble finding work.

Sure enough, Viola Huggard quickly took a job in a department store, then landed one with Bell Telephone, where she became a long-distance operator and finally started making some decent money. After six months, Dreany left Windsor, and she moved into a hostel for young women. Before long, though, Harriet Rodd, one of the hostel's directors and the wife of a high-profile barrister and the Crown attorney for the county of Essex, offered her a job as a maid. While that was not Huggard's idea of a good career move, she realized the money she'd make working for the Rodd family, along with the free room and board, would allow her to save enough for business college. Initially, her tasks included some light cleaning, doing the laundry and baking pies; when another maid left, she added heavier cleaning duties, including scrubbing the floors, in return for a generous bump in pay. A year later, in 1921, she enrolled in the business college and within nine months had her certificate. That led to a job with a wholesale plumbing and hardware company across the river in Detroit. Although she was still wearing clothes she'd sewn herself, her dream of becoming a stenographer had come true.

But after just two weeks, her boss called her into his office and let her go. He explained that he was doing so at the request of John Rodd. Her former employer wanted her back, not as a maid but as a stenographer at his nine-partner Windsor law firm. So, Huggard joined the secretarial staff at Rodd, Wigle & McHugh, where she soon began learning about contracts, deeds and other legal matters.

□

The day before Huggard started working for Harriet and John Rodd, she'd met George MacMillan at a dance. A bear of a guy with a thick head of black hair, he was a terrible dancer, but she liked his eyes and his smile. They dated for a while, but he smoked and drank, which she knew would not please her father. Besides, the Ontario Temperance Act, which banned the sale of alcohol in the province, was still in effect. They broke up and she started seeing an electrical engineer. But she missed MacMillan, and after three months apart they got back together again. He was willing to give up cigarettes for her but not alcohol. If he showed up for one their dates and she smelled booze, she called it off. He accepted her rules. "Oh, I guess I gave him a real hard time," she wrote in her autobiography, "but George was strong enough, and patient enough, to take it without losing any of his manliness."

Like Viola, he'd left school early and had never been afraid of work. Born in the Ottawa Valley town of Killaloe in 1899, he was nine when his family moved to Charlton, north of Cobalt and west of Englehart, which was as far as the Temiskaming & Northern Ontario Railway went at the time. Timmins and Kirkland Lake did not exist yet, but they soon would. And over the years, he'd get to know Sandy McIntyre, Harry Oakes and many other legendary prospectors. During his teens, he worked at a lumber camp, underground in a Cobalt mine and, too young to enlist, at a munitions factory in Parry Sound. Later, he landed at a factory in Flint, Michigan. After his family moved to Windsor, he joined them and found a job with the Canadian National Railway's express department, which handled deliveries by truck. That's what he was doing when Viola met him.

For a summer vacation in 1922, the pair went to North Bay to visit her stepsister. Seeing a one-dollar excursion fare to New Liskeard on the T&NO, they decided to do a side trip to see some of his relatives, including his Aunt Agnes. George's uncle, "Black Jack" MacMillan, stayed with Agnes when he wasn't living in the bush. As a boy, George had learned the basics of prospecting from his dad and his uncle. Though Jack had never had much luck, he kept at it, always hoping for his big strike.

While in New Liskeard, George also wanted to see a woman he'd been—and might still have been—engaged to. When Viola met her, she saw a heavy-set young woman who was not an early riser and whose sink held three or four days' worth of dirty dishes. "I thought she's not the girl for him," Viola said later. "I thought I was better for him than her, especially somebody who doesn't wash the dishes every day." She gave George an ultimatum: "Either her or me."

New Liskeard was one of three towns close together by Lake Temiskaming; the others were Haileybury and Cobalt. Huggard had been born a few months before workers building the T&NO staked the first claims in what became the Cobalt silver boom. Joe Huggard, the older brother she idolized, later left the farm for a job at the Coniagas Mine. When he came home to visit family, he told his little sister stories about working underground. She thought it sounded like a great adventure, but even if mining had been a viable career option for a woman at the time, stenography held more appeal. Joe married, had two kids and enlisted when the war broke out. Shortly after his return to Cobalt, he died of the Spanish flu. Now that she was so close to where her beloved brother had worked, she had to go see it. After getting a ride to the Coniagas property, she discovered the mine was closed for the Dominion Day long weekend. Undaunted, she found the mine captain and asked to go underground. "I can't do that," the appalled boss said. "We never allow women underground. It's bad luck."

This was a common and long-standing superstition in the industry, but Huggard was already a hard person to say no to. She pleaded and wheedled and convinced him that she was thin enough that she would look like a boy. "Just give me the right clothes and no one will ever know I'm a girl," the nineteen-year-old insisted. Somehow, it worked. She donned the standard miner's garb: coveralls, big rubber boots and a helmet, carefully tucking her hair under it. Then she descended the shaft in the cage, the elevator that took workers underground. Rather than being scared, she was fascinated as the mine captain gave her a tour. One of the area's richest properties, its name came from the chemical symbols for four elements in the rock: Co for cobalt, Ni for nickel, Ag for silver and As for arsenic. When it opened in the fall of 1904, workers just stripped slabs of silver off the walls. By the time Huggard visited, extracting the remaining silver was more difficult and the Coniagas was nearing the end of its life as a productive mine. Although she found it cold and damp underground and felt sorry for the men who had to work so hard in those conditions, the tour made a strong impression on her. "It was one of the most glorious experiences of my lifetime," she later wrote, "and I was completely hooked on the glamour of mining."

After they returned to Windsor, Viola and George continued to grow closer, especially now that the New Liskeard girlfriend was no longer a concern. Huggard thrived at her job as a stenographer with Rodd, Wigle & McHugh, and, in her spare time, she began reading everything about the mining industry she could get her hands on. That included learning about the Cobalt silver boom, the Porcupine gold rush and the Kirkland Lake gold rush, which were seminal events in Canadian mining history, and they'd all happened in her lifetime.

□

George and Viola seemed so different from each other. He was relaxed and she was driven, he was soft-spoken and she was self-assured, he was large and she was diminutive, but love doesn't depend on similarities. They were a good match. In the summer of 1923, he travelled to Windermere to ask Thomas Huggard for his daughter's hand in marriage. George later told Viola that her father had responded: "Well, if you think you can handle her, it's okay with me."

They married in October and, for the most part, he "handled" her by letting her run things. As she said, "He put up with me and so we got along all right." She'd bought a small house shortly after she began working at Rodd, Wigle & McHugh. By her own admission, it was really just a shack and had cost only a little over $1,600. But it was hers. Her brother Jim, who'd left his mine job up north for one at a forge in Windsor, moved in, helping her pay the mortgage. But now that she was married, she wanted something bigger and better. One of the law firm's clients was a building contractor who gave the newlyweds a deal on a new house in nearby Ford City. With a mortgage of more than $7,000, the couple lived on the main floor and rented the second floor, which was a separate unit, to eight or nine boarders, who each paid nine or ten dollars a week. After a while, the bank manager became suspicious of this young woman who deposited a little stack of small bills every Monday. Wanting an explanation, he invited her into his office but was too embarrassed to put the question directly. Eventually, she realized what he was driving at and angrily insisted, "I'm not that kind of girl."

Clearly, though, she was the kind of woman who was good with money. She was also good with people. The building contractor, who'd noticed how she dealt with clients at the law office, soon offered her a job selling houses. She began moonlighting as a real estate agent in the evenings and on weekends. The law partners didn't mind because her clients often became their clients. She also somehow found time to do charitable work as the secretary of a Windsor chapter of the Order of Eastern Star, an organization connected to the Masons. It was a busy life, which she liked. And it was about to get busier.

In 1926, George received a letter from his Uncle Jack. The old prospector had some gold claims northwest of Kirkland Lake, but he was losing his eyesight and couldn't do the annual forty hours of assessment work required to keep them. Not wanting to lose the claims, he offered his nephew a half interest in exchange for doing the work. The letter came at the right time: the CNR had just laid off George.

Viola's first night in the bush didn't get off to a great start. Because she was still working at the law firm, she had to wait for her vacation time before heading north. George and her brother Ed, who was living with the couple at the time, went ahead and started on the assessment work. Before she joined them, she bought riding breeches, high boots and a big suitcase that she filled with clothes and other things that seemed like necessities. Then she boarded the T&NO and requested a stop at Sesekinika. George and Ed had stocked up on provisions at the general store before meeting her at the little train station. The three of them walked into the bush on their way to the shack on one of Black Jack's claims, with Viola lugging a suitcase full of clothes she wouldn't need. "I'm sure I didn't really expect to find any gold on my holiday, but just being out there in the wilderness was thrill enough," she later remembered. "The air was so crisp and clear, and the silence so immense when we paused occasionally for a breather, that I really felt as though I was in another world, and that we were the only human beings who had ever passed that way."

The light had just about left the sky and they were almost at the shack when George stopped and said, "Mmm. It looks as though we've had a visitor." The pail he and Ed had stored their honey in was lying beside the trail. Cautiously, they kept going. When they reached the cabin, they discovered a broken window with tufts of fur stuck in the frame. Once inside, the bear had behaved like a rock star in a hotel room. Trashing the place to get at all the food that wasn't in cans, it had shredded blankets and crushed a sheet-iron stove.

One thing was for sure: Viola wasn't going to spend the night there. George knew that Art Wilson, another prospector, had a cabin a few kilometres away, so they decided to head there even though it was now dark. They didn't have a gun, but they had an axe. Viola insisted on carrying it. Bears are a fact of life in the woods of northern Ontario, and while a healthy fear of them is wise, even essential, her terror did not bode well for someone about to spend a couple of weeks prospecting. Before the night was over, though, she would be well on her way to understanding the charms of a life in the bush.

When they reached the cabin, the trio found Wilson, three other prospectors, a couple of excitable huskies and a blazing fire in an old oil drum. Despite the crowd, the newcomers were welcome to stay. After chowing down on some baked beans, George and Ed soon went to sleep, but Viola stayed up late listening to Wilson's tales. He regaled her with stories about people she'd only read about. How Harry Preston found the Dome Mine when he slipped on a rock and exposed gold. How Benny Hollinger found gold and how Noah Timmins developed it into the Hollinger Mine. How Harry Oakes found and developed his own mine. Wilson also had plenty of stories about prospectors who didn't become rich. About people like Reuben D'Aigle, who'd staked, prospected and then walked away from the claims that held the deposit that Hollinger would later find. About Sandy McIntyre, who'd found two big mines and then drank away what little he made from his hard work and good fortune. And about himself, someone who'd never made a big discovery but still loved what he did. Listening to Wilson, Viola began to understand what drove prospectors. It wasn't the dream of a big strike, though that was part of it. "It was something more than that," she realized. "The real attraction is the life itself."

Part of that has to do with the joys of spending time in nature, including the fresh air and the unspoiled scenery. The northern Ontario terrain is rugged and perhaps not classically beautiful, but it's still captivating. Eating just-caught-and-cooked fish is gourmet dining. Spending time around a fire beside a lake is exquisite, especially with friends. For prospectors, all that is an everyday experience and it never gets mundane. Of course, there's also lots of hard work, bad weather and an astonishing number of blackflies and mosquitos, as well as the occasional bear encounter. But prospectors enjoy a bossless freedom. Perhaps that appealed to Viola most of all. By the time she and Wilson had finally packed it in for the night, she'd decided to learn all she could about prospecting.

She didn't have to go far to find her first mentor. The next morning, she and George hired Wilson to help them do the assessment work on Black Jack MacMillan's claims. Viola enjoyed her time so much that she decided she wanted to go prospecting every summer. Her law firm agreed to give her July and August off. During the rest of the year, she worked hard at her job and tried to learn as much as she could about legal subjects that might come in handy later. Stenographer was no longer her dream career. She was determined to get into mining.

Over the next few summers, the MacMillans learned a lot about prospecting and accumulated all the right gear. Aside from small magnifying lenses to examine minerals in rock, the essentials included $1.50 grub hoes, which they used to dig trenches, scrape moss and chip rocks; axes; and tape to patch their canoe. They slept in a fifteen-dollar tent made out of cotton duck, another name for canvas, that was just big enough for two people. Silk tents were lighter but too dear at $84. To help combat the blackflies and mosquitos, they made their own bug juice by mixing pine tar, olive oil, citronella and carbolic acid. They called it fly oil, and although it stunk, it was somewhat effective.

The MacMillans also met some of the characters who populated the bush. One day, they came upon a shack that was home to an old prospector and eleven mangy mutts. "They won't hurt you, they're my family," he reassured them about the snarling dogs. "And great little helpers they are, too. Why, I never have to wash a single dish. I just set 'em out after I've finished eating and these fellers clean 'em up as nice as you please." Hearing that, George asked the prospector to make Viola some tea, saying that while he never drank the stuff, she "lived on it."

Although the MacMillans made no big discoveries during their summer trips, that didn't lessen their enthusiasm for prospecting. As she'd realized listening to Art Wilson, it was about more than just finding a gold mine, as much as she wanted to do exactly that.

CHAPTER THREE

THREE STRIKES

A fox was hanging around the forge and wouldn't go away. Finally, the exasperated railroad blacksmith threw his hammer. He missed. Instead, in a marvellous stroke of good fortune, the hammer chipped a rock, revealing a silver deposit and igniting the Cobalt silver boom. That's the most famous version of the legend, anyway, though there are several variations: in one, the target was a rabbit, not a fox. But mining stories, like fishing tales, are often too good to be true. What really happened in 1903 doesn't make for as tidy a story, and no foxes, or rabbits, were harmed, but railroad workers, including a burly blacksmith named Fred LaRose, were involved. Although he wasn't the first to find silver in the area, he often gets the credit.

While prospectors should have drooled over the Canadian Shield, the general impression before the turn of the century was that Ontario was not a promising region for mining. Of course, Indigenous peoples had been extracting minerals from this land for millennia, but white settlers weren't much interested in traditional knowledge. Not that the new-comers never made any finds; it's just that most of them didn't amount to much. Copper mining started north of Lake Huron in 1846. Twenty years later, the province had its first gold rush after a discovery on John Richardson's farm, near Madoc. But it led to only one mine, which closed after two years. An 1868 silver find on a small island, later named Silver Islet, in Lake Superior, led to a mine that produced for sixteen years. A small gold rush began near Lake of the Woods in the 1870s. Workers building the Canadian Pacific Railway in 1883 discovered nickel west of Lake Nipissing. Mining started six years later, but the nickel wasn't that profitable because of processing problems and an underwhelming market for the metal, which had few uses at the time. So, it took a while before anyone understood how massive the deposits in the Sudbury Basin were or how lucrative they'd become.

Even as the expansion of the railroads promised to make prospecting feasible in previously hard-to-reach areas, the province didn't look like it would ever be home to a robust mining industry. The government hoped to open up the northeastern part of the province, branding it as New Ontario, for farming in the Great Clay Belt as well as providing access to the area's abundant timber and any other resources that might be worth extracting. The politicians tried to convince the private sector to build a railway, but when the businessmen, seeing no money in a line designed to colonize the boondocks, took a hard pass, the province funded the Temiskaming & Northern Ontario Railway itself. The line was to head north from North Bay and make its way to Cochrane, where it would meet the Canadian Pacific Railway's transcontinental line. Eventually, if all went according to the government's plan, it would reach James Bay.

Construction on the first 182 kilometres of the T&NO, to New Liskeard, began in the fall of 1902. Two thousand lakes freckle this part of the country, and near one called Long Lake, workers began noticing some red rocks. Cobalt bloom, the common name for erythrite, is a mineral that varies in colour from pinkish to crimson. Sometimes where there's cobalt bloom, there's silver or nickel, and, in fact, the Algonquin and Ojibwa peoples had begun trading silver from the area at least 2,000 years earlier. But no one paid much attention to the possible presence of the precious metal until early in August of 1903 when a couple of timber cruisers named James McKinley and Ernest Darragh were working ahead of the rest of the crew. The terrain was low, with lots of rocks and swamps, but also plenty of dense mixed forest full of spruce, pine, birch, tamarack and other species. The two men were on the hunt for trees that would make good railroad ties. By reputation, lumbermen make poor prospectors because they keep their eyes on the timber, not the geology. But when McKinley and Darragh spied cobalt bloom near the south end of Long Lake, the half-brothers checked it out. They hefted some loose rocks that seemed heavy and had flakes of a black metal in them. A little washing and scraping exposed a soft, bright metal. McKinley had spent some time prospecting in California, and, remembering what an old forty-niner had told him, he bit into a rock. His teeth left a mark. The lumbermen sent one bag of rocks to the Ontario Bureau of Mines in Toronto and another to a lab at Montreal's McGill University. The former reported that the sample was bismuth and worthless; the latter had better news: the ore was about 12 percent silver.

Between the wait for the assay results and McKinley and Darragh registering their claim improperly, no one knew about their discovery when Fred LaRose made his. A blacksmith with a construction gang grading the railroad bed, he spent his days shoeing horses, sharpening drill steel and repairing equipment. But he had some mining experience and liked to do a little prospecting on the side. The side hustle was fine with Duncan McMartin, the subcontractor who employed LaRose, because he'd get a half interest in anything the blacksmith discovered. In September, LaRose came across a pinkish rock with sharp points. It was unusually heavy for something that was about the size of his hand. He wasn't sure what it was, but he knew enough to be excited. "Boss, I have a good thing," he said to McMartin. "Come with me." And off they went to have a look.

They staked two claims, and the moon-faced LaRose worked them in his spare time. The new claim holders showed samples to Arthur Ferland, who owned the Matabanick Hotel in Haileybury. Ferland thought they were copper, but by late October, the rocks had made their way to Willet Miller, who'd left his job at Queen's University in 1902 to become Ontario's first full-time provincial geologist. Determining that the samples were niccolite, or Kupfer nickel, which is similar in colour to copper, he wanted a closer look at where they'd come from; maybe Sudbury wasn't the only place in the province with a great nickel deposit. Winter was coming, but he didn't want to wait. Miller was in his late thirties, with a thick moustache and beard and a high forehead. He always wore a straw boater hat, even when he took a steamer across the icy water of Lake Temiskaming to Haileybury. The next morning, he walked eight kilometres along the T&NO right-of-way to LaRose's forge. The blacksmith showed him four veins. Three of them, Miller realized immediately, weren't nickel. They were silver—and rich in it. In addition, while focusing on the pink rocks, LaRose had ignored the black ones, some "as large as stove-lids and cannon-balls," strewn about the site. These were the result of blasting the veins, and he'd unwittingly tossed many into the nearby swamp. They were, in fact, tarnished silver nuggets.

Miller was about to head home with the exciting news when he heard from another railway worker. Tom Hébert wanted him to look at something he'd found while on his way to visit another lumberman at the other end of Long Lake. "It was a text-book vein," the geologist later wrote, "it was perfect." Miller left for Toronto armed with dazzling samples from the two sites, including a 4.5-kilogram nugget that was three-quarters pure silver. When he showed the specimens off in Haileybury, people were enthusiastic, but not much happened in Toronto even after he gave interviews to the newspapers. Half a dozen years earlier, two steamships full of miners and gold from the Klondike arrived in Portland and San Francisco and induced people to drop everything and immediately depart on an audacious trek to the Yukon. But news of the Long Lake discoveries didn't create a silver rush right away, even if an overnight train ride from Toronto was a lot cushier than a climb up the Chilkoot or White Pass trail. People weren't as obsessed with silver as they were with gold, so they were less likely to give up good jobs to pursue a dream the way so many had during the Klondike rush. Experienced prospectors remained skeptical about the finds, and many investors had recently been burned on mining deals. Even when Miller displayed his specimens at a Canadian Mining Institute meeting at Toronto's King Edward Hotel in March 1904, they generated muted interest. People were impressed, but specimens did not make a mine.

Not everyone ignored what was going on. William Trethewey was a lawyer and real estate agent in Vancouver who liked to do some prospecting in the Rocky Mountains during his summers. On his way to Cobalt, he stopped in Toronto and talked to Miller. Then he headed north in mid-May. He was an odd sight in the bush: with his starched white shirt with a diamond pin, his rubber boots and his rifle, he looked more like a member of the English gentry on a pheasant hunt than a prospector. But he knew what he was doing. Within a couple of days, he found a deposit that became the Trethewey mine. Then he found a second. It became the Coniagas.

By that time, the dealmaking had already begun. On his way to visit family in Hull, Quebec, LaRose had to wait in Mattawa before catching a train. He walked into the general store and showed his samples to Noah Timmins, who owned the shop with his brother Henry. The two merchants often grubstaked prospectors, but Noah didn't make an offer right away. After some thought, though, he wrote Henry, who was in Montreal, and told him to go to Hull, find LaRose and make a deal. This was not an easy assignment as LaRose was such a common name in the Quebec town, but he eventually found the blacksmith and paid him $3,500 for half of his interest in the claims. The shopkeepers later bought out LaRose completely for $25,000. By that point, lawyer David Dunlap had joined the partnership with the Timminses and the McMartins as payment for his work in a legal battle with some claim jumpers. The McKinley and Darragh claims were soon owned by investors from Rochester, New York, including some directors of Kodak. Ferland and two railway engineers bought Hébert's claims and then sold them to a Standard Oil executive in New York, who turned them into the Nipissing mine, colloquially known as the Big Nip, which would end up being the richest in Cobalt.

The LaRose Mine was the first one to produce silver in 1904, followed by three others: the McKinley-Darragh, the Nipissing and the Coniagas. Prospecting activity increased enough that the province installed a mining recorder in Haileybury to handle new claims. While camping by the LaRose find in June, Miller put up a sign that read "Cobalt Station, T&NO." The name stuck. And the next spring, the dreamers came to Cobalt by the thousands from all over the world, perhaps convinced by the story of the hammer and the fox that anyone could find a silver deposit. A haphazard but bustling mine camp sprang up, and the Bank of Commerce opened a branch, initially in a tent, in July. The following year was even busier, with sixteen mines operating, and Cobalt officially became a town. Eventually, it had an electric streetcar line, a stock market and a professional hockey team, the Cobalt Silver Kings.

Down in Toronto, investors wanted in on the chance to get rich. The Toronto Stock Exchange didn't welcome speculative mining companies, so people bought and sold shares on the Standard Stock and Mining Exchange. Cobalt didn't reach peak production until 1911 when thirty-four mines, all within less than thirteen square kilometres, produced more than thirty-one million ounces of silver. By 1920, when the mining camp was winding down, it had generated almost $200 million worth of the precious metal. And it left a legacy that went far beyond holes in the ground.

The silver boom was Canadian mining's Big Bang, as so many people who'd taken part in it went on to discover, develop or work in mines in other parts of the country. The Haileybury School of Mines, originally located in Cobalt, opened in 1912 and went on to educate generations of engineers, technicians and other workers. The *Northern Miner* newspaper launched in 1915, though it moved to Toronto in 1929. The Ontario government appointed a mining commissioner; introduced new legislation, including the Mines Act of 1906, to promote and regulate the industry; and updated laws concerning stock markets, labour practices and public health.

Cobalt mines also produced dozens of millionaires, including Duncan McMartin and his brother John; Henry and Noah Timmins; David Dunlap; and Arthur Ferland. Many others were financiers or lawyers or engineers. William Trethewey was a rare prospector to reap $1 million from what he'd discovered. None of the men responsible for the first three strikes—McKinley and Darragh, LaRose and Hébert—made the list.

□

The Cobalt silver boom made prospectors excited about what else might be in the northern Ontario ground. Many who'd been part of it, some successfully, most not, kept on looking elsewhere in the region. They included Fred LaRose, who by 1908 was seeking another strike, gold this time, around the Montreal River, which flowed into Lake Temiskaming. Other prospectors explored areas such as Larder Lake, Maple Mountain and Gowganda, sometimes successfully, most often not. But they didn't have to wait too long for the next big rush.

Prospectors brimmed with dreams and hunches but were low on the resources to pursue them. They often sought financing, or grubstakes, from other people in exchange for a piece of the action. William "Pop" Edwards was a Chicago plumbing contractor who liked fishing in northern Ontario. In 1909, he and a Chicago doctor grubstaked an exploration team led by John "Jack" Wilson with $1,000. That was a substantial amount, so Wilson, a T&NO superintendent, went into the bush in May with four other prospectors, including Harry Preston; three Indigenous guides, including Tom Fox; and plenty of gear and supplies. From the railroad, they canoed and portaged to the southwest corner of Porcupine Lake, where they set up a base camp and began a detailed search of the area. The crew found some gold-laden quartz but continued prospecting. Wilson's account of what happened next casts him as the hero, but others have it that Preston was moving through the bush when his foot slipped, stripping some moss from the rock and revealing a wide, gold-flecked quartz vein that, when uncovered, lead to a dome-shaped mound of gold-splattered quartz. Blasting the dome with dynamite revealed a remarkable display of the precious metal that became known as the golden stairway. One person who saw it said, "The gold was in blobs, like candle drippings . . . some of them as large as a cup." Every mine is a freak of nature, but the golden stairway was a freak among freaks.

Evidence of placer gold deposits, such as the ones common in the Klondike, is often flakes or nuggets in nearby creeks. But there's no guarantee of seeing even flecks when searching for igneous or primary deposits, where the gold can be so much finer and more diffuse that it's microscopic. According to an old prospectors' adage, "Quartz is the mother of gold." But of course, not all quartz contains gold and not all gold is in quartz. Prospectors look for rocks or rock formations that might host gold, and, if they're lucky, they might spy a few tiny flakes or grains of the precious metal, though even that doesn't ensure commercial quantities of it. More often, they must wait for an assay to reveal if any gold is present and at what concentration. But the area around Porcupine Lake offered visible gold, also known as free gold, in several spots.

Benny Hollinger was the next person to find some. He'd joined the Cobalt rush in 1905 and continued prospecting in the Temiskaming region while also working as a barber in Haileybury. Armed with a forty-five-dollar grubstake from John McMahon, a Matabanick Hotel bartender, the twenty-four-year-old took off for Porcupine with Alex Gillies, who had a hundred-dollar grubstake from another prospector. The Wilson party had staked all the land around the golden stairway, but Hollinger and Gillies went northwest and saw gold. They staked seven claims, including one for an ailing prospector. But with different backers, they couldn't share the other six. They flipped a coin and Hollinger won the ones that proved to be the most valuable.

As in Cobalt, the origin story included a third big discovery. Alexander Oliphant, a factory worker unhappy in his marriage, split for Canada in 1903 and, taking his mother's maiden name, started a new life as Sandy McIntyre. The red-bearded Glaswegian spent some time on a railroad construction crew, but mostly he liked prospecting and was good at it. He also liked to drink and make friends, and he was good at those things, too. He was in Gowganda when he heard about the Porcupine. On their way in, McIntyre and Hans Buttner ran into Hollinger and Gillies, who were heading out to register their claims. After seeing the latter pair's gold-rich quartz samples, the Scotsman and the German staked two claims. They'd planned to stake more, but that night their tent caught fire, putting an end to their expedition. Buttner turned his claims into a quick ten grand and took off for the United States; McIntyre hung around to work his.

Prospectors rushed into the region. By mid-December, 200 men had left Haileybury for the Porcupine. Some would be among those who staked 2,000 claims over the next three months; others had gone to work existing claims. The moneymen also showed up. Wilson managed to parlay his leadership of the exploration team into a director position with the Dome Mine Company. But the other prospectors did what prospectors usually do: without the financial wherewithal to develop their properties, they sold their claims cheap.

As soon as Noah Timmins, who'd moved to Montreal after his success in Cobalt, heard about gold in the Porcupine, he jumped on a train. He tried to buy McMahon's interest. The bartender, who'd sold half his share for fifty-five dollars before Hollinger had found anything, wasn't sure he wanted to sell, and if he did, he was looking for a lot of money. Eventually, he made a deal with Noah and Henry Timmins for $330,000. Later, Hollinger sold his share to a syndicate that included the Timmins brothers, the McMartin brothers and David Dunlap for $165,000. The Hollinger Mine would become the most productive in the region. The accounts of how McIntyre let his claims go vary in the details but not in the end result. One version has it that in the spring of 1910, Ferland gave the prospector a $500 deposit on an eleven-day option to buy him out for $80,000. But after that deal fell through, he made one with Weldon "Weldy" Young. A former star with the Ottawa Hockey Club, he'd moved to the Klondike in 1899 and worked as a mining recorder and miner, among other jobs, before helping organize Dawson City's failed Stanley Cup challenge in 1905. Young paid McIntyre $125 for a quarter share or, according to another version, $300 for a half share of three claims. Either way, Young soon flipped his purchase for $300,000. McIntyre sold another one-eighth interest to Jim Hughes for $25. Letting the claims go for far less than they were worth was one of many bad deals in the prospector's life, especially since the McIntyre Mine became the third richest in the region. "I have always been lucky—for others," he said later, "unlucky for myself."

Several other mines opened in the area, but none surpassed the output of the Dome, Hollinger and McIntyre properties. Initially, many people settled in Golden City and Pottsville, also known as Porcupine City, at the north end of the lake. Some Pottsville buildings were constructed of logs, others of boards clad in black and red tar paper or, in some cases, tin. A few people lived in tents. "It is a typical mining town, where there has been a rich strike—men hurrying to and fro with eager, absorbed-looking faces not exactly happy, but all hopeful," according to Edith Tyrrell. The wife of a prominent Geological Survey of Canada man, she'd visited in January 1911 and wrote about it in the *Globe*. The T&NO's decision to run a branch line south of the lake led to the growth of South Porcupine near the Dome Mine. Trains started reaching the town on July 1, 1911, but two weeks later, a forest fire swept through the area. The massive blaze killed at least seventy-three people while destroying South Porcupine, Pottsville and Cochrane and doing considerable damage to Golden City and Kelso.

Noah Timmins, who was worried about housing for the Hollinger Mine's employees and their families, had already begun work on establishing a new settlement just northwest of the mine, and the T&NO reached it a month after the fire. By Labour Day, the Timmins Townsite Company began auctioning off lots for private development. But because the mining company wanted an orderly place that would serve its purposes, it built the Goldfields Hotel, bunkhouses for single workers and rudimentary houses of four or five rooms, which were available to married employees with families on a rent-to-own basis. In 1912, the town of Timmins incorporated, began adding cement sidewalks and suffered its first, but not last, housing shortage. The nearby destroyed towns rebuilt themselves, though Golden City, renamed Porcupine, didn't fare well because it wasn't on the railway line. Close to the Dome Mine, South Porcupine thrived, soon expanding to include Pottsville. Eventually, though, Timmins emerged as the largest community in the region.

The legacy of the Porcupine gold rush also includes the birth of two companies—Dome Mines Company and Consolidated Hollinger Gold Mines—that would grow into giant corporations with head offices in Toronto. Among the prospectors, only Wilson did well, having wisely kept an interest in the Dome Mine and serving as a company director. The other two men credited with the original finds had mines named after them but failed to make millions. Neither did Preston, Gillies and Buttner. But northern Ontario's third great rush would finally make a prospector fabulously wealthy.

By the time Harry Oakes reached Dawson City, most ground along the gold-bearing creeks was already staked. The twenty-three-year-old had grown up in Maine, where he'd graduated from prep school and Bowdoin College, but in 1897, he left to join the Klondike gold rush. After staying in the Yukon long enough to get a crash course in mining, he tried his luck in Alaska. Then he made his way to Australia's Kalgoorlie goldfields and eventually landed in Nevada, where he prospected in Death Valley for several years. That's where he was when he heard about gold in northern Ontario.

On his way through Toronto, he visited the Bureau of Mines, where he could learn about the geology of the region, what had already been staked and what claims might soon be open. After boarding a T&NO train, Oakes ended up at Swastika on June 19, 1911. One story contends the conductor booted him off at the small mining settlement about eighty kilometres north of Cobalt because he had neither a ticket nor money. More likely, Oakes knew he was too late for the Porcupine rush and was intrigued by the look of the geology around Kirkland Lake, a few kilometres from the train line. After studying the rock formations, Oakes had a prospector's hunch that veins of gold ran under the lake. Others operated by staking claims, selling them for whatever they could get and then using the proceeds to look for more good ground. But Oakes wasn't interested in doing that just to make a few thousand dollars when he could make several million by developing his own mine. Although no one believed any prospector could pull that off, he was determined. "You wait," he told one doubter, "I'll show you."

The area had seen a lot of staking in the winter of 1906–07 and, later, after the discovery of two modest gold properties at Swastika. But prospectors couldn't just sit on claims; they had to work them. At the time, that meant putting in thirty eight-hour days within three months of registering claims and then sixty days in each of the next two years and ninety days in the third year. Prospectors who failed to do this "assessment work" forfeited their claims. Oakes saw that some claims were already available, and others would soon revert to the Crown. He did have some competition, though. Bill Wright, a former English butcher, and his brother-in-law Ed Hargreaves had worked in Cobalt as painters. But because prospecting seemed like more fun, they put down their brushes and headed for the bush. They'd spied some flecks of gold and done some staking on the east side of Kirkland Lake.

Oakes set about accumulating claims, mostly on the down-low so no one would notice what he was up to—or more to the point, where he was up to it. This may or may not have been necessary since no one seemed to care about what Wright and Hargreaves were doing. Collecting a lot of claims wasn't as simple as staking them because of the limit of three per licence per year. But the way around that was to pay another prospector to stake and register claims and then transfer them. Oakes used this tactic to acquire one at the south end of the lake that would prove to be particularly valuable. Meanwhile, he waited for others to become available. He made trips to the closest mining recorder's office to check the status of claims he wanted, but that was in Matheson, four dollars away on the T&NO. Despite his comfortable upper-middle-class upbringing, money continued to be a problem.

Around eight o'clock on the evening of January 7, 1912, he approached the four Tough brothers in the Swastika Hotel. Railroad contractors from Sudbury, they did some prospecting on the side, and, living up to their last name, they were big boys, strong and hard-working. The tightly wound Oakes was shorter, but he too was strong and hard-working. Although he liked to tell tales of hair-raising experiences during his wanderings around the globe in search of gold, he didn't drink much and wasn't big on socializing or making friends. Besides, years in the bush had made his manners rough and his opinions dogmatic. At some point, though, he realized he needed partners if his dreams were to come true. And if he must have partners, the Toughs would do. Explaining that he knew about some valuable claims that were about to lapse, he offered the brothers a half interest in return for the staking fees and help doing the staking. When they asked when the claims would be free, he reached for his watch and said, "In about four hours." Tom and George Tough headed into the bush on snowshoes with Oakes. The cold was bitter and the snow was deep, but the moon was bright enough to work under, though they carried tin cans with candles in them, also known as bugs. The three men finished around dawn and built a fire. That's when Bill Wright showed up. He was too late; the coveted claims now belonged to Oakes and the Tough brothers.

When Jack and Bob Tough made it to the site, the men set to work, and after three days of digging through snow, ice and frozen ground, they exposed some gold-flecked rocks. Other prospectors finally took notice. With so much ground already staked, there was no stampede like the ones Cobalt and the Porcupine had seen, but in the twelve months ending in July 1912, prospectors registered 1,000 claims. Along with the prospectors came, as usual, the moneymen. Clem Foster, a mining engineer who'd developed a successful property in Cobalt, bought into the Tough-Oakes Mine.

The Tough brothers and Oakes made for good partners. They had experience in the northern bush; he had extensive prospecting experience. And while none of them had much money, the Toughs were well known in the area and trusted enough that they could buy on credit from stores and outfitters. Meanwhile, shortly after Wright and Hargreaves had staked the claims, the latter had sold his interest to Weldy Young. Then Oakes, who'd met Wright for the first time around that early morning fire with the Toughs, went into partnership with the former butcher. But the alliances with the Toughs and with Wright didn't mean Oakes had abandoned his goal of developing his own mine on his own claims. He remained single-minded about that, and his hunch about gold under the lake had become a conviction. Uninterested in sharing a mine, he sold out of Tough-Oakes and focused on his own claims. The problem, once again, was money. In Cobalt, the ore was close to the surface and easy to extract; mining at Kirkland Lake required a lot more work. Oakes had no choice but to take his Lake Shore Mine public. Finally, in 1918, a year after discovering a second, more lucrative, vein, the company paid its first dividend. Many of the shareholders were family members who'd supported him through his lean years.

Eventually, Kirkland Lake had seven mines. Although that was fewer than in the Porcupine, their ore was richer, so the area produced much more gold. One of the other lucrative mines was the Teck-Hughes, a deposit Sandy McIntyre found after Jim Hughes hired the Scotsman to do some prospecting on claims he'd purchased. Hughes and his brother were so appreciative that they rewarded McIntyre with 150,000 shares, which were later worth $1.5 million. Unfortunately, the prospector had sold them for $4,500 long before that. When geologist Arnold Hoffman asked him what he'd done with the money, the Scotsman replied, "Why, Oi spent it on the drink an' sech. What's monaie for? Easy come, easy go, thet's Sandy McIntyre."

Wright was much better with his money. Among the things he did was buy Toronto's *Globe* newspaper. Then he financed the purchase of the *Mail and Empire* and merged the two dailies, creating the *Globe and Mail*. But Lake Shore turned out to be one of the richest gold mines in the world. By the time of his unsolved murder in 1943, Sir Harry Oakes was reputed to be the wealthiest person in the British Commonwealth and had moved to the Bahamas to avoid paying taxes. Despite all the money he made, his greatest and rarest accomplishment was finding a mineral deposit and turning it into a major mine without giving up control.

The Oakes story was just a small part of a larger, more consequential one. In less than a decade, the Cobalt silver boom, followed by the Porcupine and Kirkland Lake gold rushes, had transformed Ontario from unpromising mineral territory to the home of a flourishing mining industry—and launched Toronto as a major mining finance centre.

CHAPTER FOUR

QUEEN BEE

Viola MacMillan had been so successful selling houses on the side that she decided to leave her job as a stenographer at Rodd, Wigle & McHugh to start her own real estate agency. The move turned out to be ill-timed. By the end of the 1920s, Windsor was no longer booming, and then the Great Depression followed the stock market crash of October 1929. George hadn't had a job in a while, so they moved to London, Ontario, where she sold Christmas cards wholesale. They kept the place in Windsor and filled it with boarders while taking in more roomers in the home they rented in London. She also tried to sell houses on the side, but that proved a tough go.

Her new idea was to prospect from spring to fall and then return to London to sell cards and real estate. But she needed financing. Syndicates had become a popular way to get a grubstake. Investors bought units that could be converted into company shares if a prospector found something worth developing. Sweat equity was typically worth a third of the shares. Units might sell for ten dollars, so for investors it was a bit like buying a lottery ticket, if lotteries had been legal at the time. The MacMillans liked some gold claims they'd staked in Bowman Township, near Matheson, so Viola created the Bowman-Matheson Gold Syndicate.

Once she'd sold enough units in her syndicate to pay for a season of prospecting, she decided to go. The problem was George had finally found work at a brokerage house. He was a customer's man, another name for a stock market salesman. But she was determined to be a full-time prospector. "I'm leaving for the north. If you want to come along with me, that's OK," she told him. "If not, I'll be OK alone."

George left his new job, and then he and Viola loaded up their Model T jalopy and headed for the bush. Although her friends thought she was crazy and told her so, she would not be dissuaded. "I'd far sooner sit and listen to a prospector all night than go dancing or go to a movie," said MacMillan, who loved dancing, a few years later. "Mining is my life. It's on the books for me." That expression—"on the books for me"—was one she used a lot.

Going prospecting for gold wasn't a crazy move during the Depression. Just about every industry suffered during the Dirty Thirties. That included mining, as most mineral prices collapsed. In Sudbury, for example, several mines shut down, the population fell and the city defaulted on its bonds in 1934. The rare exception to all the bad news was gold. With the price of the precious metal set at $20.67 an ounce, there were jobs available in the Timmins and Kirkland Lake areas. But only for people with mining experience, and most of the people who joined the employment rush to northern Ontario had none. The province produced $33.6 million worth of gold in 1929. That climbed to $70.9 million in 1934. After President Franklin Delano Roosevelt raised the guaranteed price to US$35 per ounce that year, annual gold production in Ontario reached $122.6 million by 1940. Forty new mines opened in the province during the decade and at least a dozen reopened. Prospecting also increased. While there were still no guarantees, the high price of gold meant the chances that someone would want to develop a new discovery were higher and the threshold for economic ore was lower. In addition, many people turned to prospecting because they had nothing else to do. That meant Viola and George weren't the only ones headed to the bush.

Few, if any, of the others were women. Viola was a rarity in the first half of the twentieth century. Among the others, perhaps the most famous, at least in her day, was Caroline Mayben Flower. A pianist and composer who'd studied in Europe, she was a music teacher and high society manqué in Manhattan until she faced much-publicized petty larceny charges. When her doctor advised her to spend more time outdoors, he was thinking of a quiet spell in the Adirondacks. Instead, she began to divide her time between New York and northern Ontario, where she reinvented herself as "the Lady Prospector." When she first arrived in Cobalt in 1906, the thirty-seven-year-old mostly stayed at the Matabanick Hotel in nearby Haileybury, which was a far more refined town. After the claims she owned north of there didn't amount to any-thing, she staked claims in the Gowganda area before joining the rush to the Porcupine in early 1910.

Flower, who regularly fed less-than-reliable stories about herself to the newspapers, claimed to be a graduate of the Columbia School of Mines (in fact, she had taken a mineralogy course at Barnard College, the women's liberal arts school associated with Columbia University). Still, while many mining men initially scoffed at the idea that this slight, big-city woman dressed in a cowboy hat and boots could hack it in the bush, she was tough. She staked numerous claims, selling some while keeping others and doing the necessary assessment work on them. Along with helping to build her own log cabin, she proved to be a good shot, taking down deer and bear for her food. One night, when a black bear came by her cabin, she calmly shooed it away instead of killing it because she already had enough meat. One newspaper called her "the golden-haired heroine of the Porcupine."

Early in 1913, after time in New York, where she'd taken more geology classes, she came back with a vintage lute, something to play during the evenings in her cabin on the Mattagami River. But the days were for mining, not music. After a stop in Cobalt, she continued north with steel, other provisions and hired men to work her group of six claims next to a gold discovery in the Cripple Creek mining district, west of Porcupine Lake. She didn't have the same luck on her ground and soon a decline in her health led to a permanent return to New York, where she died in 1917.

Another woman who took to prospecting was Mabel Fetterly. Like MacMillan, she'd grown up in the Muskoka area. She moved to Swastika in October 1911, a few months after Harry Oakes arrived. Her late sister's four children, now her responsibility, and her mother joined her. The next year, she paid five dollars for a prospector's licence and learned the trade from Hiriam Tobico, an Indigenous man from the southern part of the province who'd come north before she did. Within a year, Fetterly had sold a claim she'd staked in Playfair Township for $6,000.

When she wasn't looking for gold, she drove a horse-drawn sleigh between Swastika and the Argonaut Mine, chopped wood to sell, worked as a camp cook, trapped with Tobico and hunted. After he gave her a rifle for Christmas one year, she became a superb shot, once taking down a moose so large that the antler spread was more than 160 centimetres. Harry Oakes bought the head for $200, had it mounted and hung it on a wall of the magnificent chateau he'd had built in Kirkland Lake. Known for smoking a clay pipe and always wearing men's clothing, she was brash, plain-spoken and proudly independent, but was well-liked in the community.

Fetterly and Tobico were best friends and long-time prospecting partners. Although they never made a discovery to rival Oakes's success, they did make money staking and selling claims, notably three properties that went into development but not into production: the Queen LeBel, the Tobico and the Cambro-Kirkland, though the Tobico later became part of the Upper Canada Mine. And Fetterly continued prospecting well into her sixties.

Roza Brown had a shorter career in the bush, but it worked out well for her. Originally from Hungary, she showed up in the Cobalt area sometime around 1906, possibly after stays in Paris and London and several Canadian towns. She ran a bakery and lived with Lieutenant Louis Brown, a British Boer War veteran. He may or may not have been her husband, though she took his name. Either way, the relationship didn't last long because he turned out to be an indolent drunkard. Known as Rosie or Rosa, she found work as a cook on T&NO railway trains, and many of the passengers she made meals for were prospectors. Around 1910, she settled in Swastika, where she opened a bakeshop and laundry. After hearing so many tales from mining men, she decided to give prospecting a try. She may not have looked the part: a short, middle-aged woman usually in a long gingham dress, apron, beaver coat, high rubber boots and a man's peaked cap. But what stood out were her idiosyncratic ideas about prospecting. "Gold has a mind of its own," she believed. "Gold is a woman. All the gold in the world is waiting for just one thing, for the right man to find it."

Or the right woman. Her theories aside, Brown had no experience. She staked claims beside those of some respected prospectors, perhaps acting on their tips. Unlike the pros, though, she didn't trust that registration with the mining recorder provided enough security. So, even as she continued to operate the bakery and laundry, she slept in a tent on the ground she'd staked to ward off claim jumpers. Her ground fetched $21,000 or $40,000, depending on who's telling the tale, from the company that would later open the Sylvanite Mine on the neighbouring claims. She invested the money in real estate, including in Kirkland Lake, correctly anticipating where the main streets would go.

The subject of many local legends, some of which may even have been true, Brown was completely bonkers about animals and the royal family. A clamorous pack of canines accompanied her everywhere, including to the movie theatre. Even as cats, chickens and other creatures shared her hovel, she regretted that her home wasn't big enough for horses. In a move that managed to combine her obsessions, she once sent a black lamb to a young Princess Margaret. Behind her ramshackle boarding house, Brown rented out tar paper shacks to bootleggers and prostitutes, which was lucrative for her and convenient for her tenants, many of them mining men. Though unable to read or write, she possessed "an inexhaustible vocabulary of higher blasphemies and the lower four-lettered words" and delighted in attacking anyone who displeased her, especially the town officials with whom she clashed over taxes and orders to fix up her dilapidated buildings. Few residents had sympathy for her battles. When she ran for council in 1935, she finished fourteenth, ahead of only two other candidates. Still, her reputation for mouthiness worked in her favour when the Ontario Court of Appeal overturned a $5,800 award in a libel suit against her, noting that she was "much given to expressing her mind publicly on all sorts of occasions and on all sorts of things."

Like Fetterly, Brown was fond of Oakes, something that certainly wasn't true of everyone in a community where his orneriness and success made him a polarizing figure. She'd met the uncouth American when he first arrived in Swastika, often feeding him when he was too broke to feed himself, and remained fiercely loyal to him. According to some accounts, she continued to buy and sell shares in mining properties and grubstake the rare prospector she trusted and may have been one of Oakes's backers when he was still trying to raise enough money to turn his claims into the Lake Shore Mine. She left behind an estate worth $75,000, nowhere near the million bucks some locals thought she was worth, but not bad for 1947.

□

Fanciful legends, such as the one about Fred LaRose throwing a hammer at a fox, make finding a mine seem more like luck than anything else. Even stories that may be true—such as the one about how Harry Preston stumbled, scraped moss and revealed a gold mine—suggest the secret to successful prospecting is good fortune rather than expertise. But Preston discovered gold because he was looking in the right place and was alert enough and experienced enough to understand what he was seeing. Still, given how many prospectors dream of a big strike and how few ever find anything of significance, chance is certainly a factor. They often talk about Lady Luck and put a lot of stock in intuition and hunches. That's part of the charm of a life in the bush. In *Not for Gold Alone: The Memoirs of a Prospector*, geologist Franc Joubin argues that there are "capricious" forces at work in the creation of rock formations. "Nature is not entirely predictable," he writes. "If it were there would be little romance in geology and prospecting."

Prospectors don't need to be trained geologists, but geology is part of the job. Experience definitely counts for something, and being tenacious is essential. Oakes was indefatigable, rarely doing anything but working, except to eat and sleep, until he found and began to develop his Lake Shore Mine. Oakes was also obstinate, which probably helped. Prospecting is all about looking for anomalies. But the first step is deciding where to look. That means unstaked ground where the presence of minerals seems likely. One source of information is the Geological Survey of Canada. Founded in 1842, the nation's oldest scientific agency maps the country and produces reports on its mineral resources.

After identifying likely ground, it's time to see what's there. Tromping through the bush is not the same as a walk in the woods. Well, it can be on some days, in some places, for a little while at least. But most of the time in northern Ontario, it means trekking long distances while fighting through thick alders, trudging through bogs, plodding up and down steep hills, climbing over deadfall and jagged rocks, skirting around cliffs and, occasionally, strolling in glades. Then there's the weather, which may be wet or scorching or frigid. Barbarous blackflies rule in spring and then the merciless mosquitos take over for summer.

And, of course, a prospector needs to know what to look for. Anomalies worth checking out include faults, shears and folds in exposed rock. Before the development of reliable geophysical instruments allowed mining people to "see" beneath the layer of soil and loose rock, known as overburden, covering the bedrock, rock outcrops were the best place to look for minerals. A quartz vein was always worth checking for visible gold. Discolouration on exposed rock could be minerals, sometimes valuable ones or associated with valuable ones. Cobalt bloom, or erythrite, might indicate the presence of nickel or silver, as it did west of Lake Temiskaming in 1903. And some prospectors claimed they could smell sulphides—which often contain valuable minerals—or had trained a dog to do so.

Once someone with a valid five-dollar mining licence found evidence of minerals, the next step was to stake a claim. A claim is forty acres and staking one was straightforward enough. Start by erecting the No. 1 post at the northeast corner by chopping down a tree and cutting a metre-and-a-half length. Use an axe to square the sides at one end and stick the other end in the ground or prop it up with rocks. On the squared end, write the required information, including the staker's name, mining licence number, date and time. Then, using a compass, walk directly south. Periodically blaze trees by slashing a bit of bark off with an axe; where there are no available trees to mark, cut a sapling and create a picket and stick it in the ground to mark the trail. Pace off 1,320 feet, or a quarter of a mile, until reaching the southeast corner of the forty-acre square. That's where post No. 2 goes. Repeat the process until reaching the southwest corner, where No. 3 goes. Post No. 4 marks the northwest corner. (Today, staking a claim is as simple as going online and clicking.)

The next step was to register the claim with the district's mining recorder and pay a fee. Ontario mining regulations—including the number of claims one prospector could register, the cost and the required amount of assessment work—changed often over the years. By the 1960s, licence holders could stake up to ninety claims a year, but no more than eighteen in any one of the province's fourteen mining divisions. Prospectors had to register them within thirty-one days of staking them and then they had six months to hammer numbered metal claim tags into the posts.

Activities that counted as assessment work included everything from collecting samples, removing overburden and cutting lines through the bush to prepare for geophysical exploration all the way up to drilling and sinking shafts. On Black Jack MacMillan's claims, Viola spent a lot of her time trenching. Using picks and shovels, prospectors dig trenches to remove the overburden and reveal a stretch of bedrock that they can study for signs of mineralization.

Most of the time, claims turned out to be "moose pasture," as mining people sometimes called worthless ground. But when a prospector found something promising, rumours started circulating, and others rushed to obtain nearby property on the theory that where there's one deposit, there may be many. That was certainly true in Cobalt, the Porcupine and, to a lesser extent, in Kirkland Lake. And all the claim-stakers around Timmins in 1964 sure hoped the Texas Gulf ore body would be the first of many. Sometimes these "tie-on" claims turned out to be more lucrative than the discovery claim.

□

When they first went north, the MacMillans struggled to make a living, as many prospectors do. Without enough money to buy sleeping bags, they made beds by piling pine boughs on the floor of their tent. They staked claims and tried to sell them, but at times they were flat broke and survived on their dreams, cadged meals from other prospectors and, one summer, a steady diet of onions. One source of free meals was Art Wilson, the man whose tales had enchanted Viola on her first night in the bush. Around another campfire, he told a story about how he and some friends had been prospecting on eight claims they'd staked west of Kirkland Lake. After finding a little gold in a quartz outcrop, they attracted some investors from Buffalo who were willing to fund further exploration on the property. The catch was the prospectors had to put the claims up as a guarantee they'd do the work. Once Wilson's group finished, the Buffalo moneymen would pay them and keep the claims. But the Americans pulled a fast one, taking title to the claims without paying the prospectors.

Hearing this, Viola became angry. "They can't do that to you, Art."

"Well, they've done it."

She didn't need to be a former law office stenographer to know he'd been swindled, but her experience at Rodd, Wigle & McHugh meant she knew what to do about it. Deciding to fight for her friend and mentor, MacMillan made the long drive down to Toronto, hired a lawyer and took the case to the Mining Court of Ontario. But the lawyer was clueless about mining, so after the first day of the hearing, she fired him and hired Kelso Roberts, who'd practised in Cobalt and Kirkland Lake before moving to Toronto. The judge ruled in favour of the prospectors, and though they never saw any money, they did get the claims back.

Winning the case was less valuable for Wilson and his friends than it was for Viola. They discovered the amount of gold on the claims was negligible. She discovered a new way to be involved in mining and help prospectors. Soon she realized she had a knack for the promotion side of the business, including buying and selling claims, raising money for exploration projects and creating syndicates to develop properties. There are two mining industries and MacMillan wanted to be part of both. One is earthbound and involves finding ore bodies by banging rocks, staking claims, drilling and, in the unlikely event that everything works out, taking the minerals out of the ground to be milled and processed. The other is a more abstract business that involves raising money—or, as the MacMillans liked to call it, "rustling up the dough"—to fund exploration as well as the buying and selling of claims and companies, often in complicated financial transactions. Although the two industries can seem completely different, they are connected and symbiotic. Prospectors and promoters are both risk-takers, and the rewards can be substantial, especially for the latter. In Cobalt, the Porcupine and Kirkland Lake, most of those who found deposits sold their claims to people with the kind of money necessary to develop a mine or someone who'd taken advantage of their need for money. The most notable exception, Harry Oakes, served as an impossible role model. Eventually, though, more and more prospectors realized they could sell their claims for both money and shares, or even a percentage of the mine's output.

Prospectors and promoters are usually two different people. Even Oakes, despite his stunning triumph with the Lake Shore Mine, never really understood the stock market. Consequently, he didn't invest much of his fortune in stocks, instead opting for real estate, something he could touch and understand. And plenty of promoters knew little about geology. MacMillan began as a prospector, and continued to spend time looking for a motherlode, but she turned out to be much more successful as a promoter, though she hated that term, preferring mine developer. She rented an office in Timmins and started MacMillan Securities in June 1933. The timing was good. The Porcupine was down to just three mines—Hollinger, Dome and McIntyre—but that was about to change, and MacMillan was available to hammer out deals between prospectors and investors, create syndicates and sell shares for companies with properties they wanted to develop.

Timmins was one of several communities the Porcupine gold camp had fathered. After the 1911 fire that destroyed or damaged so many towns in the area, Schumacher grew up around the McIntyre Mine, while the rebuilt South Porcupine was near the Dome Mine. But the town Noah Timmins founded near the Hollinger Mine in the aftermath of the fire became the largest with a population of 14,200 by 1931, and that would double in the next decade. Men still outnumbered women, though not as dramatically as before. After the First World War, a housing shortage made it hard for Hollinger to attract new workers. The company responded by building more single-family homes on the west side of town. Known as Hollinger Houses, they were clad in red or green tar paper. Most Timmins residents, many from Italy or other European countries, owed their livelihood, in one way or another, to gold. Despite the Depression, the 1934 increase in the guaranteed price of gold helped keep the local unemployment rate low because the mines could suddenly profitably extract lower-grade ore. The mining workforce in the region reached 9,200 before the start of the Second World War.

MacMillan wasn't the only person in Timmins whose goal of making a fortune wasn't just an idle daydream. The son of a Toronto barber, Roy Thomson was already in his mid-thirties when he moved to North Bay in 1928 and sold automotive parts, refrigerators, washing machines and radio sets. A large, amiable man with a big smile, he was always shabbily dressed in patched pants and a raincoat and fedora, even in the dead of winter. But he worked hard, travelling as far as Sault Sainte Marie to the west, Val d'Or to the east and Hearst to the north. The invention of the batteryless radio by Edward Rogers in 1925 promised to make the sets something every home must have, and Thomson sold them on a rent-to-own basis. The problem in northern Ontario, though, was that his customers had trouble tuning into anything but static. The solution was to buy a second-hand, fifty-watt transmitter and launch North Bay radio station CFCH in 1931, then add CKGB in Timmins and CJKL in Kirkland Lake.

CKGB operated from the second floor of an old wooden building on Spruce Street, across from a brothel and above a weekly newspaper that had failed as *The Citizen* and had recently been resurrected as *The Press*. In 1934, Thomson bought it for $200 down and twenty-eight promissory notes for monthly payments of $200. Under his undercapitalized and stingy ownership, the publication was thinner and more eccentric than its more established rival, the *Porcupine Advance*, but he managed to turn it into a daily. When the increased frequency meant the *Daily Press* didn't have enough copy to go around the ads, it ran some stories twice. Thomson was still so broke that he once spent a night on the floor of the MacMillans' hotel room. Despite his determination to become rich, he was surprisingly cheerful, and Viola liked his sense of humour and his hearty laugh. Later, she would see his young son, Ken, on the street shivering in the cold as he hawked the latest edition. Thomson went on to build an international media empire that included 180 newspapers, 160 magazines and twenty-seven radio and television stations.

Viola and George had their own lean years, but by 1934, they felt financially secure enough to order steak without a side of guilt. Even though MacMillan was committed to establishing her new business, she didn't spend all her time in her Timmins office. She still went into the bush to look for gold dressed in a mackinaw jacket, breeches and high-top boots. That same year, Viola and George and his brother Mark were working on the Bowman Township claims when she had to drive down to Toronto to handle some business. On her way back, she picked up a hitchhiker. He was about eighteen and said he was looking for adventure. MacMillan, who already had an evangelical zeal for prospecting, asked him if he wanted to give it a try. What she didn't know was that the teenager had just recovered from a bout of pneumonia that had put him the hospital. If she had, she'd have explained that spending time in a tent when the weather was cold and rainy was unwise. Sure enough, he was soon sick again. They put the shivering kid in the canoe and paddled five kilometres to the car, then drove him to the hospital in Kirkland Lake.

By the time the patient was comfortably in the care of the doctors and nurses, it was early evening, and the prospectors took the opportunity to replenish their supplies at the general store just before it closed. The owner turned out to be someone Mark MacMillan had gone to school with. Excited to see his old friend, the shopkeeper told the prospectors about how a Hislop Township farmer had just found gold while plowing his field. A small gold rush was underway. Before dawn the next morning, the three MacMillans were in the bush. Over the next few weeks, they went on a staking bee, amassing close to fifty claims near Ramore, a station on the T&NO. Viola's part in it led another prospector to dub her the Queen Bee. She liked the nickname and it stuck.

☐

At first, Viola spent most of the year in Timmins or in the bush, but she returned to London in the winter, where she continued to sell Christmas cards. Then, in 1935, she began renting a small office, "not much more than a cubbyhole," for MacMillan Securities on Bay Street in Toronto, though she was still much better known around Timmins. Meanwhile, she, George and Mark were thrilled to learn that some of the claims they'd staked in Hislop Township were adjacent to twelve claims where Golden Arrow Mining was hoping to develop a mine. The news let the MacMillans know where to focus their efforts. A decrepit old stable on their claims would serve as a place to camp while prospecting. Viola was cleaning it out when Paul McDermott, the veteran prospector who'd staked the Golden Arrow ground, came by and asked her to look at another property. He knew she was involved in the financing side of mining and hoped she might want to take an option out on it. She liked what she saw enough to return the next day with a geologist. He wasn't keen on it, so she passed. Many years later, in 1988, the Holt-McDermott gold mine opened on the property.

While she missed out on that ore body, MacMillan soon began a decades-long involvement with Golden Arrow. Promising results from exploration work on the Hislop property had led to a diamond drilling program, but then the owners ran out of money. That's when another friend of the MacMillans stepped in. Jim Bartleman had been in Cobalt during the silver boom and then moved on to the Porcupine before the fire of 1911. He was a businessman with political ambitions who started *The Press* because he was unhappy with the *Porcupine Advance*. When he tired of losing money on the paper, he sold it to Thomson. He later served one term as mayor but lost his re-election bid after his former paper backed a rival. In the autumn of 1935, Bartleman and a couple of his friends took control of Golden Arrow. They appointed George MacMillan to the board and made Viola the company's secretary. Needing money to continue the exploration efforts, they also commissioned MacMillan Securities to sell a million shares at fifteen cents, and then, the next year, put together another offering at twenty-five cents. But Viola didn't just sell shares to investors, she bought some for herself. Eventually, she'd accumulated so many that she controlled the company, which she renamed Golden Arrow Mines in 1938.

By then, MacMillan had already swung her first lucrative deal. She first met William Swallow, a Toronto builder, when he showed up in Timmins on a wintery day early in 1935. He offered to option some of MacMillan's claims. Although Viola admitted that she and George had spent all summer working them and hadn't found a thing, he offered her a hundred dollars right away and $5,000 in March. That sounded like a small fortune to her.

Swallow and a couple of friends controlled the Porcupine Quartet Gold Syndicate, which had leased four four-claim parcels on veterans' lots in Whitney Township, a little east of Timmins. Three of the parcels were near the Hollinger, Dome and McIntyre Porcupine gold mines. The fourth, called Poulet-Veteran, was adjacent to a property where the Pamour Mine was under development. After J.H. Cecil (Ike) Waite, a Toronto mining engineer, made a deal with the Quartet syndicate for an option on the Poulet-Vet claims in April 1935, Swallow asked MacMillan Securities to sell the unsold units in the syndicate. Waite's interest was enough for MacMillan to double the price to twenty dollars when she started running ads in the *Northern Miner* in May. What no one knew was that Waite had negotiated the purchase on behalf of Noranda. The incipient mining giant's desire to explore Quartet's claims was logical given that it had just added a controlling interest in Pamour to its growing portfolio.

The story of Noranda's rapid emergence as a major force in the industry begins with a prospector and a hunch. After working in a Cobalt mine and prospecting for gold in Gowganda, the Porcupine and Kirkland Lake, Edmund Horne had made a bit of money but no great discoveries. Figuring it made no sense that "all the good geology would quit at the Ontario border," Horne canoed into the wilderness of northwestern Quebec for the first time in 1911. Five years later, George MacMillan was living in New Liskeard when an Indigenous man showed up in town with some gold samples from Rouyn Township in Quebec. No one paid much attention to him or his rocks, but Edmund Horne kept making prospecting trips to the region and in 1926 found gold on the north shore of Lake Osisko, 200 kilometres of tough paddling and rough portaging from Lake Temiskaming. The Indigenous man's samples that no one cared about had been from the same spot. Horne and his twelve partners in the Tremoy Syndicate optioned the claims to the Thomson-Chadbourne Syndicate from the United States for $320,000 and 10 percent of the operating company of any mine the property begat. Even before making that deal, the Americans had hired James Murdoch, a Toronto mining lawyer, to do some legal work. To protect the members of the syndicate from liability, he drafted the incorporation papers for an exploration company called Noranda Mines in 1922. He later agreed to serve as the first president of the new entity on an interim basis, though he stayed in that position for more than three decades, helping to build one of the largest industrial conglomerates in the country.

Once diamond drilling began, it became clear that the Horne claims also contained massive amounts of copper. After the Quebec government brought in legislation to force companies that extracted timber and minerals in the province to do some processing before exporting the resources, the American owners began bailing out and Canadians started taking over. One of them was Noah Timmins, the merchant who'd turned the fortune he'd made from the Cobalt silver boom into a bigger fortune in the Porcupine gold rush and was now the president of Hollinger Consolidated Gold Mines. After becoming a Noranda director and major shareholder, he arranged a $3 million loan from Hollinger to build a copper smelter.

Noranda also began building an eponymous town on Lake Osisko, even as a more organic settlement called Rouyn exploded across the bay. Not just a company town in the sense that the corporation and its employees dominated the community and the economy, Noranda was a nascent modern city that the corporation planned and managed, avoiding the usual boomtown chaos that initially reigned in Rouyn. And rather than simply influencing local politics, the company made it clear who was in charge by appointing its own executives to the mayor's office until 1949. Murdoch was the first in the role, serving three years, though he continued to live and work in Toronto.

After Noranda began drilling on the Poulet-Veteran property, rumours and encouraging coverage in the *Northern Miner* helped push the price of the Porcupine Quartet Gold Syndicate's units to $25 in August and then to $35 in early 1936. This was good news for MacMillan, who had been accumulating units for herself from the beginning, not just unsold ones, but also buying them from Swallow and others. She had control of Quartet in March 1936 when Noranda, so encouraged by the drilling results, wanted to buy the claims a year before the option ran out. Now she found herself in negotiations with Murdoch. The two struck a deal that paid the syndicate 67,500 shares of the newly created Hallnor Mines and $25,000. With money in its treasury, Quartet explored its other claims but found nothing, so after the mine opened in 1938, MacMillan wound up the syndicate. Each unit, originally available for $10, was worth more than $125 in cash and shares. Hallnor proved to be even richer than Pamour and stayed in production for thirty-three years. "If I had known then how big that mine was going to be, I might have held out for better terms," MacMillan later recalled in her autobiography. "But Mr. Murdoch treated me very courteously, though I'm willing to bet it was the first time he had ever found himself negotiating a mining deal with a woman."

Her first big success made MacMillan a lot of money and provided an early-career social highlight: an invitation from Murdoch to be one of 120 guests at the dinner in the Pamour cookhouse to mark Hallnor's first gold brick. "I got a real thrill from that, because I believe he is one of the most outstanding men in Canada. But I'd like some day to be the original staker of a real producing gold mine," she told a reporter a few years later. Then she added, "Of at least 500 tons per day."

Murdoch's invitation was a sign of acceptance in the industry. The press took notice, with both the *Star Weekly* and the *Financial Post* running stories about her in August 1938. Headlined "Woman Wins Success in Masculine Endeavor," the *Star Weekly* article revealed that she liked horses and swimming and loved dancing. "Guy Lombardo is tops with me," said MacMillan, who was looking forward to seeing his upcoming show at the Canadian National Exhibition. But mostly she enjoyed her job. "Work is my favourite pastime," she said, attributing her success to luck and relentlessness, adding, "There's nothing I'd like better than to spend 18 hours a day at my office."

In the *Post* article, headlined "This Woman's Work—Mine-Making" she professed her determination to protect the interests of prospectors. "Of course, I'm in the market for anything that looks good. But I want to see that these prospectors get theirs out of anything they bring in," she said. The rest of what she told the reporter was more revealing: "Prospectors don't make mines. Somebody's got to have the nerve to put up money, and sell the stock. If a property comes through well, the prospector gets all the credit. If it doesn't, the broker gets all the blame. I don't think the public gives the brokers nearly enough credit for their part in mine making."

By the time she said that, she'd already made the move to Toronto. Montreal was bigger and certainly more glamorous, sophisticated and cosmopolitan than the dour Ontario city. But in 1934, the TSE became the largest exchange in the country, mostly because of mining stocks. Bay Street was the place to be for an ambitious mining promoter. And after being a rarity as a woman in the bush, MacMillan was about to enter another world dominated by men.

CHAPTER FIVE

LUCKY TEXAS

During the party at the Senator Hotel in Timmins on the night of April 18, 1964, Viola MacMillan had told Greg Reynolds to check back with her the next day. She might have a good story for the *Daily Press* reporter. Then she went back to the Empire to haggle with Rousseau and Larche. At midday on Sunday, Reynolds caught up with her in the hotel lobby. She was on her way to a late breakfast, but they had a quick conversation. The next morning, he broke the story about how twelve claims near the Texas Gulf discovery had sold for $250,000 and 100,000 shares. His numbers were wrong; either fatigue had caused her to mix them up or, more likely, he'd transposed them when he wrote them down in a rush. The buyer, according to the paper, was Windfall Oils and Mines. That wasn't true either, but it might be soon. As part of the deal MacMillan made with the prospectors, she agreed to offer the twelve claims to Windfall. But because she still needed the approval from the board of directors, she insisted Reynolds write the story without attribution. She also suggested he buy some Windfall stock.

The MacMillans had acquired a controlling interest in the company three years earlier. Originally formed as Windward Gold Mines in 1946, it became Windfall Oils and Mines in 1957. By 1961, it was inactive, though it did have a gold property, about twenty grand in its coffers and, most valuable, a listing on the Toronto Stock Exchange. Through a wholly owned company called Alexander Prospecting, George gained effective control by paying almost $68,000 for 345,000 of the 1.55 million issued shares.

The couple's plan for Windfall was to find and develop a mine. Unfortunately, $20,000 wasn't going to get them far, so they first needed more money. For most companies listed on the TSE, public financing required filing a prospectus. Resource companies were the exception. Instead of selling shares directly from the treasury, they could release unissued shares through an underwriting and option agreement. But they needed a broker to serve one of two roles. The first was as the underwriter; the second was as an agent acting as an intermediary between the underwriter and the company. Along with helping make Toronto's exchange the world leader in speculative mining shares, this method of primary distribution of shares was a great boon to the industry because it allowed companies with claims to obtain the funds necessary for exploration. But it was also an invitation for less-than-ethical promoters to take advantage of investors. Since 1958, the TSE's regulations required speculative companies to provide filing statements, but this did not eliminate mischief.

An example of this process saw the underwriter—often the promoter behind the stock—agree to buy, say, 200,000 shares at a set price with an option on another 800,000 shares in blocks at progressively increasing rates at specified intervals, often three months each. Then the trick was to push the price of the shares up, often without explaining what the company planned to do with the financing. If the price didn't rise, the promoter walked away from the options; if the stock went up a lot, the promoter made out even better than the company, which received only the set option prices for shares that were now worth much more. In that case, much of the invested money never made it to the treasury, so it wasn't the most efficient system of primary distribution, and it was prone to abuse. But promoters loved it.

Moss, Lawson & Company, a Toronto brokerage firm, acted as agent for Golden Shaft Mines and Variometer Surveys, two companies controlled by Viola, in a 1962 underwriting of a million shares of Windfall. This injected $210,000 into the treasury, enough to make seeking a mine feasible. In March the next year, George sold 300,000 of his shares to Viola for just under $57,000. Even though she was now the controlling shareholder, he remained president; the couple used similar arrangements for several of their companies at the time. Then Windfall went looking for property. In the summer of 1963, it acquired options on an old Nevada copper mine next to a large and successful open-pit operation called the Anaconda Copper Mine. The following January, Windfall added an option on ten claims in Tiblemont Township near Val d'Or, Quebec, while its wholly owned American subsidiary, Nevada Windfall, was running an exploration program and negotiating for additional properties. And then, early in April 1964, the MacMillans picked up an option on thirty-six claims in Loveland Township, north of Timmins. Now the company needed another infusion of cash.

Moss, Lawson agreed to handle a second underwriting, again acting as agent for Golden Shaft and Variometer. The MacMillans owned 69 percent of the former and 97 percent of the latter. The goal was to raise money so Windfall could continue work on the Nevada and Loveland Township properties, and the excitement over the Texas Gulf strike made for good timing. The agreement, dated April 17, 1964, set out a commitment by Golden Shaft and Variometer to buy 100,000 shares at thirty-five cents with options to purchase—or take down—another 900,000 shares at rising prices. But the Toronto Stock Exchange balked because the numbers were too far below the market. Four days later, Tom Cole, Windfall's secretary and lawyer, filed a revised version with the TSE. The new deal was 100,000 shares at forty cents with options on another 900,000 at prices climbing from forty to ninety cents over fifteen months. This satisfied the exchange.

Although Windfall was publicly traded, the MacMillans treated it as their own private holding, and despite not being an officer or a director, Viola regularly referred to it as "our company." The pliant directors they had selected helped make that possible. Along with George and Cole, they were Doris Drewe, Ronald Mills and Marjorie Oliver. Drewe had started working for Viola in 1941 when MacMillan was serving on a fund-raising committee for Women's College Hospital in Toronto and needed help with a campaign. She stayed on as MacMillan grew busier with the Ontario Prospectors and Developers Association (later the Prospectors and Developers Association, or PDA). Before retiring in 1960, Drewe had served as the group's assistant secretary and helped with MacMillan companies, even sitting on some of their boards. Oliver, who was Windfall's vice-president, had worked in journalism and public relations. She still wrote an advice column called Mrs. Thompson Advises in the *Globe and Mail* and did PR for the social portion of the PDA convention. She'd been close with Viola for a decade; the two saw each other almost daily and Oliver was a regular guest at the MacMillans' farm, spending most weekends there. The couple had bought the property close to Tottenham, about an hour north of Toronto, in 1959 and had fifty head of cattle on it. Mills was a neighbour who lived and worked on his family farm and also did some work for the MacMillans. Oliver considered him "a rather quiet young man." None of the latter three directors could claim any knowledge of mining or mineral exploration or expertise in the governance of public companies. Only Drewe had ever been on a board before. But they made up for their lack of experience with complete loyalty and willingness to defer to the MacMillans.

The day after Cole filed the amended underwriting agreement, Viola accepted an invitation to attend a board meeting in his law office. Fulfilling her deal with the vendors when she bought the Prosser and Wark Townships claims, she was now offering them to Windfall. She told the directors that if the company didn't want the property, which she'd dubbed the Lucky Texas Group, they should say so and she would do something else with them. She might even create her own company.

With no worries about independent directors, or even probing questions from anyone other than Cole, Viola had little trouble getting the board to agree to anything she wanted. And what she wanted for an option on the claims was $200,000 in cash, with $15,000 due initially and the remainder payable in instalments over five years; 300,000 Windfall shares; and a production royalty. That was a significant premium on what she'd paid for them, though just $15,000 was guaranteed if the company opted not to exercise the option on the property. But in discussions before the meeting, only Cole had expressed reservations about the high price she planned to put on the claims, mostly because, as he later put it, "the company had several other irons in the fire" and he worried it wouldn't have the money to meet all its commitments. But at the meeting, which lasted less than an hour, Oliver moved that Windfall accept the offer, and the board assented.

That was the easy part. Getting the approval of the Toronto Stock Exchange was going to be harder.

□

"Toronto?" a well-travelled American responded when asked about the city, then, after a pause, it came to him: "Ah, yes, that is the place where you change cars for Cobalt." That's what a speaker told the Empire Club in 1909. And for some people, that wasn't far from the truth. At least initially. The Cobalt silver boom not only created a new town in northeastern Ontario, it also transformed the city 500 kilometres to the south. Before long, Toronto stopped being just a place to switch trains and began to play the role of middleman between northern Ontario's mineral resources and the wealthy Americans who ended up owning many of the mines. Of course, even regular folks on both sides of the border, people who didn't have the capital to fund the development of promising claims, wanted to get rich. Many of them were willing to gamble that a tiny piece of a mine, in the form of a few shares, was a good way to do it. In 1905, a boom in mining speculation hit the New York Curb Market, which operated on the sidewalk of Broad Street. Despite many scams, investors' zeal continued into the next year. Crowds eager to bid on shares in Cobalt mines became so large that the cops showed up on horses. Three days in a row. But what was just a passing fad in New York was a seminal event in the maturation of Toronto from provincial backwater to increasingly wealthy mine financing centre.

The history of the city's stock markets began around 1840 when brokers started trading securities in taverns and coffeehouses. In 1852, a dozen businessmen created the Association of Brokers, and then, nine years later, they met in the Masonic Hall to establish the Toronto Stock Exchange. In the beginning, it was home to only eighteen stocks, and most days saw only two or three trades, so sessions were just a half-hour long. Infighting and bank failures in the late 1860s led to the exchange's collapse. It began to revive itself in 1871 and incorporated in 1878, moving into its first permanent home on King Street East the same year. In the country's biggest city, the Montreal Board of Brokers operated until 1872.

Then, two years later, the Montreal Stock Exchange incorporated. A third of its sixty-three listings were bank stocks. Most Canadian investors still did their buying and selling on the New York Stock Exchange or the London Stock Exchange.

But gambling on speculative mining securities was something they could do at home. The 1868 discovery of gold at Madoc, Ontario, resulted in the opening of a short-lived, unsuccessful mine and the establishment of the Toronto Stock and Mining Exchange, an even shorter-lived and less successful stock market. Three decades later, a gold boom at Rossland, British Columbia, led to the launch of the Toronto Mining Exchange, which began operating in January 1898. When its fifteen members refused to admit anyone else into their club, a group of excluded brokers started the Standard Stock and Mining Exchange (SSME), which opened in 1899. Two years later, the rivals merged under the latter's name. Then came the Cobalt silver boom. Although it led to the formation of 429 public companies by 1910, only forty-four of them had produced any silver and just seventeen paid dividends. Mine stocks went through the inevitable undulations over the following years, but the gold rushes in the Porcupine, Kirkland Lake and, in 1926 and 1927, Red Lake, as well as other mineral discoveries in the country, kept on giving promoters something new to sell and gamblers something new to be excited about. Money from Canadians, Americans and Britons gushed in.

Minerals weren't the only commodities that caught the fancy of speculators. On the Prairies, for example, farmers and other investors kept the Winnipeg Grain Exchange buzzing in the 1920s with their bets on wheat futures. But mining stocks held special appeal for swindlers. Grain prices largely depended on the economy and the size of the crop, which was affected by the weather and disease. That information was or would become available, which should have made prices easier to predict, though roughly nineteen in twenty gamblers on the Winnipeg Grain Exchange lost money. The value of a mine stock should have depended on the size, concentration and viability of an ore body, but most investors didn't have reliable access to that information. Usually, neither did the hustlers, so it all depended on their ability to sell dreams. And those dreams were almost always better than what was in the ground.

That's not to say speculative stocks didn't serve a vital role in the development of the Canadian mining industry. Finding and developing mineral deposits is inherently risky, which complicates the challenge of raising money. Penny stocks allowed entrepreneurs to generate funds they could use to turn promising claims into productive mines. And some people did make money buying shares in junior mining companies and wanted to keep doing it. Because mineral extraction was such a huge part of the country's emerging economy, the trick was to come up with regulations that encouraged investment while still protecting investors from fraud. The politicians would have been happy to let the stock markets police themselves, but that proved unworkable. Some members legitimately worried that too much regulation would just mean even more trading taking place outside the exchanges; others wanted no rules at all. So, it fell to governments, and they tended to err on the side of doing too little.

With minimal regulatory oversight, scam artists gleefully went about their business on the SSME. When times were good, most people were happy to look the other way. But after the markets crashed in October 1929, those who'd lost money needed someone to blame, and the usual suspects after a financial panic were the brokers and promoters. The finger-pointers found an ally in the *Financial Post*. Launched in 1907 while the Cobalt silver boom was still making things interesting on the stock markets in Toronto, the weekly paper was now billing itself as "The Canadian Newspaper for Business Men and Investors." It ran a ten-part series about unsavoury behaviour on the SSME. Though his byline never appeared, the articles were the work of Floyd Chalmers, the paper's young editor. His journalism generated an enthusiastic and increasingly wound-up response from readers, especially small investors. None of this looked good on the Ontario government, which had ignored all the shadiness and now found itself facing a public outcry, leaving it with no choice but to act.

The most notorious of the crooked brokers was Isaac (Ike) W.C. Solloway, who was the master of "bucketing" trades. In 1926, he and partner Harvey Mills, both former prospectors, formed a brokerage house that quickly added branch offices across the country, as well as in Newfoundland and the United States. Solloway, Mills & Company specialized in junior mining and oil stocks on the SSME and other exchanges on both sides of the border. While clients expected the brokers to execute trades immediately, Solloway and Mills held on to the orders—bucketed them—when they anticipated that a favourable price spread would soon develop. Instead of selling a stock at fifty cents, as instructed, they waited until the price rose to fifty-five cents. Then they sold, paid the client and pocketed an illegal profit of five cents a share. If the client was buying, they did the same thing in reverse, waiting until the price had dropped. The con was a lucrative one. After starting out with $18,000 in 1926, the firm was worth $18 million three years later. Early in 1930, though, Solloway and Mills were among the twenty-seven stock market players the cops rounded up under orders of the Ontario attorney general. By that time, they'd already been charged in Alberta. The pair racked up $600,000 in fines for theft or bucketing from courts and regulators in British Columbia, Alberta and Ontario. In addition, a Calgary judge sentenced Solloway to four months in jail while giving Mills one month. By 1931, long before their legal troubles had ended, the *Toronto Daily Star* estimated they'd paid their lawyers $400,000 and said, "The brokers rank as the most heavily fined men in the records of Canadian justice."

Ike Solloway and his ilk made the already questionable standing of the SSME sink further. And while it had a slightly better reputation, the TSE wasn't without its own dubious practices, including the selling of shares by going door-to-door or cold-calling customers on the phone. A short-lived upsurge in mining stocks starting in 1933, combined with the availability of more affordable long-distance rates, led to the establishment of boiler rooms, from which salesmen applied high-pressure tactics on people all over the continent. All the scandals and shenanigans made the need for more regulation clear. The provincial government responded by establishing the Ontario Securities Commission, the first oversight body of its kind in the country. In 1934, the SSME merged with the TSE in a shotgun wedding. George Drew, the OSC's first chairman, wielded the firearm. The value of the trading on the two exchanges was about the same, but the volume was bigger on the SSME because of all the junior mining stocks.

The merger created the largest stock market in Canada and was a crucial early step in Toronto's march to overtake Montreal as the country's most powerful business city. Not that many mining companies were listed on the MSE. For one thing, Ontario had more mines. For another, the two provinces had different investment cultures: Montrealers, especially the wealthy English burghers of Westmount, tended to be conservative and didn't have much of a hankering for speculative stocks; rural and small-town Québécois generally preferred to keep their money in local savings banks, or *caisses populaires*, or to buy real estate.

Now home to both blue chips such as International Nickel as well as myriad penny stocks, the TSE wasn't just North America's leading exchange for mine finance but the third largest on the continent. Needing a bigger trading floor, it moved into a new art deco palace on Bay Street in 1937. Behind the imposing stainless-steel doors, it featured full air conditioning, an amenity no other building in the country had, and so much new technology that traders had to go through training before the trading floor opened. But the shiny new digs didn't mean the exchange had cleansed itself of all its bad habits, especially when it came to mining stocks.

While many investors called for more, and more effective, regulation, the mining and brokerage industries wanted laxer rules. Drew, now the leader of the Progressive Conservative Party, became the premier of Ontario in 1943 and appointed a royal commission on mining in the province. Bizarrely, his choice for commissioner was Norman Urquhart, a broker and a former president of the SSME. Since Drew was at the helm of a minority government, he knew he could be going back to the polls before too long, so he was more interested in appearing to be doing something, while avoiding any controversy, than in meaningful reform. And with groups such as the Ontario Mining Association and the Canadian Institute of Mining and Metallurgy even suggesting getting rid of the OSC, rather than strengthening it, meaningful reform never had a chance.

Finding a level of regulation that would protect investors while still encouraging risk-taking remained elusive, but for all the complaining from the industry, improved performance of the junior mining companies depended on more than removing rules. Since the early '40s, once the war in Europe started to go better for the Allies, stocks had begun to recover. After the war, Canada entered a long period of economic expansion. But by the mid-1950s, mining stocks, and mineral exploration, faced tough times again. Gordon Sinclair, a veteran radio commentator and renowned curmudgeon famous for his blunt, often contrarian rants, spoke for those who blamed the regulators for being too strict. The public buys speculative mining shares, he argued, knowing "that in at least nine cases out of ten it will lose its shirt" and hoping "the one winner in ten would pay off at a rate strong enough to make the other losers fade away. But the Securities Commission looked on all promoters as thieves, bandits, ace chisellers and con men, whose slogan was 'Never give a sucker an even break.'" Easy for him to say. Despite being just a newspaper reporter when the markets crashed in 1929, he'd made a fortune on stocks in the aftermath. What did a sophisticated—and well-connected—investor care if stock market charlatans ever gave their naive marks an even break?

Maybe what the struggling industry needed wasn't more skulduggery but another big discovery. Sure enough, the Texas Gulf strike not only led to a staking rush, it revived mining stocks, much to the delight of brokers, promoters and investors. While nothing could touch gold for stoking human obsession, if people could make money off base metals such as copper and zinc, they were keen to do that, too. The claims Viola MacMillan bought in Timmins gave her an opportunity to cash in on that zeal.

□

On the Monday after her success in suite 358 of the Empire Hotel, Viola went to see Donald Lawson. She showed the vice-president of Moss, Lawson a clipping of a map from the *Northern Miner*. On it, she'd marked the three groups of claims she'd purchased on the weekend. Lawson assumed she meant Windfall had purchased them. After the board meeting where the directors had approved the optioning of the claims, she was back in Lawson's office. "All right, now the deal is set," said MacMillan, who could be as gruff as she could be charming. "This is what we are going to do."

That's when he realized that she'd bought the claims herself and the company was going to pay $200,000, plus 300,000 shares and a royalty for them. He told her the TSE would never agree to that. As a member of the exchange's Filing Statement Committee, he knew the rules governing non-arm's-length transactions well. Even though she wasn't an officer or a director or even an employee of Windfall, she was the largest share-holder and the underwriter. And when a company bought properties in a non-arm's-length deal, and the vendor had held them for less than a year, the purchase price could not be more than the acquisition cost. In other words, buying the Prosser and Wark Townships claims personally and then optioning them to Windfall for a profit wasn't allowed. "I explained this, but of course Mrs. MacMillan is a developer, she is a mining person," Lawson later recounted. "She is different in her mind from everybody else who might be dealing with these kinds of companies."

Sure enough, when Tom Cole submitted the paperwork, the TSE turned down the deal. MacMillan was indignant. After putting up a hundred grand of her own money, as well as stock, she believed she deserved something if the property became a mine. She amended the proposal so that the instalments of the second $100,000 and last 50,000 of the shares would not be payable unless the company found an ore body on the claims. In addition, she agreed to accept 90 percent of the shares going into escrow, even though none of the shares she'd paid for the claims had been escrowed. The exchange remained unsatisfied.

The sometimes-bitter negotiations dragged on, with a number of failed proposals. During this time, Lawson spent many hours talking to MacMillan. Having known her a long time, and worked with her in the past, he understood what a determined person she was. And now, during these discussions, he could see that she was worried about losing control of the company and the claims, and she wanted to make damn sure that wouldn't happen.

One day, both Viola and George were in his office. Lawson had never seen her this worked up. She railed against exchange officials and declared, "They can't tell me what I'm going to do." If the deal went through, she wanted to ensure she and George kept control of Windfall. She even threatened to call a meeting of the shareholders and delist the company. If the TSE refused her deal with Windfall, she'd form a new company for the claims. Lawson felt sorry for George. Some of the things Viola was saying made the broker worry for their marriage.

The next morning, George went to Lawson's office by himself. He was upset. As president of the company, he had a responsibility to the shareholders, and he felt caught between them and his wife. The two men came up with an idea they hoped might satisfy both sides. Their solution was to sweeten the deal for Viola by giving her a share option. The first time they tried it, the TSE said no. But, finally, in late May, Viola agreed to an arrangement that, subject to shareholder approval, would give her $100,000; 250,000 shares in Windfall, with 90 percent of them escrowed; and a royalty of five or ten cents per ton, depending on the grade of the ore. In addition, she received an option on 200,000 shares in the company at fifty-eight cents, exercisable within five years, but only if an independent geologist or mining engineer established that the property had an ore body of at least two million tons.

MacMillan certainly wasn't making out the way she'd hoped. Unless Windfall found a mine on the claims, she'd receive only what she'd paid for them, except she'd paid with free shares and now she was getting back mostly escrowed ones. Despite her disappointment over a deal she felt she had no choice but to accept, and her seething resentment of the exchange officials, she was ready to find out what the property was really worth.

CHAPTER SIX

BOYS' CLUB

As the Victorian era was winding down and Toronto's aspirations were cranking up, the city still didn't have a luxury hotel. London had the Savoy, New York had the Waldorf-Astoria and Paris had the Ritz. Montreal, the largest and most important urban centre in the country, took pride in its Windsor Hotel, which opened in 1878. Even Quebec City had the Château Frontenac. But the best Toronto could offer was the dingy Queen's Hotel. Deciding to do something about that, some of the city's wealthiest men proposed building "a palace hotel." They initially hired two architects: prominent Chicagoan Henry Ives Cobb and local up-and-comer Edward James Lennox, who'd already begun earning his reputation by designing the new city hall. Cobb didn't continue beyond the early stages of the project, but Lennox carried on. By the time construction was complete in 1903, the owners decided to name the eight-storey building on King Street East after the new monarch. The King Edward Hotel immediately became a favourite of Toronto's elite, who enjoyed attending balls and banquets in the second-floor American Dining Room, also known as the Grand Ballroom.

The rich weren't the only people drawn to the King Eddy. The investors behind the venture were businessmen, and they'd wanted a new hotel not just for their high society parties but as a place for business travellers to stay and local businessmen to meet. The two-storey Rotunda, neither round nor domed, provided a grand marble lobby with cut-glass chandeliers, murals depicting significant events in Canadian history and impressive works of art. Just off the lobby, the Bar and Gentlemen's Café, which featured antique oak panelling and soon became known as the Oak Room, was a popular spot for meetings or a glass of port after dinner in the European Dining Room, the main restaurant. The shop in the Rotunda sold newspapers and cigars and there was a grill room and a barber shop in the basement. All of this was conveniently located across the street from the Toronto Stock Exchange. Even after the TSE moved west to Bay Street in 1913, it was still only a few blocks away.

The King Edward opened a few months before the discovery of silver at Cobalt, and the mining industry took to the hotel right away. The Canadian Mining Institute held its annual meeting there in March 1904. Over the following years, more and more companies, consultants, engineers, stockbrokers and financiers huddled around the TSE. But downtown suits weren't the only people who patronized the hotel. Unwashed prospectors checking in with muddy boots and packs laden with rock samples were a common sight. According to one legend—no doubt burnished over the years—in 1907, several prospectors showed up in the bar with mules in tow. The unseemly side of the industry also came: as early as 1910, according to one journalist, it was impossible to go into the King Eddy "without seeing scores of crooks at work trying to separate victims from their money, flashy fellows and big spenders." Of course, he observed, in hotels across the country "'strong arm' salesmen were at work endeavouring to bamboozle ignorant men and women out of their savings."

□

The addition of an eighteen-storey tower in 1921 briefly made the King Edward the largest hotel in the country. But the Depression left much of the building empty, and Viola and George MacMillan lived in a two-room suite for just fifty dollars a month when they first moved to Toronto in the spring of 1936. Although affordable luxury in a hotel, especially one that was so popular with mining people, should have been the perfect arrangement, MacMillan was still a farm girl at heart and downtown Toronto didn't feel much like home. Wanting some open space with trees, fields and a river, she and George bought a sixty-hectare farm on Sixteen Mile Creek, north of Oakville, and hired her brother Reg to help run it.

Now in the centre of mining finance, MacMillan quickly proved an adept operator. One of the businesses she created in 1936 was Airquests, an exploration company with a federal charter to operate an airline. For a time, she and George did have a private plane and two pilots on the payroll. They flew around checking out properties and pursuing deals until they realized owning their own aircraft and paying pilots to hang around while they worked made no sense. Viola sold the plane but held onto the company because the airline charter was such a valuable asset.

In 1937, in the wake of the Hallnor Mine deal, the MacMillans finally felt flush enough to go on a real holiday, the first either of them had ever taken. They bought a new car and set off for California, stopping at all the tourist attractions, including the Grand Canyon, which stunned them, and the Hoover Dam, the engineering triumph that had been completed two years earlier. They rented a place south of Laguna Beach and stayed for a few months. When a movie starring Olivia de Havilland, George Brent and Claude Rains began filming near their house, Viola had fun mingling with the cast and crew. The flick was called *Gold Is Where You Find It*.

George, in particular, fit right in with the laid-back lifestyle, and he mused about selling everything in Canada and staying in California. "Oh, no. Canada needs us," Viola said. "We need to go back and help find more mines in Canada." The couple returned to Toronto before Christmas, and as her profile grew, the *Financial Post* took note of her "sizable fortune and a rapidly growing reputation as one of Canada's smartest young mine promoters."

She continued to work in the bush, often for months at a time. By the end of the 1930s, she'd prospected in New Brunswick, Quebec, Ontario, the Northwest Territories and the Yukon. But as a mine developer, she was now based in Toronto, and as much as she liked the Oakville property, which she insisted was a farm, not a country estate, it wasn't convenient for doing business downtown. At first, she and George kept their suite in the King Eddy, but eventually realized they needed something more permanent in the city and decided to get an apartment. Suggesting a house made more sense, her real estate agent drove her to a large brick one on Oriole Parkway on the edge of Forest Hill, a wealthy enclave just north of downtown. MacMillan marvelled at how beautiful it was, and while still in the car, she asked, "How much?" Constructed in 1926 for $18,000, the house was now available for just $7,500. She agreed to buy it before she even went inside.

One of the things she did to furnish it was pick up some Oriental rugs that had decorated a reception for a royal visit. She didn't know anything about rugs but figured good enough for a monarch, good enough for her. The house was bigger than the MacMillans needed; the third floor had three bedrooms and a bathroom. By then, they knew Viola would never bear children because of a miscarriage in the summer of 1935. They had taken the train from Timmins to Toronto for a business trip and borrowed a car to drive to London to pick up some things at their house there. Shortly after beginning their return trip, Viola fell ill and began hemorrhaging. George turned the car around and then carried her into her doctor's office. After being rushed to the emergency room, she underwent surgery. She'd put off having children as she threw herself into her career, and now that they had some measure of financial security, they learned a family would not be possible. The news was shattering for both of them, but their marriage survived.

□

After working in British Columbia and Michigan, Walter Segsworth made his reputation as a mining engineer in Cobalt. He struggled for months to get the Seneca Superior Mine into production in 1912, even as he fell deeper and deeper into debt. But his faith in the property paid off and the mine eventually yielded six million ounces of silver. Twenty years later, the consulting engineer in his early fifties grew alarmed when the government wanted to make engineering a profession in Ontario, as was the case in all the other provinces except Prince Edward Island. Under the proposed legislation, the only people who could call themselves engineers were those who'd studied the discipline at university or had five years of experience. The act had the enthusiastic support of four engineering branches—chemical, civil, electrical and mechanical—with only those in mining opposed. Fearing that such a law would be bad for business, they argued that mining was unlike the other disciplines. Requiring a professional engineer made sense when building a bridge, for example, but not for finding mineral deposits.

Prospectors would be especially hard hit. Once they staked a claim, they had to do forty hours of assessment work on it every year or lose it. But, if the bill passed, claim holders would need an engineer's approval before filing a report on their progress. Even if that were a reasonable policy, few prospectors had the money to pay a professional engineer for a signature. Instead, they'd just stop looking for minerals. That would be disastrous for mining in Ontario.

On the morning of February 29, 1932, Segsworth gathered a dozen prospectors to discuss ways to stop passage of the Professional Engineers Act. He was savvy enough to realize that the objections of prospectors could help sway the government. But as people who tended to work in far-flung parts of the province—often alone or in pairs—they had no collective voice. Organizing them during the summer, when they were in the bush, would be all but impossible. Even those who continued working in the woods during the winter, sometimes by turning to trapping, usually came out for spring breakup. The timing for rounding up a lot of them couldn't have been better.

Segsworth and the others acted quickly. They formed the Ontario Prospectors Association and picked Arthur Cockeram to be president. After starting out in Cobalt, he'd gone on to the Porcupine; Kirkland Lake, where he'd staked some of the ground that became Harry Oakes's Lake Shore Mine; and Noranda. At a meeting the next afternoon at the King Eddy, well over one hundred people showed up. Predictably, chaos ruled at first with "a lot of hashing and chewing by a bunch of highly independent and strong-willed prospectors." But eventually, they realized they had to come together to fight the proposed law. They even chipped in a total of $168.45 for the cause. Cockeram presented a petition with 400 names on it to a legislative committee and claimed that if he had more time, he'd have been able to collect 9,000 signatures. By mid-March, the bill was dead, but a new organization, soon renamed the Ontario Prospectors and Developers Association, had been born. (In 1957, it would become just the Prospectors and Developers Association, or PDA.) After defeating the Professional Engineers Act, the group lobbied politicians and bureaucrats on a number of existing and proposed laws and regulations, often with success.

The MacMillans joined the group early on, though Viola later admitted, "It took these old-timers about three years to accept the idea of having a woman member." One day in 1941, the couple invited eight or nine men, including Segsworth, to the house on Oriole Parkway for an informal meeting. The guests assembled in the living room to plan the upcoming annual meeting, and finding a new president was among the items on their agenda. The membership was open to prospectors, developers, engineers and anyone else connected to mining. But Segsworth, who was a mining engineer, was adamant that the organization needed to be led by a prospector. His voice carried a lot of weight, given that he was so well-respected in the industry and had been instrumental in creating the group. One of the other men in the room was Murdock Mosher. Born in Nova Scotia, he and his family moved to Cobalt in 1907, and, like his older brother Alex, he went on to be a leading prospector. He suggested George for the job. Having gone into the kitchen to get a tray of sandwiches for her guests, Viola returned in time to hear Segsworth's cranky reaction to that idea. "No, we haven't had a real good president yet, and you won't do either, George," he said. "You're too soft." Known for his blunt talk and less-than-delicate manner, he apparently had no qualms about insulting his host.

But soft wasn't quite the right word to describe George. No one who'd spent that much time in the bush was soft. Certainly, he was easygoing, and even though he was a big guy, especially next to Viola, some people thought he was meek. He knew his stuff when it came to looking for gold, but he was not a driven man. Fortunately, his wife had more than enough drive for both of them. Upon hearing the brusque assessment of her husband, she looked Segsworth in the eye. She wasn't intimidated by him. "George will make a very good president," she declared. "I'll see that he does."

That was enough for most of the others in the room. A few weeks later, at the annual meeting, George won the presidency by acclamation. Viola was unopposed for the secretary-treasurer position. Although she and Segsworth continued to have a difficult relationship, she kept her vow to him by taking care of most of her husband's responsibilities.

With the tenth anniversary of the association coming up in 1942, the board wanted to do something a little more elaborate for the group's annual meeting. Previously, members had gathered once a year at the King Edward to briefly discuss industry matters before enjoying drinks. Viola MacMillan arranged a day-long session with speakers that included government ministers and senior bureaucrats, followed by a four-course banquet and dancing in the hotel's Oak Room. To help raise the group's profile, she also let the press know. During its first decade, the PDA never had a membership fee, and MacMillan found sponsors to pay for printing the program. But realizing the growing organization needed its own funds, she announced annual dues of one dollar (despite the inevitable grumbling, by the end of the year, 600 members had paid up). The whole event was a great success.

The only hitch was the women. Although most members had been against inviting wives to the event, MacMillan overruled them. "Wives have their rights, too," she reasoned. "They're the ones who have to keep the home fires burning, and they'd like to meet their husbands' friends." While 150 people attended the banquet, three chairs at the head table sat empty. The men who were to sit in them had staged a boycott. As usual, MacMillan remained undaunted by the sexism. While cutting the ceremonial cake after dinner, she gave three large slices to the waitstaff to save. The next day she delivered a piece to each no-show in his office and received apologies. The men had missed a good party in a futile effort to make a point not worth making.

Before that unpleasantness, the convention speakers had included Gilbert Monture, pretty much always known as "Slim." The first Indigenous engineer to graduate from Queen's University, where he studied mining and metallurgy, he was now a senior civil servant. His speech, called "The Battle of the Metals," was about how the Second World War had increased the need for more than a dozen base metals, including copper, molybdenum and tungsten, few of which had ever been mined in Canada. The problem was most prospectors, who'd spent their careers looking for gold, knew nothing about finding these strategic metals. But they were keen to find out, especially because demand for gold had dropped off since the early days of the war. MacMillan travelled to Ottawa to convince the Geological Survey of Canada to send experts to give lectures at a workshop the PDA would host in Toronto. Once the GSC was in, the Ontario Department of Mines offered additional speakers. By the time more than 150 prospectors attended the three-day workshop in Toronto, MacMillan had already arranged sessions in Kirkland Lake. When that didn't satisfy all the demand, she set up a repeat performance in Sudbury.

The workshops enhanced the reputation of the organization. If the bureaucrats had been skeptical when MacMillan first pitched the idea of training prospectors, that was no longer a problem. As the minister of munitions and supply in Mackenzie King's Liberal government, C.D. Howe was in charge of Canada's industrial policy, earning him the informal title of the "Minister of Everything." He'd named George Bateman to the powerful position of metals commissioner. Bateman was a mining engineer and the former secretary-treasurer of the Ontario Mining Association. In 1942, he appointed three PDA members to the new War Metals Advisory Committee. MacMillan was the only woman on it.

The next year, the organization hosted expanded prospecting workshops across the country, and the 1943 convention ran for two days. Although not everyone had come around on the inclusion of women, at least the head table was full. The annual gathering had become so popular, especially with the group's membership closing in on 1,700, that MacMillan realized the King Eddy was no longer big enough. The solution was to move the convention to the Royal York, which had opened on the site of the Queen's Hotel in 1929. The new hostelry was, it liked to remind everyone, the largest in the British Commonwealth. But the manager was skeptical the group would be able to pay for such a sizeable event. MacMillan balked when he suggested she ask one of the big mining companies to provide a guarantee. Instead, she came up with her own security deposit: the life insurances policies she and George had and a wedding ring someone had given her to settle a debt.

Everything worked out well in the new home. The sessions were well-attended, the banquet was a blast again, and MacMillan didn't lose the security deposit. After a representative from Ontario's Department of Mines spoke to a packed room about new geological studies in the Kirkland-Larder Lake region, MacMillan told the press, "I could feel they were itching to rush right out and stake some claims." Her instincts were right on; that summer was the beginning of a prospecting boom in Canada.

Although George was still the president, Viola had been doing all the work, including signing his name to letters. He regularly received thanks for work he didn't know he'd done. She was also better at getting the organization's message out to the public. When the *Star Weekly* profiled her in May 1941, she said, "We have 75 per cent of the pre-Cambrian shield in Canada and our country hasn't even scratched it. Instead of half a billion dollars a year from mining we should be turning out two or three billions."

Tired of being a puppet ruler, George was happy to cede the job to the puppet master and become the organization's secretary-treasurer. While most of the members may have finally accepted Viola, being its president didn't mean a universal welcome in the industry. For the next ten years, the Canadian Institute of Mining and Metallurgy barred her from joining because she was a woman.

☐

Not being part of that boys' club wasn't going to stop MacMillan from pushing politicians and bureaucrats at Ontario's Queen's Park as well as in Ottawa and Washington. She lobbied them to introduce laws that were good for the mining industry and drop potentially harmful legislation. There were plenty of issues to work on, including tax policies and financing rules such as regulations regarding syndicates as well as a request for more mapping by the GSC and provincial departments. She also fought for more government money.

Her most consequential success was helping to ensure the passage of the Emergency Gold Mining Assistance Act in 1948. Initially, Canadian miners and prospectors had welcomed American President Franklin Delano Roosevelt's decision in 1934 to peg gold at US$35 per ounce. After all, that was a big bump from $20.67. But as costs rose over the next decade or so, more and more gold properties became uneconomic. The industry began to falter. Collapse would be bad for prospectors, miners and the communities such as Timmins and Kirkland Lake that relied on the jobs. The Ontario economy was most at risk because the province produced almost 60 percent of Canada's gold. But across the country, more than 22,000 people worked in mines and mining companies paid over $4.5 million in taxes. Along with colleagues, MacMillan made many trips to Ottawa to convince federal politicians to provide financial assistance to keep high-cost and marginal mines in operation. In the first year, the Emergency Gold Mining Assistance Act injected over $9 million into gold mines. The government originally set the subsidy to expire after three years but continued it until 1971 when another president, Richard Nixon, ended the international convertibility of the US dollar to gold, allowing the market to set the price of the precious metal.

MacMillan was committed to raising public awareness about mining and alerting people to the job opportunities. The industry was the second largest in Canada, after only agriculture, but few people knew that. In 1946, she created Mining Day, which she hoped would be celebrated on the second Wednesday in March. Acceptance of the idea was slow, but she didn't give up. Eleven years later, she told CBC, "One of my greatest ambitions is that someday Canada will have a Mining Day, a day in which every teacher in every school in Canada will teach something about mining and that everyone will be conscious of what the prospectors and developers are doing for Canada."

Although Mining Day never became a big deal, she certainly did a good job building the PDA. When George began his presidency, the association had seventy-three members. In an early effort to attract more people, Viola arranged a mailing to the 20,000 Canadians with a mining licence. Printing and folding, stuffing envelopes and affixing stamps took a lot of work, only to have nearly half of the letters come back return to sender because the addresses were no longer good. Prospectors are a transient lot. But if the organization couldn't find them, they soon found the organization, especially after the war when many returning soldiers wanted to give mining a try.

More than a few veterans visited MacMillan at her office or even her home to seek her advice on staking claims, finding financing or some other aspect of the business. She explained how to get started—and preached patience. "Mining's not like the fruit business that's going to spoil overnight," she'd say. "Don't try too hard. Always realize there's another day, and maybe your luck will be much better." One vet she helped was Carl "Moose" Fummerton. A bush pilot before the war, he'd also prospected a little. After the war, he devoted more time to prospecting but was getting frustrated about his lack of success. His luck improved as soon as he visited MacMillan's office. She'd just received a telegram about a strike at Rush Lake. They immediately headed to a department store to buy a canoe. Then Fummerton boarded a train with it. Later, she helped him form and finance a development company for the claims he'd staked. He did well enough to build a house in Toronto with his English bride.

MacMillan, who'd been committed to education ever since the first workshop on strategic metals in 1942, also arranged lecture tours across the country and convinced the University of Toronto to offer an extension course in prospecting. But almost all the people joining the field were men. Even by the late 1940s, no more than a dozen other Canadian women prospected, and none of them made their living doing it. Most went into the bush with their husbands for just a few weeks in the summer, though MacMillan knew a couple who'd gone out on their own. Still, twenty-five women from various fields within the industry had joined the PDA. Although she was no longer alone, she was the head of what remained an overwhelmingly male organization, and she made great copy, regularly doing radio interviews and talking to reporters from newspapers and magazines. She was ready with lively quotes and entertaining tales of life in the bush while also skillfully promoting the PDA, the industry and herself. Although MacMillan talked quickly and liked to get down to business right away, she was always happy to discuss mining at length.

The conventions were an annual triumph. What had started out as a small group's yearly meeting had become a four-day event featuring technical sessions, a trade show and innumerable informal discussions. Along with learning about new technology and new techniques, prospectors shared gossip about recent strikes and promising areas and met with promoters to sell claims and raise grubstakes. For the promoters, it was a chance to make deals; for companies, it was a place to snap up talent; for students, it was a job fair; for the media, it was a source of colourful stories.

One reason for the success of the conventions, which required a lot of planning, was that MacMillan liked to be in control of everything, from the menu to the speakers. "Choose your subject, but make it short, make it snappy and make them like it," she advised one man, "or they'll all go back to their rooms and continue the evening's festivities without you." She also instructed him to not smoke his cigar while he was talking. Meanwhile, MacMillan worked to make wives more welcome at the convention with lunches, lectures and other events that, as she put it, were "designed to keep them occupied and interested while their menfolk were attending the technical sessions." The inclusion of women helped make the convention a legendary annual bash as people who spent much of the year alone in the bush relished a chance to socialize. And MacMillan, who loved a party, enjoyed it as much as anyone.

She ran the PDA from her office at 67 Yonge Street, a spartan space that made it clear she was there for business, not lounging in comfort. In fact, the closest thing to extravagance was a swivel chair at one of the two old desks. The top shelf of the glass-fronted bookcase held ore samples and framed photos of prospectors in the bush. Geological maps served as additional decor. And since the presidency was a volunteer position, her staff donated their time.

The group celebrated its twenty-fifth anniversary in 1957 and, to acknowledge its national presence and scope, finally dropped Ontario from its name. The paid membership had climbed to 2,000, reflecting the growth in the Canadian mining industry. Although prospectors had picked over most of the United States, plenty of unexplored regions remained north of the border. Beyond the swelling membership rolls, MacMillan had turned the motley collection of mining men into an organization that offered effective training and information for members and was increasingly influential with politicians and bureaucrats. By the mid-'50s more women were joining and attending the convention for the technical sessions instead of just going to the social events as their husbands' plus one. In 1959, 1,400 men and 360 women showed up.

Along with her energy and organizational skills, MacMillan genuinely liked prospectors. She went out of her way to meet as many as possible at the conventions and was always quick to offer advice to the inexperienced and to help those in need. When the manager of a seedy hotel called her and said an old-timer named Smokey was seriously ill and had locked himself in his room, refusing to see a doctor unless he talked to MacMillan first, she responded, "I'll be right over."

Every year at the convention, prospectors and other mining people repaid her support by serenading her with a boisterous rendition of "Let Me Call You Sweetheart." In 1957, the PDA presented MacMillan with a silver tea service and tray, but it was not a farewell gift. With a knack for doing a lot of tasks quickly and efficiently, she never considered giving up the role, even as her own web of companies grew. Over the years, the position helped her build her standing in the industry, make more and better connections and strengthen her reputation as an honourable businesswoman, even as some members began to grumble that she had too much control over the organization, and the Queen Bee moniker took on another, less flattering meaning.

By the early 1960s, with prospecting and indeed the whole mining business in a slump, MacMillan and the PDA wanted to open up provincial and national parks to exploration. "There's nothing more beautiful than a good mine," she argued in 1963. Despite the sluggishness, the next year's convention attracted a record 1,900 registrants. After winning re-election yet again, MacMillan started her twenty-first year as president by declaring in a speech that "Red tape, taxes and apathy are destroying the Canadian mining industry." Her solution was a ten-year plan that included more tax breaks and generous subsidies for prospectors. But the mood in the industry was about to change. A little more than a month later, Texas Gulf announced its discovery of a massive base metals deposit near Timmins.

CHAPTER SEVEN

LONGER CHANCES

S hortly after Viola MacMillan acquired the twelve claims in the Timmins area, she and George pulled out a map and showed Marjorie Oliver how close their new property was to the Texas Gulf discovery. Clearly excited about the Prosser claims, Viola talked about how hard she'd worked to get them. But Oliver, who was a Windfall director as well as a close friend, noticed that George seemed less enthusiastic. Before long, though, he appeared to be over any reluctance he may have had because he wasted little time getting started on the exploration. He even gave Don Lawson, the brokerage executive, the impression that there was a fifty-fifty chance of finding something on the property.

The couple hired Sui Shing "Rocky" Szetu, a consulting geologist who'd helped on some of their projects in the past. After getting his undergraduate degree in China and working there for five years, he studied in England, then did a doctorate in geology at the University of Toronto. He also had a decade's worth of experience in geophysics. He'd known the MacMillans since the Prospectors and Developers Association convention in 1947 when he was still a student. Even before he first visited the Windfall claims with the couple in early May, he'd met with them to go over government maps, one showing the geology and another showing the results of an airborne magnetic survey.

Dense boreal forest, dominated by a mix of coniferous trees, surrounded the many lakes, streams, swampy ground, rocky shores, stray boulders and outcrops that punctuate the rugged terrain around Timmins. Studying the geology here was more difficult than in some other places because most of the bedrock was underneath so much soil and loose rock. After the last continental glacier receded nearly ten millennia ago, a massive lake covered much of the Canadian Shield. As the water level dropped and the big lake became many much smaller lakes, it left behind a thick layer of clay—as much as ninety metres deep in places—on top of the bedrock, hiding a bounty of minerals and leaving few outcrops to help prospectors and geologists find them. That was one reason the mining industry had been slow to discover northern Ontario. Even after the Porcupine gold rush, exploration remained limited in the area because of all the overburden.

"Seeing" beneath the surface had long been one of mining's challenges, and, for most of history, few effective tools existed. Versions of the magnetic dip needle, also known as a miner's compass, had been around for centuries and continued to be used until the 1930s to find magnetic ore bodies. But other options were limited, which inevitably encouraged a parade of inventors and con men to claim they'd developed new devices that would locate minerals. During the Klondike gold rush, Nikola Tesla promoted a gold-detecting X-ray machine (much of his previous work, including developing the alternating-current electrical supply system, proved more successful). During the Cobalt silver boom, newspapers carried ads for divining rods and other conjuring methods. For Leo Daft and Alfred Williams, two British mining engineers, the Cobalt discoveries seemed to come along at just the right time. They'd invented the Electrical Ore Finder, which used electrodes to send low-frequency alternating current into the ground and then read the current distribution with a receiver attached to two electrodes on the surface. But the gadget never quite worked as well as Daft and Williams had hoped, and their company went bankrupt in 1905.

They had the right idea, though, and geophysics, which is the study of the physics of the Earth, began to play an increasingly prominent role in mineral exploration a few decades later. Advances in electronics during and after the Second World War gave prospectors instruments to reliably detect and measure magnetic fields, electrical conductivity, specific gravity and radioactivity. By the late 1940s, aerial geophysical surveys were feasible. As the technology continued to improve in the '50s, the adoption of these instruments increased, which accelerated a trend to more companies, and fewer lone prospectors, in the bush. Companies could more easily afford the new equipment and to hire people who knew how to use it. Geophysics became an increasingly frequent subject of the technical sessions at the annual PDA conventions. MacMillan had sensed opportunity early on; in 1946, she and geologist Willis Ambrose formed Variometer Surveys to do geophysical exploration for her projects as well as for other mining companies.

By helping reveal what was beneath the glacial debris, geophysics represents a useful early step in the exploration process. Texas Gulf had performed airborne surveys over the Timmins region, though it wasn't sharing its research, and Aeromatic Surveys had completed airborne geophysical surveys in 1953. What was less well known was that Norman Keevil, a respected exploration geologist, had paid for a more recent aerial survey with up-to-date equipment. Shortly after Viola acquired the claims, Keevil's son called George and said, "I think I have some information you might want." George paid the $2,500 asking price. The maps indicated that Windfall's Prosser Township claims were in a zone of electrical conductivity. An electromagnetic anomaly, also known as a conductor, might indicate the presence of sulphides, which may or may not contain valuable metals, or just be graphite, which was so plentiful that it was practically worthless. (Today, it is on Canada's critical minerals list.) The odds of a conductor being a mineable ore body were long, but the potential payoff was huge.

Following up on the ground was the next step. To prepare for geophysical surveys, Szetu had a crew set up a camp with three tents. One of them, a short distance from the others, was for the MacMillans. That done, the crew began cutting lines, which required clearing trees and brush to create dead-straight paths. First, they cut a baseline, and then, every hundred feet, they cut a perpendicular line, marking every hundred feet with a picket made by cutting a small tree. This allowed the geophysical exploration team, which began work June 9, to carry instruments through the bush and take a grid of readings that would help Szetu outline the anomaly and determine whether it made sense to drill and, if so, where.

Szetu wanted to do two surveys. The first, completed by Evald "Monty" Hall and Dennis Lavalle, was an EM survey to identify electromagnetic anomalies. Walking down the lines the crew had cut, Lavalle wore a harness that held a transmitting electromagnetic coil, which surrounded him like a small hula hoop and was attached to a 200-foot cable. At the other end of the cable, Hall carried a receiving electromagnetic coil and wore headphones to listen to the signal. Every hundred feet, Lavalle stopped and pushed a button to send electromagnetic waves through the ground. At his end, Hall recorded the reading, which indicated the presence of conductive material. Another man handled a second survey using a magnetometer, a hand-held device that measured the strength of a magnetic field. That can be useful if a base-metal deposit contains iron sulphides such as pyrite or chalcopyrite, though not all do. He took readings on every second line. Although the magnetometer survey showed a weak anomaly, Hall and Lavalle hadn't picked up anything. Szetu called George and said, "I think we have to change our methods."

□

Back in December 1963, it had occurred to Marjorie Oliver that Viola would be an ideal guest on *What's My Line?* The CBS television game show featured a panel that tried to guess the occupations of guests with unusual jobs. Without telling her friend, Oliver wrote the show's producers. They didn't think MacMillan was right for *What's My Line?* but liked the idea of her appearing on *To Tell the Truth*, another of the network's programs.

In June 1964, MacMillan flew down to New York to film the show. After she returned, on June 12, Windfall Oils and Mines held a shareholder meeting in the Board of Trade's council chambers. Viola sat beside the *Northern Miner*'s Graham Ackerley, one of the reporters in attendance. He found her in a chatty mood. When he asked if the ground geophysics had found the anomaly indicated by the airborne survey, she told him that the geophysics crew was still at work, but they'd found two anomalies. Drilling would start soon. She also invited him to a wedding, promising the guests would include "all sorts of very important people." He wasn't the only reporter to receive an invitation to the nuptials. MacMillan also invited Frank Kaplan of the *Financial Post* over the phone. Both men declined.

Among the other items on the agenda were an update on the exploration work, votes on some transactions related to the Nevada property, the new round of underwriting and the optioning of the twelve claims owned by Viola. Even though they still owned most of the 250,000 shares they'd received in the deal for the claims, John Larche, Fred Rousseau and Don McKinnon weren't there. In fact, other than Viola and the board members, the only registered shareholder who showed up was a man with 1,000 shares.

When it came time to vote on optioning the claims, the MacMillans and the companies they controlled abstained as part of the deal with the TSE. The one exception was Consolidated Golden Arrow, which was a publicly traded company. In addition, the couple had the proxies of other shareholders, including from Larche, Rousseau and McKinnon. The motion passed unanimously. A short report on the meeting ran in the *Northern Miner* under the headline "Windfall Meeting Routine." Three nights later, Viola and George attended the wedding at which Marjorie Oliver became Marjorie Humphrey. That evening, the episode of *To Tell the Truth* featuring MacMillan aired. If she'd hoped the publicity would boost Windfall's stock, it didn't work. The next day, the trading volume was low, and the share price slipped two cents to fifty-five cents.

But the stock did receive a small bump on June 18 when Texas Gulf issued a statement that boosted the excitement, and the envy, in the Timmins area. The company had been busy drilling, and after twenty-six holes, it now realized the Kidd Township ore body was bigger and richer than it had originally thought. The new information put the deposit at fifty-five million tons, more than double the original estimate, with higher concentrations of copper, zinc and silver.

For the MacMillans, the news provided even more incentive to start drilling on the Windfall claims. As if they needed any more motivation. Ken Darke had swooped into the Porcupine district and quickly found a massive deposit for Texas Gulf, and they respected him for it. In fact, the same weekend Viola bought the Wark and Prosser Townships claims, she'd dropped by Darke's room at the Bon Air to congratulate him, even though they knew each other only slightly. But the discovery stung. "That also made us people feel a little silly after being around here for twenty-five, thirty, years and not being able to find that ore body," George later said. "It also made us very anxious to find one."

Although no Canadian prospectors could afford to spend the $2 million the American company had devoted to its search, the MacMillans and their bush colleagues didn't have to go far for evidence that mineral strikes can happen in bunches. Viola and George weren't the only people hoping the Texas Gulf find would be just the first of many. By the summer, as many as forty diamond drill rigs were operating in the area.

□

George MacMillan had held off on showing Keevil's airborne survey to Rocky Szetu because he didn't want the exploration efforts to focus on just one part of the property. But now he did. No wonder they hadn't been able to pick up anything on the ground, thought Szetu. The conductors were weak. He asked Hall to redo the survey using a 300-foot cable to allow the EM instrument to take deeper readings. This time, the equipment identified a conductor that appeared to be a good size, though not especially strong. MacMillan asked him, "Would you drill that conductor if you were two hundred miles in the bush?"

"I certainly would," Szetu said.

The information also helped determine where to drill the first hole, at what angle and to what depth to get through to the other side of the conductive material. On June 28, the two men went to the property and spotted the first drill hole. Szetu marked it on a map: "D.H. No. 1, forty-five degrees, five hundred and fifty feet."

Weeks earlier, the MacMillans had spoken to Edgar Bradley about reserving a drill. The couple often hired Bradley Brothers to do their drilling. Owned by Edgar and Wilbert Bradley and Frank Spencer, the company was experienced and well-respected. The head office was in Noranda, Quebec, but with so many new projects in the Porcupine, Edgar Bradley had set up a Timmins office on Second Avenue. On June 20, the MacMillans signed a contract for 5,000 feet of drilling at $3.25 per foot.

Over the last few days of June, a crew moved the drill rig onto the site and set it up. They also created a camp, including building platforms for the tents that would be home to the cookhouse and sleeping quarters. Drilling started Wednesday, July 1, and continued around the clock with two shifts.

Diamond drilling has been an important part of mining exploration since the latter part of the 1800s. By extracting a continuous tube of rock, called core, it provides information about the depth, dimensions and concentration of an ore body. The size of the core depends on the drill, but the one Bradley Brothers used on the Windfall site produced core that was one and a quarter inches in diameter. The process works like this: a circular bit encrusted with a matrix of small industrial-grade diamonds rotates at the end of a series of drill rods. As the hole gets deeper, the crew adds more rods. The rig pumps water down the inside of the rods to cool and lubricate the bit so it's less likely to get stuck and to reduce the chances of overheating. The lowest rod is the core barrel. As the bit bores the hole, rock moves up into the barrel. Once the barrel, which on the Bradley rig held up to fifteen feet of core, is full, the crew raises it to the surface.

A crew typically included a runner, who operated the drill, and a helper. On most jobs, they removed the core from the barrel, but sometimes mining companies hired their own person, known as the core grabber, to handle the task. Often this was because the drillers had hit something promising or were working in a sensitive area and the company was keen on maintaining secrecy. Both shifts at the Windfall site had core grabbers who worked for the MacMillans. The drill had closed barrels that hid the extracted rock, though during removal of the bit, a small section—at most about four inches—became visible. When the crew raised the barrel, the core grabber took it from the drill and carried it away from the rig. Then he removed the rock and placed it in the trays of the core boxes, making sure to keep it in the proper order. Each box was one and a half metres long with five trays running lengthwise. Once he filled a box, he put a top on it, nailed it shut and marked the footage. At the end of the shift, a tractor took the boxes to the main camp, about a kilometre and a half away. This system limited how much of the core the drillers could see, although they couldn't miss the colour of the sludge, a slurry of finely ground rock and water that's a byproduct of drilling.

When Viola returned to Toronto on June 29, George had stayed behind to keep an eye on the drillers' progress. While in the Porcupine over the next few weeks, he occasionally slept at the Empire Hotel but mostly at the office in Timmins or at Windfall property. He and Viola were frequently in different places and had always seemed an unlikely match. But whether it was a case of opposites attracting or two people who wisely chose partners who provided something they lacked, they loved each other. Despite the added complication of often working together, as well as rumours that Viola had affairs with other mining men, the marriage appeared to be a good one. A revealing moment occurred when they made a television appearance on a CBC current affairs program called *Graphic* in 1957. During the interview, George called host Joe McCulley by the wrong name, leading Viola to shoot her husband a stern look and quietly but firmly correct him before turning back to the camera and flashing a charming smile. The MacMillans were Canadian mining's power couple, though given how few women were in the industry, they didn't have much competition. And she was always the more powerful of the two. "George was very proud of me and I didn't have any trouble with him not taking the lead," according to Viola. "He was willing to follow."

Certainly, he was more experienced in the bush. Two uncles, Black Jack and Alex, had joined the Cobalt rush, and as a teenager, George had gone prospecting with his father and helped with assessment work on some Larder Lake claims. But even in the bush, she was more motivated. In 1936, they'd joined a gold rush near Larder Lake after a discovery by Kerr-Addison Gold Mines. One day, Viola saw a small hill that reminded her of her father's gravel pit at Windermere. She'd help move the output to scows on Lake Rousseau when she was growing up. She checked it out. "I hauled enough gravel as a kid to know a gravel hill when I see one," she later said. That night, she suggested to George that they get up before dawn to stake some claims. If there was a possibility of gold, he'd have readily agreed, but not knowing anything about gravel, he dismissed her plan and said he had no interest in getting out of his warm sleeping bag in the dark to do that. By this point, the couple was driving a Graham-Paige roadster that they'd bought second-hand and painted dark red, so Viola offered their old Model T jalopy to Art Wilson in exchange for help staking the claims. Once the Kerr-Addison property went into production in 1938 and needed a lot of gravel for backfilling mined-out areas, Viola's investment of an old car and an early morning staking session proved shrewd.

She and George had complementary skills. He knew more about geology and prospecting, but when it came to evaluating a property's value and figuring out how to realize it, even he said, "It's Viola's show." One thing they had in common was that they were easy to underestimate: she just because she was a woman; he because he seemed to live in her shadow. In 1953, a magazine writer described him as "white-haired and slow-speaking" and said, "George likes to hide behind her driving personality." Friendly and cheerful, he had a big, warm smile and a gentle laugh, but even Viola saw him as "laid back" and "a very quiet, easygoing guy, not at all one to push himself forward." When she wasn't in the office, he'd put his coat and tie on the back of a chair, take off his shoes and walk around in his socks. She had too much energy to relax like that.

While he worked, and relaxed, in her office, they weren't business partners. This wasn't because they didn't trust each other. One reason: she wanted to be a success on her own and not be known simply as Mrs. George MacMillan. Another reason: he was a big worrier and not much of a gambler when it came to investing money, which she believed was essential for success in mining. He was, by his own admission, a wildcatter, someone willing to speculate on properties that big miners had walked away from or even dismissed before doing any serious exploration and development work. "We have to take longer chances than established companies," he later said, "and in taking these chances we hope to be right about thirty percent of the time and if we are, we are solvent." But he was so risk-averse that he didn't even like borrowing from banks. With her higher tolerance for financial precarity, she didn't want to make him anxious. While they often had some involvement—executive role, board membership or ownership position—in each other's companies, they continued to operate as two independent business entities and kept separate sets of books. But, as Viola's friend Marjorie later said, "Well, can you separate George and Viola MacMillan?"

Still, they had different responsibilities: he handled the mining side, she took care of the money side. They had the same goal, though. As she told the *Financial Post* a couple of weeks before drilling started on the Prosser claims, emphasizing each word, "I've gotta have another mine."

CHAPTER EIGHT

PINK PENTHOUSE

Viola MacMillan hadn't intended to rent a downtown apartment, let alone a penthouse. But in 1954, she realized she needed more room because she and her staff could barely move in her Yonge Street office. She found what she was looking for in the Knight Building, a fancy new brick-and-aluminum tower at 25 Adelaide Street West, which offered her more room and a prestigious new address. After she leased suitable office space, she discovered that there was a penthouse apartment on the thirteenth floor with a fifteen-metre wall of glass that offered a view of Lake Ontario. At first, she laughed when the building's owners suggested she rent it. "Why, my home is only ten minutes away from here by cab," she said, perhaps indulging in a little exaggeration. But she soon came to see the wisdom of the idea: a handy place to stay when she worked late and a distinctive venue for entertaining clients..

MacMillan had fun decorating the penthouse, but most of the mining men who visited must have been shocked. The apartment had a terrace and the standard comforts of the middle-class home—including a small piano and a hi-fi phonograph—and the gadget everyone wanted, a television set. But it also had two mirrored walls, a mirrored column and pink broadloom. Actually, aside from a little beige, just about everything in the place, including the ice bucket and paper napkins, was pink. Perhaps

MacMillan just liked the colour; she did like feminine things. Or maybe she wanted to make a point. She was, after all, a success not just in the man's world of 1950s Canada but in mining. And she was the president of a respected organization that was practically a fraternity, given how few women were part of it.

Being able to indulge her more feminine tastes didn't mean she was ready to stop spending time in the bush. Despite her money and success, despite her responsibilities with her companies and the PDA, despite having reached her fifties, she kept bedrolls, tents and other gear at the ready for whenever she had the urge. "I'm not going to spend all my time in the office," she told a reporter in 1955. "You can bet on that. I'll be out in the field whenever I get a chance."

When she was in Toronto, MacMillan usually made it to her office by seven or seven thirty in the morning. Once there, she was a non-stop whirlwind of restless energy. One journalist who interviewed her was impressed by how she could juggle so many things: "As she talks she answers the telephone, pours coffee, signs cheques, issues vouchers for thousands of dollars' worth of mining equipment, and never for a moment loses the thread of the conversation."

She usually left the office at five o'clock, but that was rarely the end of her workday. She'd often take the elevator up to the penthouse, where she'd meet with people from the mining or financial industries. Depending on how late things went, she sometimes just crashed in the apartment. If she went home, all the extra rooms in the big house on Oriole Parkway—sometimes referred to as a mansion in the press—came in handy when she hosted senior personnel from her properties or other out-of-town mining men, which meant the shoptalk might continue until after midnight. The house was a great place for entertaining, and the MacMillans took full advantage of it by throwing many lavish parties. The guest lists were typically full of business associates, as work was never far from Viola's mind.

Even though she stayed in the penthouse more than she'd originally expected, it lacked personal touches. There was only one painting, which she'd selected because of the colours, and some plants, but otherwise a distinct lack of clutter. When journalist Christina McCall visited for a 1957 magazine article, she saw only one book: a Department of Mines publication called *Out of the Earth*. Explaining that she kept the apartment that way so if she had to leave it behind, she could do so without a second thought, MacMillan insisted, "I'd be every bit as happy in a tent."

The pink penthouse was a long way from the struggling farm where she'd grown up as the thirteenth of fifteen children. It was also a long way from the bush, where she'd so often stayed in a tent when she started out as a prospector, and even from one of her mine sites, where she regularly stayed in bunkhouses with the men who worked for her. Naturally, she wanted a journalist to believe she hadn't changed a bit. She may have believed it herself.

While MacMillan had done well since settling in Toronto, a crucial move in her ascent to the penthouse was the 1945 incorporation of ViolaMac Limited. She used it to buy and develop the first mine of her own, and it would become the most successful of all the companies she created or acquired. As was often the case for her, its success started after someone she knew presented her with an opportunity. One of the benefits of her PDA position was a chance to meet many mining men, even if she sometimes had to win over those who were reluctant to have a woman in their midst. These new connections regularly paid off. So did old ones. Art Cockshutt, whom MacMillan had known since her early days in the bush, approached her in 1947 with an intriguing opportunity. The prospector had an option on the old Slocan Rambler Mine in the Kootenay region of British Columbia. Although long closed, it had opened in 1895 and was for many years an excellent producer of lead, silver and zinc. Cockshutt asked MacMillan if she'd be interested in buying an interest in the property. She sent Willis Ambrose, another PDA connection, to have a look. After graduating from Yale with a PhD in geology in 1935, he found work with the Geological Survey of Canada and was one of the speakers at the association's first strategic metals workshops in 1942. He left the GSC three years later to work as a consultant and to lecture part-time at the University of Toronto and Queen's University.

After checking out the Slocan Rambler, Ambrose returned with a favourable report. With gold mining in the doldrums and few encouraging signs about the viability of Golden Arrow's property in Hislop Township, MacMillan was ready to pursue something other than gold. She incorporated B.C. Slocan-Rambler Mines (1947) as a subsidiary of Golden Arrow and paid Cockshutt and his wife 300,000 shares each. As part of an underwriting deal, she bought 200,000 shares at ten cents to "put some money immediately in the treasury and get the ball rolling." Then she began a drilling program to see if reopening the mine made sense. If it did, she could exercise her options on another 800,000 shares over the following two years at prices ranging from ten cents to fifty cents.

The drilling wasn't generating any results to get excited about when she heard about another possibility. One of the many old mines in the Slocan region was the Victor. George Petty had discovered the deposit in 1921 and opened the mountainside mine two years later. Ernest Doney, who'd been leasing it from Petty's daughter since 1931, was extracting ore by hand from a modest vein. He told MacMillan the mine might be available for the right price. Turned out, she could have the Victor as well as the nearby Lone Bachelor and the Cinderella properties for $50,000, half up front. But she'd also have to pay Doney $15,000 to buy him out of the lease. In 1948, acting on a hunch that the deposit had richer veins than the one the old prospector was working, MacMillan sold a large chunk of ViolaMac shares, emptied her bank account and raised the final $1,000 from a financier she ran into in Calgary. When she handed Doney his cheque, he said, "I hope you make a million, Mrs. Mac."

Ambrose mapped the property, which had five adits, the horizontal openings in mines, in a column on the side of the mountain. After MacMillan picked up a used air compressor on the cheap, six miners who'd been working for her at the Rambler began drilling underground. Before long, they stopped. MacMillan had gone to San Francisco for a mining convention and George called several hotels before finding her in Vancouver, where she'd stopped to pursue a possible deal for yet another Slocan mine. His call woke her up. "We've finally hit the main vein at the Victor," he said. "You better get back here as soon as you can."

Viola walked into the mine with George and Doney, and when they reached where the drillers had stopped, their miner's lamps shone on a blueish-grey wall. It was galena, a mineral that's the chief ore of lead and often contains silver. MacMillan squealed with delight. Throwing her arms around the old prospector, she said, "Oh, Mr. Doney, I'm so sorry it wasn't you that found it. You should have found it."

"Now Mrs. Mac," he replied, "I told you I wanted you to make a million."

The main vein was rich in silver, lead and zinc and contained some gold, copper and cadmium. After four months, a truck delivered the first load of ore to a smelter. It was worth $3,500. "We nearly dropped dead when that beautiful cheque came in," she said later. The money allowed her to pay her workers and buy dynamite and blasting caps. More cheques followed as the five adits became nine, with the last one on the adjoining Cinderella property. MacMillan's first producing mine did indeed make her a millionaire.

She bought a fruit ranch near New Denver, not far from the mine, and she and George thought they might eventually retire there. But she wasn't ready for that yet. Instead, she invested much of her earnings in other projects. She liked making money, she liked spending money, and she liked working in the mining industry best of all.

□

MacMillan often took the bus downtown to the Knight Building. One day, she found herself riding the same one as a man she knew who worked in exploration for Noranda. Since she wasn't one for social chit-chat—she was all business, all the time—the conversation quickly turned to work. She told him about her plans for a property in the northwest corner of Saskatchewan. The MacMillans had spent the summer of 1953 there, living in a tent and prospecting as part of a big uranium rush in the area. They went back the next year, again without success. But in the fall, they took a liking to some ground owned by Lake Cinch Uranium Mines and started buying up shares through ViolaMac and a financing subsidiary called Deebank. The location was certainly promising. The eight claims sat between the Eldorado and Gunnar Mines, both of which would be among the top uranium producers in Canada. She knew that Noranda was one of two companies that had checked out the Lake Cinch claims and taken a pass, so she couldn't have been surprised when the exploration man was dismissive of her hopes for the claims. "Oh, you're going to be disappointed there," he said. "We did a lot of work on that property and didn't find anything worthwhile."

When she explained that she was going to drill by the lake, he said the fault wasn't there. Although even George had advised her against pursuing the project, MacMillan thought she knew better, or at least she trusted her intuition. "There was something about the geology down toward the lake that just gave me a hunch we would find a fault down there," she recounted in her autobiography. Sure enough, the first drill hole hit good ore. Subsequent holes were so promising that MacMillan exercised her remaining share options early.

Lake Cinch was remote, reachable only by air in the winter and by air or water in the summer, but MacMillan kept close tabs on developments from Toronto as well as making the occasional visit. One day in 1955, for example, she flew in early; changed from city duds to bush clothes; toured the property with senior staff; looked at core samples; talked about the location for a bridge across a creek; agreed on the shaft site; arranged for the drillers to begin a hole; discussed locations for the bunkhouse, cookhouse and other mine buildings; and mused about where some private homes might go. Then, at the end of the day, she flew back to Toronto. Her attention to detail paid off: after she sank a shaft in the fall of 1956, the underground results were even better than the drilling had promised.

The dawn of the nuclear age had turned uranium into a strategic mineral. In June 1942, C.D. Howe received a visit from a British delegation that included the high commissioner and two scientists. During a two-hour meeting, the Liberal minister of munitions and supply learned about the development of a new weapon based on the power of the atom. The device required uranium, a radioactive mineral that Gilbert LaBine's Eldorado Gold Mines had plenty of in a pitchblende deposit in the Northwest Territories.

Lean and square-jawed, LaBine was an ambitious and adventurous guy who was, like MacMillan, both a prospector and a promoter, though he was even more successful than she was. As a kid growing up on an Ottawa Valley farm, he was fascinated by tales of the Klondike gold rush. As a teenager, he'd worked at Cobalt's University Mine for less than a year before turning to prospecting. He staked some silver claims and sold them for $5,000, then joined the Porcupine and Kirkland Lake gold rushes. In 1926, he and an older brother, Charlie, started Eldorado to develop some gold claims near Red Lake, Manitoba, a project they eventually abandoned after sinking a shaft and cutting several drifts, as miners call the underground tunnels that follow ore bodies. Despite that disappointment, the company still had money in its coffers and the shareholders agreed to let the LaBines look for another mine.

Gilbert went prospecting for copper and gold on the east side of Great Bear Lake, not far from the Arctic Circle, in 1929. While flying out in August, he'd spotted cobalt bloom from the air and resolved to return the next year to check it out. The result was Canada's first discovery of a commercial deposit of pitchblende. Also known as uraninite, it is the host ore of uranium, radium and other minerals. LaBine was one of the few people in the country who could identify it because he'd taken some mining classes in Haileybury, and one guest lecturer was Willet Miller. The provincial geologist showed off some pitchblende samples he'd collected in Europe and said he believed there might be some in the Cobalt area. Once LaBine, the prospector, found the deposit, LaBine, the promoter, had to find a way to finance a mine. The latter proved harder than the former, but eventually, Eldorado worked the ore body for radium and built a plant to refine it in Port Hope, Ontario. Uranium was initially just a waste product. Its main commercial use was in paint for ceramics, but the company hadn't been able to tap that market. LaBine believed uranium might be worth something someday and stored some of it, but plenty ended up in Lake Ontario. The radium was already valuable for cancer treatments. In fact, its potential to save so many lives and its high price—$70,000 a gram—led the then-opposition Liberals and others to begin calling for nationalization of the mine as a social justice measure as early as 1931.

The mining industry has always liked to bill itself as a beacon of free enterprise, conveniently ignoring its reliance on government assistance, encouragement and technical expertise. For decades, prospectors had been taking advantage of the maps and reports generated by the exploration work of the GSC. Most provinces had bodies that helped and encouraged exploration and the development of minerals, and the federal Department of Mines offered plenty of free advice and services. That's how Eldorado could succeed with no professional engineers or geologists on its payroll. During the winter of 1930, LaBine had gone to Ottawa to consult GSC research before returning to Great Bear Lake. After the discovery, the Department of Mines even conducted a radium refining pilot project. Still, owning a mine was too much for R.B. Bennett's Conservatives. Good thing, too. Operating in the remote subarctic was expensive, and radium prices sank lower and lower during the '30s as Eldorado's production smashed the monopoly on the world's supply held by a Belgium syndicate with mines in the Congo, and the Second World War ended sales to Europe. Deeply in debt, Eldorado shut down operations in 1940.

Two years later, the company quietly reopened the mine to provide uranium to the US government for the Manhattan Project, the top-secret program to develop an atomic bomb led by Robert Oppenheimer. Similar experiments were underway in the United Kingdom under a program code-named Tube Alloys. Concerned about maintaining the supply, pricing and security of uranium, the British delegation that visited Howe recommended that the Canadian government take control of Eldorado. The Liberal Minister of Everything readily agreed. With the country at war, he had a different attitude toward the nationalization of mines than his Conservative predecessors. Within weeks, the government began secretly purchasing stock from shareholders. "I haven't any regrets," LaBine later said about the takeover. "Sure it was high-handed burglary. But it was war. After all, what you lose on oranges, you gain on bananas." Howe also asked him to stay in charge of the new Crown corporation, renamed Eldorado Mining and Refining. Most of its uranium oxide went to the Americans, much to the displeasure of the British. One consequence of this was that minerals from the Canadian North helped develop the devastating atomic bombs that the United States dropped on the Japanese cities of Hiroshima and Nagasaki in 1945.

Earlier, to ensure that the Crown corporation maintained its monopoly, the government had banned prospecting for the mineral by the private sector. Under LaBine's direction, Eldorado dispatched teams of prospectors to various parts of the country starting in 1944. This led to the discovery of uranium ore bodies near Beaverlodge Lake in northern Saskatchewan two years later. LaBine stayed at Eldorado until 1947 and then continued his career as a prospector and promoter with an older company of his called Gunnar Gold Mines. When the government rescinded the moratorium against private-sector uranium prospecting in 1948, prospectors began scouring the Canadian Shield, and a staking rush erupted in northern Saskatchewan. Once again, LaBine had more luck with uranium than gold. In 1952, a prospector working for him found a large deposit on the north shore of Lake Athabasca. Eldorado's Beaverlodge operation, which included the Ace, Fay and Verna Mines, opened in 1953. LaBine's nearby Gunnar Mine began production two years later. Smaller mines followed, and Uranium City exploded from an outpost full of tents to a thriving boomtown.

During the 1950s, uranium mining also flourished in other parts of the country, including in the Northwest Territories and in Ontario at Bancroft and, especially, Elliot Lake. Helping fuel this new mineral rush were the Canadian government's contracts with the United States and Britain to supply uranium at a guaranteed price until 1962. And, like many others, MacMillan saw opportunity in the radioactive mineral. "I particularly wanted to get into the uranium business," she said later, "because in the annals of history, I wanted to have something to do with the atomic age." If Lake Cinch didn't work out, her holdings in the Beaverlodge area included interests in Uranium Ridge, a property beside the Lorado Mine; Glencair Mining, which had property next to the Gunnar Mine; and Gateway Uranium. ViolaMac also still had substantial non-uranium interests in the rest of the country.

By the mid-1950s, the Victor was generating a profit of more than $1 million a year. That allowed MacMillan to go on an acquisition spree to increase the size and diversity of her holdings. She now had controlling interest of or significant stakes in Lone Bachelor Mines, a promising property near the Victor; Camarillo Oils, a company participating in the development of oil fields in Alberta's Grand Prairie region; Lithia Mines and Chemicals, which had a lithium property in Manitoba's Cat Lake area; copper claims at Cirrus Creek, near Manitouwadge, Ontario; and base metal claims at Bathurst, New Brunswick. Her other businesses included MacMillan Prospecting and Development; Variometer Surveys, the geophysics firm she'd started with Willis Ambrose; and Airquests, the exploration company with the airline charter. She also had a controlling interest in Golden Arrow, which she'd reorganized as Consolidated Golden Arrow in 1953. She was reputed to be the only woman to be president of a company listed on the TSE. This portfolio removed any doubt that she'd established herself as a serious member of the $2 billion Canadian mining industry. Meanwhile, under her leadership, the Prospectors and Developers Association had become an influential national organization with a famously wild annual convention every March. No wonder she was flying close to 50,000 kilometres a year.

One of those flights was down to Washington on a lobbying mission. The US wanted all the uranium Canada had to offer but had negotiated terms that called for a ceiling on the price, as well as two deadlines that mines needed to meet: to sign a contract by April 1, 1956, and to go into production by the same date a year later. When it looked like Lake Cinch would miss the second one, MacMillan convinced the Americans to allow a little wiggle room. She didn't need much of the extra time, as the mine opened in May 1957, initially producing 75 tons of ore a day. By the end of the year, it had ramped up to 200 tons daily. Like several other mines in the area, it was too small to make building its own mill economic, so the ore went to the one at the nearby Lorado Mine. The supply contracts, which ensured a steady market, and the mine's higher-than-expected ore concentration meant paying off the $1.5 million investment didn't take long. In 1958, Lake Cinch Mines had a net profit of more than $1.7 million. "The dream of every prospector is to see a new mine brought into production," observed *Globe and Mail* mining editor James Scott in a story about the opening. "That dream came true for Viola MacMillan, the dynamic bundle of energy who is a prospector, promoter and company president all rolled into one." Her hunch, and her confidence to pursue it despite the naysayers, had given her a productive mine. Though dwarfed by Eldorado and Gunnar, Lake Cinch was a good moneymaker for MacMillan.

After her success in northern Saskatchewan, MacMillan returned to the Porcupine camp, as she and many others called the Timmins region. And as the end of the 1950s edged closer, she still wasn't satisfied. Production at the Victor Mine dropped in 1957 and plunged the next year. She knew she needed to add new properties to replace the ones that would inevitably reach the end of their natural lives. She'd been trying to do that, but despite her high hopes, nothing had come of the base metal claims in Bathurst. She couldn't find any buyers for her lithium, and with no sales contract, work had stalled at Uranium Ridge. Lake Cinch was a rare bright spot. But once again, her connections came through for her when she received a phone call from George Jamieson, a prospector she'd known since her early days in the Porcupine.

Working for a local syndicate in the 1920s, he'd staked some claims northwest of Timmins in Robb Township. He'd also staked some for himself. After Hollinger bought the syndicate's claims and identified enough copper and zinc to sink a shaft, it decided against putting the Kam-Kotia property into production. During the war, the company allowed the Canadian government's Wartime Metals Corporation to mine copper from an open pit on the site. After the war, Hollinger lost interest in the property again, but MacMillan, who'd served on the War Metals Advisory Board, didn't. She couldn't convince the company to sell, though Jules Timmins, who'd succeeded his Uncle Noah as president of Hollinger, said he'd do the deal if she could convince Jamieson to sell his adjoining claims. The problem was that, for years, the old prospector had stuck to one answer for everyone who asked: they weren't for sale.

One Friday morning early in 1959, MacMillan was in her Knight Building office when Jamieson called. "You're going to be in Timmins, aren't you, you and George?"

Viola had no plans to be in Timmins; in fact, the MacMillans were going to Chicago to spend the weekend with friends. But she said, "Yes, George, we are."

"Good," he said, "I'll be looking for you to come out and see me."

Instead of boarding a plane bound for Chicago, they flew to Timmins. When the MacMillans woke up Saturday morning, they looked out the window of their room in the Empire Hotel and saw a huge dump of new snow. George MacMillan wasn't keen on driving in that, so the reclusive Jamieson came into town. By one presumably exaggerated account, he snowshoed thirty kilometres to get there. As she'd guessed when he'd first called, he was ready to sell the claims. They quickly made a deal in the hotel room. She drew up the papers and Jamieson signed them the next morning, with two hotel maids as witnesses because her husband was still asleep. Then she phoned Jules Timmins in Montreal. He remembered his promise and agreed to sell Hollinger's 82.5 percent of Kam-Kotia Porcupine Mines to ViolaMac for $198,000.

Lots of mining people thought she was crazy and that the property, which included an old open-pit mine and a mill, would never amount to anything. But MacMillan was convinced there was a valuable ore body there, and after doing a geophysical survey, she started a drilling program in 1958. One day, George was at the site when some men from Texas Gulf showed up in a helicopter. One of them said, "You have fine copper ore there." The MacMillans later contended that the American company would never have been in the Porcupine if it hadn't been for them.

By the summer of 1959, the drillers had completed eight holes, and the results were better than expected. Viola was increasingly excited about the property as she and George drove out west. The road trip was to combine business in Vancouver and a vacation at their fruit ranch near New Denver.

While in British Columbia that summer, MacMillan began to feel unwell but wasn't sure what the problem was. Although resting at the ranch would have been prudent, the fifty-six-year-old was determined to make the trip to Vancouver for a business meeting. During the drive, her condition deteriorated, and she told George she wanted to go back to New Denver. She was so ill that they stopped to see a doctor in Nelson. He rushed her to the hospital. She stayed for a month. When she was finally well enough to fly home, she had to go on a stretcher, accompanied by a doctor.

As sturdy as she was, MacMillan had faced some health challenges, including the miscarriage in 1935 and a heart murmur diagnosis in 1953. And then, when she made it back to Toronto, her doctor gave her bad news:

she'd had a heart attack and needed to stop working. Given the fortune MacMillan had amassed, she could have resolved to enjoy retirement, spending time in her downtown penthouse, in her big house uptown, on the farm near Tottenham, at the New Denver property and in her apartment at the glamorous Surf Club in Miami. Or seeing the world. Or doing just about anything she wanted. But leaving the career she loved and was good at was not an appealing prospect.

Nor was it the best time to sell. Her Victor Mine wasn't worth much by this point, and even Lake Cinch was less profitable than it had been because the ore coming out of it was now lower grade. Worse, the United States had found enough domestic supplies of uranium so it wouldn't be renewing its contract with the Canadian government once it expired in 1962. Britain soon followed suit. Lorado closed. It wasn't all bad news, though. The government paid Lake Cinch $2.5 million in compensation, which meant ViolaMac had a lot of cash on its books. In addition, the drilling program at Kam-Kotia had found another copper deposit, making a profitable mine even more likely.

In July 1960, MacMillan sold controlling interest in ViolaMac to New Dickenson Mines. Run by Toronto mining promoter Arthur White, it had a producing gold property in the Red Lake area. The nearly 1.5 million shares she relinquished represented 42 percent of the company, which had been trading at around $1.35. But she kept some shares—"for old time's sake"—and stayed on as vice-president. Although she no longer owned a significant interest in any active mines, she held on to several of her smaller private companies, including MacMillan Prospecting, Variometer Surveys and Airquests. And she liked being president of the PDA too much to give that up; in fact, she said, "I will have more time for the prospectors association." In other words, she may have reduced her workload and stress, but it was hardly retirement.

Serving as White's vice-president wasn't enjoyable. After all, she'd been her own boss for three decades. She lasted a year. More than that, even stepping back from mining only partway was too difficult for her, and she admitted, "We thought we would slow down a little bit, but I was never happy about it." When White was looking to raise some money for ViolaMac, he agreed to sell her enough shares in Consolidated Golden

Arrow Mines to give her back control, though he kept a sizable chunk. The company had sentimental value because her association with it went back to the 1930s in Timmins, and she'd regretted losing it in the ViolaMac sale. It also had some potentially valuable assets, including interest in a Slocan property and thirteen claims near Dogpaw Lake in the Kenora area. MacMillan commissioned a drilling program on the latter.

That wasn't all. In December 1961, she and George took over Windfall Oils and Mines. Now with control of these two public companies, and plans to find and develop mines, Viola had definitely returned to the industry she loved. "I suppose I knew I was going against my doctor's orders," she later recalled, "but it felt great to be back in business again."

CHAPTER NINE

BLACK SLUDGE

C old for July, with rain showers and fog, Friday the third was not a pleasant day at the Windfall site. Damp weather seemed even more miserable on the Prosser property because it was mostly swamp, except for one granite outcrop. Looking at the core, George MacMillan saw a small amount of mineralization. He grabbed a four-inch piece and put it in the pocket of his raincoat. But by seven o'clock in the evening, the crew had drilled 300 feet and still had not encountered a conductor. Disappointed, MacMillan drove back to Timmins. Early the next morning, he called Szetu, who was still in bed in Toronto. The geologist explained that he'd estimated the conductor would start at 300 vertical feet, and since the hole was at a forty-five-degree angle, they weren't there yet. Go another hundred feet, he assured MacMillan, and you'll hit it.

During the night, the drillers had watched the sludge coming up from the drill turn black. Walter Turney, the core grabber, had never done the job before so he didn't realize the significance of the change in colour. But Fernand Boucher, the runner on the night shift and the crew's foreman, was a veteran driller. He'd worked on half a dozen MacMillan projects in the past, including at Kam-Kotia when Viola had owned it. He said that black sludge was a good sign and reminded him of what he'd seen there.

As soon as MacMillan showed up at the site Saturday morning, he heard about the sludge turning black. That indicated the drill bit was now boring through either sulphides or graphite. MacMillan laid the core boxes on the ground and examined the cylinders of rock while on his hands and knees. Some minerals, such as gold and silver, may not be visible in host rock. But an experienced eye can usually tell just by looking at a length of core if it contains base metals such as copper and zinc—and often make a good estimate, within less than 1 percent, of the concentration. Although he wasn't a trained geologist, MacMillan had been a prospector and mine developer for decades. He'd looked at core countless times in his career and was certainly capable of telling whether the first drill hole contained anything of interest. He liked what he saw.

The drillers had gone through 68 feet of overburden before reaching 300 feet of volcanic rock called andesite. MacMillan spotted some flecks of chalcopyrite, a brassy yellow mineral associated with copper, and brown and black-jack sphalerites, which are associated with zinc. He could see no native silver or free gold in the core, though that didn't mean much. After that, there was a fifty-five-foot section of what he thought was probably rhyolite breccia, which is common and wouldn't necessarily be of much interest, except that it indicates geological disturbance. Rhyolite is a brittle volcanic rock and brecciation is the process of breaking up into fragments and then being cemented together again. "When I see brecciation anyplace," he said later, "I immediately pick up my ears." Even better, he believed Texas Gulf had rhyolite breccia next to its ore body, at least according to the rumours he'd heard because the company wasn't sharing that information. At 416 feet, the Windfall drillers had entered graphitic shale with pyrite, an iron sulphide sometimes called fool's gold because it looks like the precious metal. None of the mineralization suggested economic ore yet, but MacMillan was encouraged. The drillers had hit what he considered the target zone, and he was hopeful the mineral concentration would increase as they went deeper, maybe even show commercial values.

The problem was snoopers. This was a common concern in an industry where everyone took it as a given that large companies hired people to keep an eye on drilling activity on other properties. Several people had already walked in along the camp road to take a gander and ask the drillers questions. Others hovered over the drill in helicopters. Noranda's Mel Rennick, who'd tried to acquire the claims for his company back in April, first checked out the drill site in a chopper on July 1. As a fieldman for the mining giant, one of his responsibilities was to gather information about other operations in the Timmins region. Noranda had a helicopter on charter to deliver some men to the bush in the morning and pick them up late in the afternoon. Several times a week, during the middle of the day, the chopper would take Rennick and cruise around so he could note the location of drills. Other companies' fieldmen did the same thing. It was all an indication of the fever in the industry after the Texas Gulf discovery.

Boucher was completely fed up with the choppers and told MacMillan so. Aside from being worried about the safety of the men on the day shift, the foreman was unhappy because the noise disturbed the sleep of the guys on the night shift. The choppers annoyed MacMillan, too, though he found it amusing that when he left his tent and walked toward the drill rig, they apparently recognized him and flew away. But he was worried about security. Even from thirty to fifty metres up—and they often hovered lower than that—people in helicopters could get a good look and determine the direction and angle of a drill. They could also determine the depth by counting the number of rods as the crew removed them from the hole when bringing up the core barrel. And now they might see that the sludge had turned black.

Many drilling operations will build a core shack, a small, lockable building. Inside, someone, usually a geologist, can work in secret and out of the weather, putting the boxes on a table, opening them, washing the core with water, then doing a close examination of it before logging it, noting and recording attributes such as the depth, rock type and any signs of mineralization. Anything that seems promising gets split in two longitudinally, with half being smashed into chunks with a hammer, then packed into labelled bags and sent to a lab to be assayed. The other half stays intact and stored in the boxes, locked in the core shack. But unless it's a big or sensitive project or on a property that's easily accessible by the public, most companies will hold off on building a core shack as long as possible. Even Texas Gulf didn't build one until April when it had four drills going. Darke kept the core from the discovery hole in his tent, then moved it off the property.

At the end of each shift on the Windfall site, the crew took the core boxes to the main camp by tractor and the core grabbers put them in a tent left over from the line-cutting crew. Throughout his career, MacMillan had always liked to look at his core again and again, each time seeing something a little different. And he was always careful with it, fearful of tampering. He didn't build a core shack on every project, but all the snoopers complicated the situation here. He'd never had choppers above one of his drill sites before. Without a shack, he had no safe place on the site to store the core the drill crew continued to extract. Nor did he have a core splitter. Early Saturday afternoon, he asked the drillers to use the tractor to move four full core boxes to his Ford Falcon station wagon, which was parked out on the road. He covered the boxes with raincoats in case anyone looked in.

After driving back to Timmins, MacMillan left the core in the basement of Windfall's office on Pine Street. Then he went to the Bradley Brothers office and asked for acid. He didn't say why, but he planned to use it to do a field test for copper. Edgar Bradley sent an employee to go to the service station to pick up some battery acid. By this point, Boucher had told Bradley the drill had hit mineralization, and Bradley had told his partners in the Noranda office. Frank Spencer and Wilbert Bradley had already been planning to drive to Timmins on Sunday to visit their sons, both of whom were working for the drilling company at another site. The three men would have a chance to talk more about Windfall in person then.

Inevitably, in an industry that thrives on speculation and scuttlebutt, MacMillan's actions on Saturday encouraged people to think he had something. His decision to remove the core boxes from the site suggested what was inside them was so good he didn't want anyone to see it. And his request for acid gave the impression that he was eager to test the core. After George left the drilling contractor's office, everyone gossiped about the good-looking core. Soon, word of a Windfall strike reached John Angus, the manager of T.A. Richardson's Timmins office.

As the rumours he'd unwittingly ignited spread, MacMillan went about his business. He received a call from Szetu, who asked, "Did you find anything yet?"

"Oh, yes," said MacMillan. "I found a conductor."

"What is it?"

"Graphite and sulphides."

That evening, George phoned Viola and told her they'd hit mineralization. She'd already been planning a return to Timmins to speak to a contractor about converting the second floor of the office into an apartment she could stay in. Her husband's news gave her a reason to head up north right away.

□

The broad streets of Timmins paid homage to its roots as a frontier town while also seeming to be waiting for the new economic boom. The north-south ones downtown bore the names of trees—Elm, Maple, Birch, Balsam, Cedar, Pine and Spruce—while the main east-west road was Algonquin Boulevard. The Empire Hotel, which had opened in 1925, sat at the corner of Spruce and Algonquin, across the street from the train station. Timmins had 650 hotel rooms, but in the days and months following the Texas Gulf announcement, any accommodation was hard to come by. During the height of the April frenzy, the Empire was turning away forty to fifty customers a day. Many visitors considered it the best place to stay in town. For those in the mining industry, though, the Empire was more than that: it was the unofficial clubhouse.

Other popular haunts were the Senator Hotel, only a couple of years old and half a dozen blocks to the west at Elm and Algonquin, and the Bon Air Motor Hotel in the other direction, just the other side of the railway tracks from the Empire. The Bon Air was a classic roadside motel with a large, colourful sign and seventy rooms that opened out to parking spots. Geologists, geophysicists and others who were staying long-term had taken it over; Texas Gulf occupied a wing of the place for living quarters and offices. At night, several helicopters parked in a field behind the low-slung building, ready to take people back to the bush first thing in the morning.

Bon Air residents regularly made the short walk to the Empire for meals or drinks. The hotel was home to a pair of the twenty-seven drinking establishments in a town of 29,000 residents. Even before Larche,

Rousseau and McKinnon had finally checked out of suite 358 in mid-June, the two bars served as prime spots for shop talk. Prospectors, drillers and timbermen dominated in the taproom, an unfussy saloon with swinging doors where, according to one journalist, they "sturdily battled upstream against rivers of beer." The Fountain Court, a slightly fancier cocktail lounge, tended to be the first choice of a slightly better-dressed crowd that included geologists, bosses and brokers. One out-of-town journalist paid a visit shortly after the Texas Gulf announcement and found the hockey game on the television, a young woman singing on a spotlit stage and two patrons wagering over who could toss the other in the large fountain in the middle of the room. "In the end," he reported, "both men were splashing on their bellies in six inches of water!"

A lot of rumours also spread in the Empire's lobby, over drinks in the rooms at the Bon Air and in the restaurant at the Senator. But gossiping took place anywhere mining people gathered. William Robertson, the manager of T.A. Richardson's Noranda branch, first heard about mineralization in the Windfall core when he dropped by a tournament at the local golf club Sunday morning.

That afternoon, Robertson was in his office when a client called with a more specific rumour. Richard Edwards, a geologist with Noranda, said that Windfall had hit a substantial length of sulphides. He hadn't heard anything about the width of the mineralization or the values, just that there were sulphides. Accumulating as much information as possible was an essential part of the job for a stock salesman. That meant speaking on a regular basis with numerous contacts in the mining and investment industries. Trading intel, or just gossip, with competitors was commonplace. One of the people Robertson called on Sunday was Ted Jones. The two had known each other since the 1940s when Jones was a partner in Jones & Bradley, the precursor to Bradley Brothers. After his departure from the drilling contractor in 1950, he went into the investment business and was now a director at Houser & Company, a Toronto brokerage firm. Robertson hoped that past connection to the Bradleys would mean Jones was aware of what was going on at the Windfall site. When Jones said he knew nothing, Robertson told him about the rumours that the MacMillans had hit sulphides in their first hole.

Frank Spencer and Wilbert Bradley didn't realize that the Windfall rumours were already spreading when they arrived in Timmins mid-afternoon on Sunday. They looked for Edgar Bradley at the Bon Air Motel and at the office, but he wasn't around. Roch Grignon was in the office. Edgar's son-in-law handled the bookkeeping and ensured supplies made it to drill sites. "George MacMillan sat right here at this desk and told us that he had sixty-five feet of good-looking core," said Grignon, adding, "He wasn't keeping it quiet. There were a number of boys around and he was talking loud enough so that they would all hear."

That evening, the three principals of the drilling company met in Edgar Bradley's room at the Bon Air and discussed whether they should buy some Windfall shares. On the one hand, they figured they could make some money; on the other, they had reservations about acting on inside information. Plus, they knew that once other people heard the drill contractors were buying shares, everyone would think the first hole was a good one, even if the MacMillans wanted to keep it a secret. Spencer suggested that Edgar call Viola and see if she was okay with them buying stock or if she would sell them some of hers privately. But Bradley couldn't reach her. In the end, they agreed that each man would make his own decision.

After receiving the call from George on Saturday, Viola decided she didn't want to drive up to Timmins at night on her own. She also thought it would be a good idea for a director to be there if the mineralization amounted to anything. She asked Ron Mills, the Tottenham neighbour who was on the Windfall board, to go with her. July is a busy time on the farm, but he agreed as long as she could wait until after he'd finished his chores. They left a little before midnight and headed up Highway 11 to Timmins in her Cadillac. When one drove, the other slept, and then they switched. They made it to the Empire Hotel around seven o'clock Sunday morning.

George was still in bed. Viola woke him up and they went for breakfast. Then, because George had arranged to meet Mike Clancy, the day shift core grabber, at nine, they waited for him in front of the hotel. When Edgar Bradley came along, the couple told him they were thinking of shutting down the drill for a few days and asked if that was okay. It would be an expensive move, given that they'd still have to pay the drillers while they waited to restart, and the couple said nothing about building a core shack. But it was no problem for Bradley, who said, "You're the boss."

The MacMillans and Mills showed up at the Windfall property close to noon. The drillers had reached 570 feet by the time the night shift finished on Sunday morning. The day shift did not take over. Most of the year, the drillers worked seven days a week, but they liked to take Sundays off in the summer. The day shift had already left camp, and the night crew was still asleep. George woke them up and everyone chatted over coffee. Four core boxes sat on a tent platform, and George opened one and lifted an end of the lid to give Viola a peek. "I think we have got some rhyolite breccia," he said. She was happy to hear this. George quickly nailed the core box closed again and didn't say more because there were people around. He asked the crew to get the tractor and move some core boxes out to the car. These samples were from just below the section he'd taken away the day before. Then the MacMillans, Mills and Turney piled into George's station wagon. Because Boucher's car had broken down, he and his eighteen-year-old helper rode with them, making for a tight squeeze. Only the cook stayed behind to look after the property.

The prevailing mood in the car was buoyant during the twenty-minute ride into town. The rear gate of the station wagon was down so the core boxes would fit. At one point, Viola turned around and asked the three men in the back seat if the core was still there. "Don't lose my gold mine," she said. Because Boucher was smaller than the other men, he sat in the front seat between the MacMillans. Despite her concern about the core, Viola was clearly delighted and asked the drill foreman if he'd bought any Windfall stock yet. Then she threw her arms around him, kissed him and thanked him for finding her a new mine.

CHAPTER TEN

LEADING LADY

Two years after Viola sold control of ViolaMac, a drill crew hit a rich zone of copper mineralization just ninety metres from the Kam-Kotia open-pit mine, and the stock reached $3.70 a share on the news. This prompted the *Toronto Telegram* to run an article with the headline "Drops $2 Million Feels Wonderful." Of course, MacMillan had not lost $2 million. She hadn't even missed out on such a payoff unless she'd held onto the company for two years, pursued the same exploration process and sold her shares just when they briefly hit $3.70. Still, it was an excuse to publish an interview with a minor celebrity—"Canada's leading lady of mining"—and run a photo of her. The media-savvy MacMillan played along. "Maybe I lost a few dollars on the deal. That's what makes mining intriguing and wonderful—if you can stand it," she told the paper, noting the success she'd had with the Victor Mine after Ernest Doney had worked it for nineteen years.

The afternoon paper's story seemed even goofier because the last paragraph noted that the stock had opened at just $1.90 that morning. But Kam-Kotia was suddenly worth a lot more, and while most people were excited about that, MacMillan was privately unhappy because if George had drilled another fifty feet, he'd have hit the ore body. She rued not holding on to the company a little longer and making more money. Still, no one ever went broke selling at a profit.

Besides, she continued to own a significant number of shares in ViolaMac and was convinced more good fortune would come her way. Although she later claimed that she never liked using her name for companies and blamed George for talking her into it (she'd also formed Virita Gold Mines from Viola and her middle name, Rita, in the 1930s), MacMillan told the reporter something that revealed the strange contradiction that afflicted so many prospectors: a trust in both science and superstition. Convinced ViolaMac's favourable results augured well for her, she said, "When something named after you has some success, it's good luck. There are more mines in Timmins, and I'll have one."

As all the socializing she did with journalists in Timmins in 1964 suggested, MacMillan was comfortable with the media. She rarely turned down a chance to agree to a magazine or newspaper profile, go on the radio or, once television broadcasting began in Canada, appear before the cameras. And she had long kept in regular contact with mining reporters, often trading information with them, and was willing to go off the record.

Her relationships with reporters went only so far, though. When they asked specific questions about her properties or businesses, they found she could be far less co-operative. And in some of the interviews she gave, it wasn't always clear whether she was speaking as the Prospectors and Developers Association president or as the president of one of her companies. Similarly, her lobbying efforts helped the industry and her businesses. In 1953, she combined a trip to London for the Queen's coronation with a chance to promote Canadian mining to European investors in France and Switzerland. While there's no question she did admirable work for the PDA, she frequently benefited personally from the organization's campaigns. The potential conflict of interest never seemed to bother her.

Finding and developing mines depended on a knot of disparate characters that included grizzled prospectors; slightly less-grizzled geologists

and geophysicists; professional engineers; clean-fingered corporate executives; lawyers, increasingly of the Bay Street variety; and most colourful
of all, promoters. "In Canada during the years 1947 to 1967, a unique
group of entrepreneurs of the mining industry, celebrated as promoters
or brokers and described as 'buccaneers' by some American commen-
tators, and 'angels' by some of the beneficiaries, flourished in Toronto
and Montreal," Franc Joubin wrote in his autobiography, *Not for Gold
Alone: The Memoirs of a Prospector*. "These were the money-finders for
the highly speculative penny stock companies that specialized in raising
the money prospectors required to carry on their work." Without that
money, he argued, the mining boom Canada enjoyed during those two
decades would never have happened.

A regular practice was for a promoter to advance some money to
a prospector who wanted to check out some ground. The discovery
of something promising, followed by the staking of claims, led to the
incorporation of an unlisted public company with, typically, three to five
million shares. A vendor's block, often 25 or 30 percent of the shares,
went to the promoter, who'd split it with the prospector, according to
their agreement, though 90 percent of the vendor's block was escrowed.
The rest of the stock went into the company's treasury. To fund diamond
drilling and other development costs, the promoter found a broker to act
as an underwriter, who'd buy the stock wholesale at escalating prices and
sell it to the public at retail prices.

Penny stock promotion required convincing others that a property's
potential was real—in other words, selling dreams of great wealth buried
in the ground. Sometimes, the company was making a legitimate attempt
to develop a mine, and the share price rose on encouraging reports from
the exploration program or news from nearby properties. But too often,
the promoter and the broker were one and the same, and adept at generating rumours to manipulate the share price. The people who played the
market, and there were many of them, often helped out by sharing tips
and rumours with one another. This created buzz about a stock. The more
buzz, the more buyers, the higher the price. If it all ended in a producing
mine, everyone did well. But economic ore bodies are rare, and, in most

cases, the stock price quickly crashed, though not before the promoters had sold most of their shares.

Chicanery was commonplace. An extreme move was to "salt" samples by adding rich ore from another property before sending them for assay. For five years, shares of Hedley Amalgamated Gold Mine, which had a property in the British Columbia Interior, traded for between eight and fifteen cents on Vancouver's Curb Exchange. But in February 1937, on published reports of assay results indicating commercial ore, the stock quickly jumped to more than $1. After insiders cashed out, the price plunged, leaving outraged investors. A popular theory was that someone had tampered with the drill core. In April, a government investigation found that although "untruthful and misleading information" had been published about the company, and the president had made an estimated $50,000 in profit, no fraud had occurred. But by May, police decided the samples had been salted and arrested the mine's superintendent and foreman and issued a warrant for the company president. As was so often the case in the aftermath of scandal, the premier of the province promised securities reform.

A less sinister, and more frequent technique was wash trading, which is the buying and selling of a block of shares by the same person. A promoter might have one of his companies sell stock to another of his companies. Such transactions create the false impression of a lot of market interest in a security. This would push the price up, but when hapless penny stock investors tried to unload some shares, they often found there were no buyers. Although wash trading was illegal, prosecutions of it were rare and convictions even rarer.

Promoters were invariably men, and slick was a common adjective to describe them. MacMillan considered herself a prospector and a mine developer rather than a promoter; in fact, she and George objected to being called that, though for many in the industry, the two terms were synonymous. She insisted she always wanted to end up with a mine rather than just taking advantage of the hopeful and the misguided. "There is a difference between stock manipulation and attempts to fill company treasuries," MacMillan told reporters when she was in Timmins the weekend after Texas Gulf announced its discovery. "Unfortunately, some of the groups in this area appear to be more interested in manipulations."

The official opening of ViolaMac's Lake Cinch uranium mine in September 1957 was surprisingly well-attended for an event in such a remote place. Through savvy planning or good luck, MacMillan had scheduled the ceremony for when delegates from the Sixth Commonwealth Mining and Metallurgy Congress were in northern Saskatchewan to visit the Gunnar and Eldorado Mines as part of a cross-country tour. So nearly 300 people from around the world, most of them men, watched MacMillan smash a bottle of champagne against the gears of the hoist. Though Lake Cinch was not a major mine, the *New York Times* covered the opening. "Tiny, vivacious, attractive and looking a good fifteen years younger than her age, which is 54, Mrs. MacMillan dominated the scene in a red silk cocktail dress, her mink jacket draped loosely over her shoulders," the paper reported. "She looked strangely out of place against the background of machinery and surrounded by men in work clothes and bush jackets." Even though the story, which appeared under a "Woman Opens Uranium Mine" headline, had been written by a woman, it was an example of how much of a rarity MacMillan was, as well as the sexism she faced.

The focus on her appearance was common. In one of the first stories about her, in the mid-'30s, the *Mail and Empire* described her as "short, slim, dainty and pretty." A 1941 piece in the *Star Weekly* described her as "wearing a schoolgirl-like dress of soft blue wool" and observed, "She is an attractive young brunette who looks like any modish young woman whose days might be spent arranging flowers and festivities in the home whose interior she designed herself." Even *Chatelaine*, the Canadian women's magazine, couldn't resist. "In the first place she's easy to look at," noted a 1945 article. "She's a little woman, about five feet one, and 110 pounds, a neat figure from her slim ankles to her dark upswept hair." Then, after comparing MacMillan to an Irish urchin, the writer continues, "Her smile is ready and pleasant. Her eyes are navy blue with dark lashes and beautifully arching brows. She dresses well in suits that are tailored but soft and brightly colored. She goes in for a little of the frou-frou—a small jewelled glamour pin, a medium-bright nail polish, expensive high-heeled shoes." As late as 1964, *Time* magazine called her "the dark-haired darling of Canada's mining men." The same year, the *Financial Post* wrote: "Viola MacMillan is a trim, very slight, attractive woman appearing much younger than her 61 years and looking more like a member of the high-fashion set (which she is in Canada and the U.S.) than a prospector, financial and mine-maker (which she also is)."

Given the times, the fascination with her looks was hardly a surprise. She may even have enjoyed that kind of attention. What bothered her was how people dismissed and underestimated her because she was a woman. When the *Financial Post* profiled her in 1938, it teased the story on the front page with, "Girl promoter is a new feature of the Canadian mining world." The article talked about her experience as a prospector and claimed, "She didn't know quartz from greywacke, so she did the cooking." While she did pay her dues by handling the cooking when she first started, there was no way she'd stay back at camp to prepare meals while the men went looking for gold. And she quickly developed a good grasp of basic geology, ending any possible confusion between quartz and greywacke, a hard, dark type of sandstone. From the beginning, she'd taken part in the claim-staking, line-cutting and rock-banging. During the Hislop Township staking rush in 1934, when she earned the Queen Bee moniker, she covered eleven kilometres a day through thick bush and swampy ground with a fifteen-kilogram pack on her back. Sometimes, she went prospecting on her own, though she never stayed in the bush overnight by herself.

By 1951, another reporter wrote, "She doesn't go along just as a cook, either. She does her share of the cooking but is able to do any task required in prospecting men can do." In fact, the headline on the article was "Woman Prospector Became Expert at Using Explosives." At the time, it was newsworthy that a woman would find dealing with dynamite and blasting caps no big deal. "She says that if you know what you are doing and take all the necessary precautions," the story said, "it's just as safe as puttering around the kitchen."

The reporting about her invariably had a wide-eyed tone. One story from 1957 entitled "Canada's Mining Boss Looks Pretty," and written by a woman, said MacMillan "is as much at home in the northern bush as she is in a mink coat in the smartest Miami fashion spots." Another described her as "a pretty woman, with black hair and flashing blue eyes, and she's equally at home on the dance floor or at a society salon." As if there weren't plenty of mining men who were comfortable in both the bush and black-tie social events.

A lot of those mining men started to take notice of MacMillan after she gained control of the Porcupine Quartet Gold Syndicate in 1936 and then negotiated the deal that gave Noranda the Hallnor property. And not everyone was happy about a woman crashing their frat party. Initially, some in the industry could dismiss her presence in the bush as a lark, but no longer. "I wish people in this business would just ignore the fact that I am a woman," she said. "All I ask is that I be treated like a man. I don't ask any favours. I think I can take it. In fact, I know darn well that I can."

Although her ability to compete with anyone seemed obvious to MacMillan, she was one of only 3,720 Canadian women who made more than $10,000 in 1953. Still, her complaints about the way mining men treated her were rare, perhaps because they weren't her biggest problem, or at least they were easy enough to win over. "She is just plain in love with mining," a 1955 *Saturday Night* profile quoted an old prospector saying, "and you know how it is with a woman in love—she gets carried away. Viola carries us all away with her." When the Canadian Institute of Mining and Metallurgy denied her application to be a member because she wasn't a man, some PDA members wanted to quit the CIM, but she convinced them not to. Her staff framed the letter denying her membership and hung it in the office. In 1953, after the organization relented on its men-only rules, MacMillan was one of four women admitted. She also had to fight with the telephone company and other businesses to receive bills in her own name, not as Mrs. George MacMillan. And she definitely wasn't happy during a staking rush near Val d'Or, Quebec, when she and George had each put claims in their own names. After finding a buyer for some of her ground, she discovered the deal couldn't go through because women weren't allowed to hold property, including claims, in the province. The mining recorder would approve the transaction only if they were in her husband's name. Furious, she went back into the bush and dragged George out so he could register the claims that she had staked.

She never thought it was weird that she became a prospector, though she acknowledged that a lot of journalists did. To his credit, George always supported and encouraged her, never expecting her to stay home to cook and clean. While some people may have assumed that she kept getting elected president of the PDA because no man wanted to do it, she saw her re-elections as evidence that mining men accepted her. And she never complained that the members serenaded her with "Let Me Call You Sweetheart" at every convention—in fact, she clearly revelled in it—though obviously they would never sing that, or anything like it, if she were a man. To a reporter who asked about leading a group as rough and tough as prospectors, she insisted, "Prospectors are not tough." Then she added: "All you've got to do to get along with them is talk their language. That means not complaining about your losses. You can't be a cry baby and be a prospector too, I have arguments with them sometimes, but I never consider arguments trouble."

At a time when few believed it, and even fewer were brave enough to say it, she maintained that a woman could do anything a man could do if she worked hard enough. "I see no reason why girls can't take their places beside the men in the field," she said on a 1948 radio show about careers for young women. "Of course, they can't be crybabies when things don't go too well, when it rains and the fire goes out or when the blackflies make life miserable." Although MacMillan's success in an unconventional career may have encouraged other women to enter mining or other male-dominated fields, making her something of a role model, her comments about crybabies offer a good sense of her attitude toward most other women. She may have denied, and possibly even bristled at, the suggestion that she was a feminist. After all, she never talked about women's rights, let alone publicly fought for them. She didn't expect men to change or treat women better. She'd succeeded on male terms, and while she'd have been happy to see other women join her in the mining industry, they'd need to suck it up and accept the men's terms, just as she had.

Despite her willingness to tough it out in the bush, MacMillan liked to buy and wear glamorous clothes, shoes and jewellery, and, of course, she did pinkify her penthouse. She also wore that red silk cocktail dress to the opening of a mine in northern Saskatchewan, so she wasn't above wielding her looks and style to promote herself. While she'd fought to get wives invited to the PDA banquets and then organized social events for them, she preferred the company of men. "I think Viola made better friends with men than with women," Doris Drewe, her friend and long-time employee, said many years later. "She seemed to have a sense of how a man talked and thought." Along with loving the attention of men, she was also comfortable hearing—and uttering—profanity. No doubt her ability to speak their language helped her feel at ease with men, whether she was going into the bush or negotiating deals. She appreciated their help. "People have often asked me if men resented my success in the business world. Some of them may have. Success doesn't come easily, and often those who don't find it become envious of those who do," she said in her autobiography. "But on the whole, most of the men I met encouraged me in whatever I tried to do, and many of them helped me a great deal along the way."

She did lament one barrier she was never going to break: the ability to join men at stag parties. "That is when they are at ease and they are talking shop. It is probably the best place to discuss business," she said. "But you can't be everywhere."

Life in the bush: Viola MacMillan wields a fry pan over a fire in winter.

Musher: For a faster way to get around, MacMillan drives a dog sled team.

Prospector: Armed with a rock hammer and a big packpack,
MacMillan is ready to go on snowshoes.

Queen Bee: MacMillan carries a post to mark the corner
of a claim in Hislop Township.

Proud of her ground: MacMillan points out some of
her claims on a map in the early 1940s.

Undaunted by all the testosterone: MacMillan was, as usual, surrounded by men at the 1950 Prospectors and Developers Association convention.

In her element: MacMillan speaks at the 1956
Prospectors and Developers Association banquet.

After the crash: Viola and George MacMillan attend the
Windfall royal commission hearings in 1965.

CHAPTER ELEVEN

GAMBLING SHOES

On the afternoon of Sunday, July 5, the MacMillans and Ron Mills headed back to Toronto in Viola's Cadillac, taking turns driving and sleeping. Eight core boxes sat in the trunk: the four they'd removed from the drill site earlier that day and four they picked up at the Windfall office in Timmins. Stopping for fuel and coffee at a gas station near Temagami, George used the pay phone to call geologist Willis Ambrose but couldn't reach him. Around ten o'clock, they dropped in at Doris Drewe's cottage near Novar, north of Huntsville. Even though she was tired, Viola was excited and told her friend, "We have the core from the property in the back of our car and it has mineralization in it."

Before getting back on the road, the couple tried to phone Ambrose again. Although he'd joined the full-time faculty at Queen's in 1948, he continued to do some consulting on the side. Highly respected in the industry, he was now the head of the Department of Geological Sciences at the university. The MacMillans had called him back on April 23, hoping he would look at their new property. He explained that there wasn't much point in going up to the site right away because the ground was covered in snow, but he hopped on a train to Toronto. When George met the geologist at Union Station on Friday, he agreed that a trip to Timmins wouldn't be valuable now. Ambrose stayed the night at the MacMillans' house and returned to Kingston the next evening. He learned later that they had hired Rocky Szetu, with his expertise in geophysics, to handle the exploration program, a choice Ambrose considered sensible given all the overburden on the property.

Although they hadn't spoken to Ambrose since April, the MacMillans now wanted him to look at the core they were bringing back from Timmins. Despite calling several times, they had no luck because he was at his cottage. They stayed overnight at their farm in Tottenham after dropping Mills off at his. In the morning, they drove the final fifty-five kilometres to Toronto. George parked the car and then pulled four core boxes out of the trunk, put them in the garage and opened them for when Ambrose showed up. The MacMillans had finally spoken to him around seven o'clock that morning. Normally, the geologist preferred to take the train, but sensing some urgency, he decided to drive.

A little after 8 a.m., Viola and George drove downtown. George wanted to drop two samples off at the Technical Service Laboratories on King Street West. He'd taken one from the site Friday and grabbed the other on Saturday. Both were from above the conductor. When he couldn't find a place to park, he asked Viola to run in with the samples, which were in a paper bag, and a note asking the lab to call George when the results were ready, later that day if possible. Then he drove his wife to the Knight Building before going home to wait for Ambrose.

□

Ever since the Cobalt silver boom, Canadians have dreamed of buying a small piece of a big mine for pennies. Stephen Leacock, who somehow managed to be both a respected economist and a beloved humourist, published *Sunshine Sketches of a Little Town* in 1912 when Cobalt was still thriving and the Porcupine gold rush was underway. He didn't know about Kirkland Lake yet but gleefully satirized the mania over mining stocks he'd seen. "All day in the street you could hear men talking of veins, and smelters and dips and deposits and faults—the town hummed with it like a geology class on examination day . . ." he wrote, later adding, "The fever just caught the town and ran through it! Within a fortnight they put a partition down Robertson's Coal and Wood Office and opened the Mariposa Mining Exchange, and just about every man on Main Street started buying scrip."

At the time, and for the next several decades, gambling was illegal. The exceptions were few. Canadians could place a parimutuel bet on a horse at a racetrack, play a game of chance at a fair or buy a ticket for a raffle to benefit a church or charity. Friends could wager between themselves on, say, the outcome of Saturday night's hockey game, as long as a third party didn't profit. And that was it: no lotteries, no casinos and certainly no legal sports betting. Many people considered gambling immoral.

But laws and moral judgment have always had a hard time eradicating vice. Anyone who wanted to gamble found a way. Illegal bookmakers thrived, for example. And while it was technically breaking the law to enter the Irish Sweepstakes, most people considered it a minor transgression. In 1938, one-third of Toronto residents bought tickets, which had been smuggled into the country and cost a little under three dollars each. Despite watching all this money leave the country, the federal government resisted calls to allow domestic lotteries, so the Irish Sweeps, as well as the French National Lottery, remained popular until Criminal Code reform in 1969 loosened the laws.

Another option was to invest in penny stocks, which wasn't illegal but was definitely a gamble. Hoping to talk a client out of acting on rumours to buy shares in another iffy mining company, one stock salesman asked how much he'd lost speculating in the previous half-dozen years. The answer: $12,000. The salesman then asked what was the most he'd made on any one company. The answer: $400. The unappealing math did little to stop people from buying penny stocks.

Advocates for and against gambling called out the hypocrisy of outlawing lotteries while allowing stock market speculation. Both sides noted that lotteries tended to appeal to the working class while wealthier people, who were more likely to have the freedom to visit the racetrack during the day and to call their brokers, liked to bet on the ponies and play the market. Either way, some people wagered themselves into trouble, sometimes leading to ruined marriages, bankruptcy or even suicide.

While gambling and speculating on penny stocks are both risky, owning shares does give the investor a small piece of a company and shareholder rights. Lotteries pay out only a portion of what they collect, and racetracks and casinos take their cut; stockholders keep all their winnings, minus brokerage fees (Canada didn't introduce a capital gains tax until 1972). And while a losing lottery ticket is worthless, mining shares are unlikely to go to zero even without an economically viable ore body. Selling at a loss is a disappointment, but something is better than nothing. And sometimes prices do rebound. A well-told story in the 1930s had it that one Toronto broker bought 20,000 shares of a mining company at one-eighth of a cent each. For his twenty-five dollars, he received several large-denomination stock certificates that became Christmas gifts. But what started as a lark became an unintentional act of generosity when the share price jumped to eighty cents. Most penny stock investors weren't so lucky, though. They usually bought high amid the excitement over a potential mine, often based on unfounded rumours and the bluster of promoters. Then they sold low when there proved to be nothing there.

And there was usually nothing there. A writer for the *New York Times* who visited Cobalt in 1906 met men claiming to have made huge strikes who were willing to let shares go for little. "Strange as it may seem, these men sell stock in properties from which a pound of silver has never yet been taken. One can drop money in Cobalt as quickly as in Wall Street, unless he knows what he is buying," noted the reporter. "The really good stocks are not sold at 10 cents a share." And yet, occasionally, companies with shares initially worth pennies do find mines.

□

Although Frank Spencer wasn't overly surprised when he answered his phone at eight o'clock Monday morning and Ted Jones was on the line, what the broker said came as a bit of a shock. Spencer had often bought stock through him, but he didn't expect the pitch Jones delivered: "Frank, if you have your gambling shoes on this morning, you might like to make some money on Windfall."

It was an easy sale. Spencer, who'd purchased 2,000 shares in the company back in June, had already decided to buy some more that morning despite the ethical concerns he'd discussed with Wilbert and Edgar

Bradley the night before. An hour after giving Jones an order for 10,000 shares, Spencer saw Wilbert in the office and told him about the call. He said it meant they no longer needed to be concerned about acting on inside information: if the Toronto brokers knew about something, it was public knowledge. This was a rationalization, of course, but it was true that conjecture about Windfall had already begun to spread.

The history of Cobalt, the Porcupine and Kirkland Lake suggested one discovery would lead to more, especially given the size of the Kidd Township ore body. Ever since April's staking rush, many people had been expecting someone to get another strike. And given that the MacMillans had managed to get four claims that Texas Gulf had wanted, it wouldn't have been a surprise if they were the lucky ones. Even mining people who knew the region well thought highly of the Windfall ground. Veteran geologist Fenton Scott's take was, "It, of the many properties in the area, seemed to be the only one with a real chance of coming up with a Texas Gulf deposit." So, when the rumours emerged about mineralization in the Windfall core, mining people weren't as skeptical as they might have been. By Sunday evening, Noranda fieldman Mel Rennick was surprised at how far the story had travelled. "Everybody was wondering what was going on," he said later, "and the thing was getting a lot of good sidewalk publicity."

No wonder Monday morning was hectic in T.A. Richardson's Noranda office. Manager William Robertson took call after call from people seeking more information. He could offer nothing other than the scuttle-butt about sulphides that most of his clients, many of whom were in the mining industry, had already heard. Some wanted to buy anyway. The broker decided to see if he could get a block of 100,000 shares for his clients. When Wilbert Bradley phoned and said he wanted 30,000 shares, Robertson said, "I don't know if you can get it. I have orders for 100,000 ahead of you." He'd placed a limit of one dollar on those shares. Bradley gave him a slightly higher limit.

Bay Streeters were baffled. Although there had been some interest in the stock late the previous week, it hadn't lasted. "Why Windfall now?" someone in Richardson's Toronto office asked. "You couldn't give it away at the close on Friday." All the buy orders piling up created a problem on the TSE's trading floor. Shortly before ten o'clock, Cecil Lecour and

Harold Field, two of the exchange's floor governors, conferred for five minutes. When buy orders swamped sell orders, they had the power to set the opening price for a stock. Lecour was a partner with T.A. Richardson and had been a floor trader with the firm for more than three decades; Field was a floor trader for Breckenridge, McDonald. Although Windfall had closed the previous week at fifty-six cents, they decided it would open at $1.01. By eliminating all the orders with a limit of $1 or less, the floor governors hoped supply would meet demand. Within minutes of the start of trading, 258,000 Windfall shares changed hands.

Jones didn't know what Lecour and Field were deciding, but there was enough enthusiasm for Windfall shares that he called Spencer back four minutes before the market opened. He kept his client on the line until it was clear what the stock was trading at. Before hanging up, Spencer bought another 10,000 shares despite the big jump in the price. Overhearing the conversation in the office, Wilbert Bradley asked him to put in an order for the same amount for him.

Jones called other clients, and some of them also wanted in. Robertson and other salesmen were also taking orders. Many of the initial buyers were associated with the MacMillans or the drilling company. Within half an hour, Wilbert Bradley owned a total of 60,000 shares, including 30,000 through Robertson, 10,000 through Jones and 20,000 through a Rouyn bank branch. Although he'd been investing in speculative stocks since 1937, sometimes making money, sometimes losing it, this was a substantial position for him.

Earlier in the morning, in Timmins, Edgar Bradley had called Reuben Brant of the John C. Allen brokerage. Brant said there were lots of rumours about Windfall in Toronto and agreed to phone back once trading had begun. Just after ten o'clock, he called and said, "The stock is active, selling at $1.01 to $1.02." Bradley bought 15,000 shares for himself and 2,000 for his wife. Fernand Boucher, the drill foreman who'd been the source of at least some of the rumours, didn't buy any stock because he didn't have any money and never played the market. But the three most senior people at the drilling contractor had quickly purchased roughly $100,000 worth of Windfall.

Before long, the brokers jumped in. Within half an hour, 400,000 shares had traded, and 87 percent of the buyers were connected to the drillers, the town of Noranda-Rouyn or Bay Street. They must know something, other people figured, and that's when the unconnected speculators began buying. The zeal spread as the penny stocks of other companies with claims near the Texas Gulf property saw their share prices climb. No one seemed to have any interest in waiting for assay results to know if Windfall's core samples contained anything worth investing in.

For some buyers, what was in the hole didn't really matter. Many of those who bought early on Monday, including Spencer and the Bradleys, were not expecting to hold on to their shares for long. They planned to start selling once the price rose. Before trading ended for the day, Jones was advising his clients to begin taking a profit by selling.

When he wasn't in the bush, John Larche made a habit of dropping by the Doherty, Roadhouse branch on Pine Street in Timmins around ten o'clock in the morning. On Monday, July 6, he walked in and looked at the chalked prices on the quotation board. He saw that Windfall shares were trading at $1.01, and, as he later recounted, "I pretty near fell flat on my back." Larche, who still had almost all the 83,000 shares he'd received from the sale of twelve claims to Viola MacMillan, had heard none of the rumours and had no idea what could make the stock price spike so dramatically. His regular prospecting partner, Fred Rousseau, another daily visitor to the brokerage house, had arrived earlier and was just as surprised. Don McKinnon was fifty kilometres north of Cochrane, about to head into the bush for work, when he heard the news on the radio. He found a phone and called Doherty, Roadhouse, hoping to find out what was going on. But no one seemed to know anything for sure. McKinnon drove back to Timmins to sell some of his stock.

Rousseau went into the branch manager's office and phoned Viola MacMillan in Toronto. Too busy to talk, she returned the call about twenty minutes later. "The stock is moving," he said. "What have you got in the core? Did you pull a good core?"

She told him that the drillers had hit rhyolite breccia and graphitic mineralization, and he asked, "Have you got copper and zinc in the hole?"

"We will get it assayed for that," she said.

Meanwhile, word soon reached the *Daily Press* newsroom. As a municipal and political reporter, Greg Reynolds had far more experience covering city council than the mining industry. But after first meeting MacMillan in April, he'd continued to follow developments with Windfall and talked to her and her husband several times, though he didn't write anything about the company again until drilling started.

He'd also regularly seen Larche, Rousseau and McKinnon in their suite at the Empire Hotel, until they'd finally given it up a few weeks earlier, or around town, often in one of the brokerage houses or in a restaurant. He'd been with them the previous Friday, in fact. A CBC documentary television show called *Telescope*, which was doing a piece on the mining rush in Timmins, had arranged a shoot with the three prospectors and Ned Bragagnolo. Seeing an opportunity to get some photos of them in the bush, which the *Daily Press* didn't have, Reynolds invited himself along. The TV crew was running behind, and Rousseau was to meet them later, so the four other men decided to grab lunch in the dining room of the Senator Hotel. As they ate, McKinnon was called to the phone. When he returned, he said a manager at Abitibi Power & Paper Company's Sturgeon Falls mill had heard from his broker in Toronto that Windfall shares were about to move. McKinnon told him he knew nothing about it. Back at the table, the conversation turned to the stock, though no one admitted to having any information the others didn't already have. But Reynolds had interviewed George MacMillan the day before, and the resulting story said the drillers were at seventy feet. Larche said MacMillan had told him that they were deeper than that. "You know darned well, Greg, that they don't tell you everything. They only tell you what they want published," one of the men said. "George has been in the mining business long enough not to blab his business through the newspaper."

Since George MacMillan had seen nothing of interest in the core by Friday, perhaps the rumour the Abitibi manager had heard was just a result of the start of drilling on the property. Still, it was an indication of the mood of heightened anticipation. When Reynolds heard about the stock price on Monday morning, he decided to pay a visit to the brokerage houses. All but empty of customers the previous week, they were now packed with excited people amid an uproar of ringing telephones, shouts and laughter. No one knew anything, but that did nothing to dampen the mood, and CKGB was again providing live updates from Doherty, Roadhouse. After Reynolds went for a coffee, the stock was still going up. Given that the three men who'd sold the claims to MacMillan were now large Windfall shareholders, they might have some reliable information. Just before eleven o'clock, he found Larche, who appeared to be in great spirits. Reynolds asked, "How does it feel to be rich?"

"It is great," Larche said with a huge smile.

The reporter wondered what was making the stock go crazy. Although the prospector said he didn't know for sure because they hadn't been able to reach the MacMillans, he gave the reporter some information but said he should check it with Rousseau. Reynolds went back to the newsroom and wrote a story for the final edition. The headline splashed on the front page that afternoon announced, "Windfall Shares Zooming on Reports of New Strike." The article noted the crowds at the brokerage houses and stated, "Although Windfall president George MacMillan was unavailable for comment, a large shareholder said that 175 feet of sulphides were hit on the first drill hole sunk by the company."

After filing that story, Reynolds found Rousseau, who said he hadn't talked to the MacMillans, but had it on good authority the core showed 160 feet of sulphides. Other than that, he confirmed what Larche had said. The reporter's next story, which ran Tuesday morning, included the revised number.

Reynolds had wanted to visit the Windfall property as part of his reporting. And choppers hadn't stopped hovering over the site just because the drill crew had stopped working. If anything, all the stock market activity increased the curiosity. Around lunchtime on Monday, he heard that Ned Bragagnolo had chartered a helicopter and was flying out to the site. Reynolds asked if he could ride along, but there wasn't enough room.

Seeing no one around the drill rig, Bragagnolo asked the pilot to land by the cookhouse. He talked to the cook, the only person left on the property, and asked if the crew had pulled a good hole. The cook said he didn't know. After flying back to Timmins, Bragagnolo regretted not being more thorough. He hired another chopper and returned to the site. This time, he saw a helicopter at the drill, along with two men. One of them had white hair, and, from a distance, Bragagnolo assumed it was George MacMillan. But as his chopper drew nearer, he saw it was Patrick Heenan from Conwest Exploration.

After checking out the site, Heenan had taken a sample of the sludge from around the collar of the drill hole. The geologist knew that the top of the pile would be from the lowest part of the hole. But when they saw another chopper approaching, the Conwest men climbed back in theirs and took off. With the site now clear, Bragagnolo asked his pilot to land. Seeing some empty core boxes near the drill rig, he wondered if the crew might have carelessly left some samples behind. He found a small piece of core and then took some sludge from the pile before taking off again.

Heenan drove to Swastika Laboratories, just outside Kirkland Lake, to get his sludge sample assayed for gold, silver, copper and zinc as soon as possible. Bragagnolo showed his core chip to Ken Darke. Of course, taking samples from someone else's drill site wasn't exactly ethical, but hardly unusual amid the fever that had gripped Timmins since April. And that fever had now spread to Toronto.

CHAPTER TWELVE

MANIC MONDAY

After Viola took the core samples into the lab and George left her at her office, neither of them was expecting anything unusual to happen that day. But shortly before the market opened, George Hunter called. Viola had maintained accounts with the partner at T.A. Richardson in Toronto off and on over the last fifteen or twenty years. Back on April 24, she'd opened an account with him in the name of Vianor Malartic Mines, one of her companies, and said she'd supply it with all the Windfall shares the brokerage firm needed to fill orders for the stock. Although she did trade in two or three other companies, she used the account primarily to buy and sell Windfall shares, though never for more than seventy cents.

Now Hunter needed stock from her. Cecil Lecour, Richardson's floor trader, had called him at 9:45 to say he had buy orders for over 100,000 shares of Windfall. Since MacMillan had only 1,400 shares in her account, he hoped she'd be able to provide more. When she was reluctant to sell any, for fear of losing control of the company, he said, "I think you should try and maintain some kind of orderly market and supply some stock." Although maintaining an orderly market wasn't his responsibility, Hunter believed it was in everyone's best interest to say it. She agreed to make up to 100,000 shares available, as long as they sold for ninety cents or more. Ten minutes later, the stock opened at $1.01.

From then on, MacMillan spent most of her manic Monday on the telephone. She received about 150 phone calls as brokers, lawyers, investors, reporters, friends and acquaintances scrambled to get in touch with her. She returned the important ones and ignored the others. Hunter spoke to her a few times to let her know how many shares had sold from the account and for how much. She agreed to sell additional shares through T.A. Richardson and sold more through other brokers. MacMillan later maintained that she'd tried to record the sales and the firms, but it all happened so fast that she soon lost track and was no longer sure how many shares were going out, at what price or where her accounts stood. She claimed, "It got out of control."

Amid this chaos, she had other responsibilities. She called Edgar Bradley to say she wanted him to build a core shack right away. Since mining companies typically brought in other employees or kept at least one shift drilling while the other handled the construction, the contractor still didn't really understand the decision to shut down the drill. But she was the client, and he was happy to do as she asked.

MacMillan also had to contend with inquisitive friends and acquaintances. She spoke to some, including Fred Rousseau, who was in the Timmins office of Doherty, Roadhouse. But others didn't wait for MacMillan to call them back. August Schlitt, a former prospector who now owned the Geotechnical Development Company, knew that drilling had started on the Windfall site but had been unable to reach MacMillan when he phoned her at her farm on Saturday and Sunday. So, on Monday morning, on his way to work, he went up to the penthouse suite of the Knight Building, which now also served as an office for the MacMillans. He rang the bell half a dozen times, but no one came to the door, so he left. After the market opened and he saw what was happening to the stock, he decided to try again. While he was at the door ringing the bell, Edward Chisholm, a geologist with the Southwest Potash Corporation, showed up. His broker had called him with news of Windfall's opening and asked if he knew anything. Chisholm didn't, but he wanted to. MacMillan finally answered the door, though she didn't invite the two men in and said there wasn't anything she could tell them. Chisholm thought she seemed nervous and assumed it was due to the barrage of phone calls she was facing. When he said he'd heard the drillers had hit 200 feet of sulphides, she responded, "That's good, eh?" He asked if they were drilling an anomaly and she answered yes. After Chisholm left, Schlitt asked if the anomaly compared to the one at Kam-Kotia, and she said it did. He congratulated her and expressed his hope that she'd find a mine, which seemed to please her.

□

Don Lawson woke up Monday morning at his cottage on Lake Simcoe and headed to the golf club. He was in the middle of a two-week vacation, though he was keeping in touch with the office in case anything urgent came up and was only an hour away. A little after ten o'clock, his wife found him on the course and told him that Moss, Lawson had called. He walked over to the pro shop to use the phone. When he learned about Windfall's opening, the broker asked a partner on the trading floor to keep MacMillan informed and make sure she received all the service she needed. Then, because the share price seemed to have settled at $1.05, he went out and played the last four holes of his round. When he finished, he learned that the office had called again. The stock was now trading around $1.45. But believing the situation was under control, he didn't jump in his car and drive back to the city.

As the underwriting agent, Lawson's firm did have an obligation to maintain an orderly market. Although the exchange had no formal definition for that term, it wanted to see continuous offers when a stock was going up, and continuous bids when it was going down, rather than big gaps in the price. For the underwriter, that could mean buying if the stock price was falling and selling if it was rising. Lawson had the power to sell shares from the underwriting accounts, if necessary, but he preferred to get MacMillan's approval first. And even though he was away, he was confident that his colleagues would give her good service. She already enjoyed access to a direct line that allowed her calls to go straight through the switchboard to the trading floor without being intercepted by an operator, a benefit no other client had (and was against TSE rules without the board of governors' approval). But she wasn't happy, grumbling later, "I couldn't get hold of the Moss, Lawson boys fast." It was, after all, a hectic day on the market, and everyone was overwhelmed, but the firm also had trouble reaching her. The traders had to wait until she called them. Eric Watson, the head trader at Moss, Lawson, liked MacMillan a lot and thought she was brilliant, though often confusing to talk to, but said, "Oh, she is the worst person in the world to get hold of at times."

The lack of communication was a bigger problem because of her insistence on control. "She seemed to always want to mastermind each trade," Lawson mused. At one point, Watson suggested she provide 50,000 Windfall shares and give him the discretion over selling them. "I would not do that at all," she responded. "Five thousand shares would be all I would ever give anybody to handle."

Although Lawson remained at his cottage, he stayed by the phone. During a call with Mansell Ketchen, the TSE's vice-president in charge of administration, he was surprised to learn that MacMillan had sold 200,000 shares. He knew his firm had handled nowhere near that number for her. He did manage to speak briefly with MacMillan "but not long enough to get any information about what was going on, except that she didn't know what was going on." He could hear the phones ringing in her office, and she said she had to go and would call him back, but never did. She never explained why she was making a spate of trades through his competitors, even though the normal practice would be to give the business to the underwriting agent. Some of her sales were through a new account with Breckenridge, McDonald, a brokerage house she'd never dealt with before.

Robert Breckenridge was a former president of the exchange who knew MacMillan socially from various industry functions over the years. He'd last seen her at April's mining convention in Montreal and had asked her to let him know if she ever had a property that looked like a good bet. She'd called him the day after drilling started. "I don't often do this," she said, though she was telling everybody to buy Windfall, "but I think that Windfall mightn't be a bad buy at this point." He bought 7,500 shares that day, but on Monday, when he heard from his firm's floor trader that the stock might open at around one dollar, he took advantage of a chance to make a quick profit and sold them.

A couple of hours later, she called him. After grousing about Moss, Lawson, she asked if his firm wanted to do business with some of her companies. When he said it would, she wanted to know if there was someone who could give her personal attention. "Yes, Mrs. MacMillan," he said, "I would undertake to do that myself." He sensed that she was surprised by all the market activity, but he had one request: "Now, I would prefer not to hear anything about what is going on at that property." He had many mining clients, and he wanted to be able to say he knew nothing. Her first move was to open an account in the name of MacMillan Prospecting and Development and put in an order to sell 5,000 Windfall shares at $1.80, with five-cent discretion. By the end of the day, Breckenridge would make several trades for her, selling a total of 68,000 shares.

Not all her calls that afternoon were with brokers. A chemist from the Technical Service Laboratories who'd tried to reach George at home phoned her with the assay results. Neither piece of core showed anything of value. She also talked to Tom Cole. He'd been receiving queries from people wondering what was making Windfall stock go up so dramatically. She told him George had stopped drilling because of all the snoopers who were showing up in helicopters and on foot. She said the core looked good, with some interesting structure, before adding in an offhand manner, "We sent a couple of samples for assay."

After MacMillan paid such a high price for the Prosser and Wark claims and then optioned them to Windfall, the investment community took notice. But trading in the stock remained sensible even after drilling started. On Friday, 42,000 shares of Windfall changed hands. On Monday, almost 1.6 million did, including the 433,900 MacMillan had sold, accounting for more than 27 percent of the activity on the TSE that day. MacMillan complained that brokers forced her to sell stock to keep an orderly market. Although doing so made her money, it diluted her position, and she didn't know who was doing the buying, which fed into her angst about losing control of the company. And yet, she'd initiated sales through several brokers, including T.A. Richardson and Breckenridge, McDonald, as well as through accounts at Tom & Barnt, a broker-dealer firm. The stock reached a high of $2.02 before ending the day at $1.95, more than triple its closing price on Friday.

Later, when Marjorie Humphrey, who had been trying to reach MacMillan since Saturday, dropped by 303 Oriole Parkway, the first person she saw was Ron Mills. He told her about the trip to Timmins and how they brought back core. Then MacMillan appeared. Humphrey thought she seemed tense and excited and asked her, "What about the core?"

Although MacMillan was enthusiastic about the possibility that they were going to hit something, she wouldn't give her friend, who was also a Windfall director, any details. All she said was, "We are to keep quiet and say nothing."

□

Most reporters who tried calling MacMillan on Monday had no luck, and the few who did heard different things, not all of them completely truthful. Robertson Cochrane, a financial reporter with the *Toronto Daily Star*, spoke to her shortly after noon. He'd never talked to her before, and it was a quick call, but she told him George was at the drill site and added, "We have definitely got some mineralization there and assays are being done." Cochrane thought she sounded excited, and he asked how she was feeling. She responded, "George and I are very happy."

When Richard Roberts of the *Toronto Telegram* managed to speak to MacMillan after the market closed, he said, "I heard the rumour of sixty feet of mineralization."

"Oh, it's much more than that," she replied.

When he asked about the copper and zinc values, she said, "Well, it looks pretty good." But she quickly added that they had no assays. She also claimed that George was up north, the drill crew was still working, and they expected to hit the target by the weekend.

A story in Montreal's *Gazette* quoted a company representative saying, "Everybody is in the bush, but last Saturday the drill was close to the target area. If a hit was made, it would have been on Sunday, and communications from the area are poor."

Although George was not in the bush, he enjoyed a quieter day than Viola. She called him to tell him about the jump opening, but neither of them could explain it. Then he went back to waiting for Willis Ambrose.

After the geologist arrived, the two men sat in George's study and looked at two four-inch samples. They talked for an hour. The pieces of core showed graphitic slate and pyrite. There was no visible copper or zinc, but that didn't make it impossible for there to be some present. The fine dusting of grey material in the black rock was possibly tetrahedrite, which is a copper sulphide and can also indicate zinc. It also often contains silver. In addition, pyrite sometimes contains gold.

Next, they went to the garage. Taking anything more than small samples to Toronto was an unusual move, but MacMillan explained that the site had no safe place to keep the core. When Ambrose heard about the helicopters hovering overhead, he found it extraordinary and unethical. Looking at the four core boxes that were already out of the Cadillac, the geologist agreed that before reaching the graphite and pyrite, the drill had gone through a section of rhyolite breccia. That was intriguing because it can be a good host for silver and gold. Another four core boxes remained in the car, but the two men didn't look at them because MacMillan said they were more of the same. Ambrose suggested drilling the hole deeper and picked out three small samples from the open boxes to take back to Kingston for further inspection. MacMillan put the covers back on the core boxes and nailed them shut before placing them in the trunk of the car. Later, the two men and Viola went out for dinner, and the next morning, Ambrose drove back to Kingston.

□

Back in April, ticker tape had descended on Bay Street as Toronto celebrated the Maple Leafs winning the Stanley Cup. The event wasn't that unusual in the days of the six-team National Hockey League; in fact, it was the club's third championship in a row. The other team that held the town in thrall was the Canadian Football League's Argonauts, even though they hadn't won the Grey Cup since 1952. But in May, the whole country was riveted by Northern Dancer, who won the Kentucky Derby and the Preakness. Canada's top thoroughbred missed out on the Triple Crown when he finished third in the Belmont Stakes, but still had the Queen's Plate to run on June 20. Ned Bragagnolo ran into George MacMillan at Woodbine Racetrack that day, where they were among the more than 31,000 excited fans who cheered as Northern Dancer won his last race in dramatic fashion.

For the first three weeks of July, "Memphis," Johnny Rivers's cover of a Chuck Berry song, ruled the CHUM Radio chart. But two Beatles songs would debut on the chart that month; both were from *A Hard Day's Night*, the band's first album of all-original material. After the Fab Four had appeared on *The Ed Sullivan Show* three times in February, Beatlemania spread across the continent, and Torontonians waited eagerly for the group's two shows set for Maple Leaf Gardens on September 7. The band's arrival in North America also represented the start of the British Invasion, the musical trend that would influence the decade's countercultural upheaval.

Any upheaval seemed a long way off in Toronto, an overwhelmingly white and Protestant city. The laws against gambling and lotteries were just the start of the war on fun. The attitudes toward sex could be seen in everything from the federal laws against homosexuality to Ontario's draconian film censorship system. In January, Elizabeth Taylor and Richard Burton checked into a five-bedroom suite—a "love nest," according to the newspapers—in the King Edward Hotel while he played the lead in a pre-Broadway production of *Hamlet* at the O'Keefe Centre. The two movie stars, who were married to other people, had fallen in love while filming *Cleopatra*. By the time they made it to the King Eddy, his divorce had gone through, but hers hadn't. And now they were shacked up in a Toronto hotel, which was too much for the delicate sensibilities of some in the city. Protestors showed up to express their outrage at this scandalous lifestyle.

If sex was too much for Torontonians, so was alcohol. The provincial liquor laws were puritanically strict. In a 1937 story on the TSE, *Time* magazine reported, "Because hard liquor is banned in Ontario restaurants Toronto has developed a 'Broker's Cocktail,' a startling yet appropriate combination of beer and champagne." Even in the 1960s, buying a bottle of wine or spirits was a bizarre experience at a Liquor Control Board of Ontario outlet. The government agency put the emphasis on control, requiring customers to select what they wanted from a list and then write down the name, brand number and price on a piece of paper before lining up to hand the slip and money to a clerk, who then fetched the bottle from the back of the store and hid it in a paper bag before handing it over. Cocktail bars finally became legal in 1947, but even in the '60s, rigid rules for bars and restaurants still applied; ordering a drink on a Sunday, for example, was only possible when also eating a meal. Actually, under Ontario's Blue Laws, little happened in public on Sundays other than churchgoing. Shopping was still forbidden on the Lord's Day, though professional sporting events were legal by then. No wonder Torontonians who had enough money took weekend trips to Detroit and Buffalo, where the shopping and the nightlife were better.

Politically, the Progressive Conservative Party of Ontario had been in power at Queen's Park since 1943, and Toronto seemed immune to the turbulence elsewhere. In the US, President Lyndon Johnson signed the Civil Rights Act of 1964 on July 2. In Quebec, the Quiet Revolution, a blossoming of nationalism along with social change, was underway. The rest of Canada was sleepier, but Prime Minister Lester Pearson was busy creating a more modern nation. His Liberal government introduced legislation to create a new Canadian flag, leading to an acrimonious debate. During his five years in office, Pearson would be responsible for the introduction of universal health care, the creation of the Canada Pension Plan, the start of bilingualism, the legalization of homosexuality and several other progressive measures. None of them sparked nearly as much public dissension as the idea of a flag devoid of any reference to Britain.

Perhaps the best place to look for hints that uptight Toronto might become more than a parochial midwestern town was in its architecture. The city had never had much tolerance for ambitious buildings, but by 1964, several were in the works. The province had just hired architect Raymond Moriyama to design an innovative science museum, one of the first in the world to let visitors interact with exhibits, which would sit atop a ravine in the suburbs. More dramatically, a futuristic-looking city hall, with the council chamber in a spaceship-shaped structure between two curved towers, was nearing completion. Finnish architect Viljo Revell had also designed Nathan Phillips Square, Toronto's first great public space, in front of the hall. The project would not escape an embarrassing controversy over the installation of a Henry Moore sculpture.

A few blocks south, beside the TSE building, construction began on the first tower of the Toronto-Dominion Centre, designed by Ludwig Mies van der Rohe, a starchitect before the term became popular. The new bank headquarters, at the crucial corner of King and Bay Streets, was another reminder of the city's ascendance as the country's business heart. Montreal could have its sophistication; Toronto was happy with its growing wealth.

Amid all this change, what wasn't changing much was the TSE itself. It remained an old boys' club where the rules were lax and the oversight sporadic. Insider trading, for example, was routine. That permissiveness invited promoters to finesse the system. But, of course, the exchange did have some regulations and sometimes did enforce them. One of them was about to squeeze Viola MacMillan.

□

Don Lawson regretted not returning to the office on Monday. His firm had sold 76,000 Windfall shares for various clients during the day, but the underwritten stock accounted for only 4,000 of them, and those had been owned by Moss, Lawson. MacMillan had made some trades through the firm but had not sold any from her underwriting accounts. "If I had been there and been talking to her," Lawson admitted, "I think I would have been in a position to force her, to say, 'All right, look it, let's stop this nonsense. You have got to sell here.'" The next morning, concerned about another crazy opening, he drove down to Toronto to spend the day at the office. Surprised he hadn't heard from MacMillan, he tried to reach her without success. But Lawson was determined to maintain an orderly market even without her approval. Expecting a strong opening, one of his partners on the trading floor asked, "How much should I sell?"

"Fifty thousand, or more if you have to."

Around the opening, MacMillan finally called and asked what was going to happen. When Lawson explained what the firm would do, she was horrified. As it turned out, Tuesday's market was tamer, and the price of the stock drifted down a bit, so Moss, Lawson didn't sell much from the underwriting accounts. But MacMillan was still in for another manic day.

Shortly after ten o'clock, Mansell Ketchen called to inform her the underwriting was due and payable. Under the exchange's rules, underwriting agreements contained an "acceleration clause" that made outstanding options due when the stock traded above a "limit price." The limit price was typically double the option prices, which in the April 21 underwriting agreement ranged from forty to ninety cents. The triggering of the acceleration clause meant Golden Shaft and Variometer Surveys had to take down 900,000 shares right away, instead of buying them over fifteen months. Although she knew it was coming, having spoken to Ketchen the day before, she initially tried to argue with him. The good news was the two underwriting companies would acquire Windfall shares for far below the market price; the bad news was they would be subject to crushing taxes. But MacMillan's immediate problem was coming up with $490,000.

That was a lot more money than she had readily available. She needed cash fast and had two choices: sell stock or borrow money. At ten thirty, she called the Bank of Nova Scotia's head office branch, where she had a current account with $600 in it and a loan account with just over $80,000 owing. Preferring to handle the matter in person, the bank asked her to come in, which she did an hour or so later, and it became clear she needed the money that day and it wasn't for her personally but for the two underwriting companies, Golden Shaft and Variometer Surveys. Since getting signatures from all the required corporate officers wasn't going to be possible on such short notice, the bank agreed to lend her $274,000 in her own name. Her loan account already had some collateral, in the form of $313,000 worth of securities, but needing more now, she agreed to provide the bank with 795,000 shares of Windfall, which was trading around $1.90 at the time. She told the assistant branch manager that she intended to repay the loan in a few days.

A little after one o'clock, MacMillan dropped by the Moss, Lawson office to deliver a cheque for $490,000. She'd successfully completed the Windfall underwriting, putting money in the treasury, while two other companies she controlled, Golden Shaft and Variometer, had both acquired 450,000 more shares for far less than the market price. That made for a profitable day, though, as she later said, "It is a terrifying experience to have to rustle up a lot of money in an hour or two."

CHAPTER THIRTEEN

RUMOUR MILL

When the Windfall stock opened at $1.01 on Monday, July 6, James Scott took notice. Recently appointed as the *Globe and Mail*'s assistant business editor, he'd spent many years as the paper's mining editor and had often dealt with the MacMillans. He'd never heard of Windfall, but a jump in the share price like that suggested the company had found something. He was curious. Visiting brokerage firms to glean intel was a regular practice for him, and by late morning, he was at the offices of Davidson & Company. That's where he ran into Claude Taylor, a former newspaper reporter who handled public relations for Harry "Bud" Knight's Consolidated Mogul Mines. Knight and his father, Harry Sr., were successful mine financiers and stockbrokers. On the side, Taylor did some PR for other companies and was a special correspondent for the *New York Herald Tribune*, writing a weekly piece about activity on the Toronto stock market. Since Taylor had worked for MacMillan companies in the mid-1950s and had continued to do PR for the Prospectors and Developers Association convention, Scott considered him well-connected to Viola and George.

Within half an hour of the market opening, Taylor had purchased 2,000 Windfall shares at $1.04, using his wife's account with Davidson & Company. Then he took the Knight Building elevator up to the top floor, where MacMillan was on the phone. Eventually, he had a chance to talk to her, but she didn't say much and didn't seem to know what had goosed the stock. At eleven forty, Taylor sold 1,000 Windfall shares at $1.43. Later, he went back up to the penthouse and said, "Come on, there must be something to this. Stock isn't moving to this extent without some reason for it."

Finally, MacMillan said the drillers had pulled seventy-eight feet of mineralization. When he asked if it contained anything of value, she was evasive at first, before telling him there was copper and zinc in the core, but George would not commit to it being commercial. She refused to say anything more until they'd done assays. Later, in what may have been a case of broken telephone, Taylor told Scott that Windfall had hit ninety feet of copper-zinc mineralization. "George feels it is ore," he said. "Viola would prefer to wait for the assays."

After Scott made an unsuccessful call to the MacMillans, he assigned a couple of reporters to chase them. The next day, the paper ran a story with the headline "Timmins Rumour Revives Buying in Speculatives." Scott's contribution to the article was a paragraph that noted, "a source close to the company said a width of 90 feet of copper and zinc mineralization had been encountered. It was not known if the material contained high enough values to make commercial grade ore."

Another journalist keen to speak to the MacMillans was Graham Ackerley. As much as he liked and respected George, the *Northern Miner* reporter wasn't all that fond of Viola. Still, he spoke to her regularly. It was his job, after all. He often called her seeking information; she often called him offering information. Five days earlier, he'd noticed some activity with the stock and wanted to ask her about it. When she called him back at three in the afternoon, she wouldn't offer anything for publication and wouldn't even confirm that drilling had begun the day before, though he knew that from other sources. What she did say surprised him: "I cannot tell you why, but you should own some stock." That was weird. She'd never recommended a stock before, but Ackerley acted on her advice, buying 5,000 shares. Her tip did not endear her to him when the price went down the next day and he sold for a loss of $250, plus his broker's commission. He was even less happy when the stock opened at $1.01 the next week.

And now she wouldn't return his calls. Every hour or two since Monday morning, he'd been leaving messages for her and for George and Cole.

As reluctant as the MacMillans were to talk, they realized that the reporters weren't about to leave them alone until the company gave them something. Viola called Cole. "George thinks we ought to have a meeting," she said, "and get out a release." On Tuesday morning, George dictated material for a press release to Viola, who took it down to Cole's Bay Street office. She told the lawyer that her husband was in the bush and the draft was based on information from Willis Ambrose. George did not attend the board meeting to discuss the draft announcement at two thirty that afternoon. (Later, he couldn't remember what he was doing instead but thought he may have started driving back to Timmins and then, for some reason, turned around near North Bay and came home.) Doris Drewe also missed the meeting, but although Viola still wasn't a director, despite Cole's urging that she become one, she sat in. She was more than simply an observer.

With George absent, Marjorie Humphrey, who held the title of vice-president, chaired the meeting. Although the technical aspects of mining were beyond her, she'd spent eight years writing press releases for Eaton's, the department store chain. She thought the company was being vaguer than ideal, especially since she and Cole were now receiving calls from journalists desperate for more information. She'd already advised the MacMillans to be more forthcoming with details for the public, but they'd pointed out the risks of talking at the wrong time. There was, for example, a neighbouring property they might want to buy, and the price would go up if the owners knew Windfall had something valuable on its claims. At the meeting, Humphrey and Cole discussed the matter at length. They were both dissatisfied, but the draft release contained all the information they had. Humphrey moved that as soon as more information was available, the company should release it. The motion passed unanimously. After she suggested a minor tweak to the wording to make the draft read better, the board approved the press release. It would go out after the markets closed.

Viola had told the directors that she'd completed the underwriting a half hour before the meeting. She thought the company should now seek permission to sell stock from the treasury, and the directors approved the sale of not more than 400,000 unissued shares at not less than $1.75. This would put money in Windfall's coffers without her having to sell any more stock. In addition, she hoped to get 225,000 of her shares released from escrow. The directors unanimously agreed and instructed Cole, as the company's secretary, to write the TSE relaying this request.

Later that afternoon, Viola finally phoned Ackerley back. She said she hoped he had bought some stock, but she wouldn't say anything for publication. Off the record, she said that drilling "was coming in on a target," which didn't tell him much. When he asked about the core, she said she'd seen only two small pieces, and they were mineralized, but gave no other details except to say assay results might be available in the morning. That evening, Ackerley received the press release. Although Ambrose had told George nothing to get excited about, the company president had put a positive spin on the situation. "The drill entered a mineralized graphitic shear zone at 416 feet and has remained in it to 530 feet," the release said, though the latter number should have been 570. To the general public, this probably sounded impressive, but it didn't really indicate anything special. Hitting minerals is one thing; hitting mineral values rich enough to be ore is another. The announcement also stated, "The core is being sampled." This line, which hadn't been in the draft George had dictated to Viola, was open to misinterpretation. Although anyone could be forgiven for thinking it meant the core was being assayed, it could just mean the company was splitting core and preparing samples for assaying. The release ended with, "Officials are encouraged because of the proximity of this area to the recently discovered copper-zinc-silver ore body of Texas Gulf in the neighbouring Township of Kidd."

Ackerley now had more questions than answers. The reference to "mineralized graphite shear" could indicate ore, as it had at the Texas Gulf property, but it didn't necessarily mean that. On Wednesday, the reporter, who was on deadline, made repeated efforts to speak to the MacMillans, Windfall directors and anyone in Timmins who might be able to clarify the information. He phoned and dropped by Viola's office, called her home, dispatched a cab driver there and tried to reach her at the Empire Hotel. Nothing worked.

Once the abnormal activity of Windfall's stock began, the MacMillans became especially hard to reach. They used the City-Wide answering service, and during the day there was always someone at the office to take messages, but George rarely returned calls or even bothered to check with the service. When he was at their home in Toronto and people called, he just let the phone ring until they gave up. Viola would prove to be only slightly more reachable, and even then, not exactly frank.

□

T.F.C. Cole, QC, was a respected and experienced lawyer. The QC, for Queen's Counsel, was an honorary title the province bestowed on leading members of the profession. A partner at Roberts, Archibald, Seagram & Cole, a Bay Street firm with many mining clients, he'd first acted as solicitor for various MacMillan companies in the mid-1940s, and sometimes for Viola and George individually. He became a director and the secretary-treasurer of Windfall after the couple bought control of the company in 1961. At first, his involvement was largely uneventful, but that changed in July of 1964. First, journalists started phoning him. Then friends did.

The day after the press release went out, Cole received a call from Dick Pearce, the president and general manager of the *Northern Miner*. The paper's editorial team had been trying to speak to the MacMillans without any luck. The Windfall press release had cooled off the share price a bit but had done nothing to stanch the gossip. With the paper's noon deadline getting closer and closer, Pearce offered to phone his friend to seek more information, or at least check out the rumours that the drillers had pulled sixty feet of ore and that a core shack was under construction. Cole confirmed that the directors had authorized a core shack. In fact, a carpenter had arrived at the site that morning to begin building one with the help of the idle drillers. But the lawyer expressed surprise at the contention Windfall had any evidence of ore. For his part, Pearce was struck at how an officer of the company was so puzzled by the stock's elevated price.

Cole found the conversation upsetting, and later that morning, when Viola called him, he said, "Now, what is this about sixty feet of ore?"

"That's a lie," she replied. "I never said there was sixty feet of ore in that hole. I said there was sixty feet we hoped would make ore."

That was a relief. Before Cole could get back to Pearce, his friend called him and said, "I have double-checked with my man and it is a mistake. This is what he said: 'There was sixty feet of core in the hole that she hoped would make ore.'"

Cole didn't know that George would arrive home that afternoon to find an envelope waiting for him. It contained the results of the assays from Technical Service Laboratories. One of his samples contained no silver, a trace amount of zinc and very low levels of copper and gold. The lab didn't do an analysis of the copper or zinc in the second sample and found no silver and only a trace amount of gold in it. MacMillan did not give those results to the press.

The issue of the *Northern Miner* that hit newsstands the next morning contained Graham Ackerley's carefully worded story. Though the article offered no details about the core, it said, "What intrigues exploration people is the real probability that Windfall has confirmed the same geological horizon which plays host to the Texas Gulf ore body."

Any hopes Cole had that the rumours about the core would now go away ended with two phone calls he received that day. The first was from Jim Booth, head of Canadian Superior Explorations. The two men had met for lunch the day before because the geologist wanted to express his company's interest in buying control of Windfall, or at least a piece of it, based on the proximity of the claims to the Texas Gulf find, the indications of an anomaly from aerial surveys and the geological structure described in the press release. Now Booth was on the phone asking about the exciting assay results he was hearing about. The second call was from Murdock Mosher. The respected prospector, who'd helped found the Prospectors and Developers Association and gone on to be the president of several mining companies, was one of Cole's clients. He cited copper and zinc percentages that were almost identical to the ones Booth had heard.

"I just don't get this," Cole said, "because I understand there were no assays."

These calls alarmed the lawyer. A flurry of speculation when a company started drilling was not unusual, but rumours of specific assay results certainly were. And while Viola had told him two samples had gone for assaying, his understanding was that there were no results yet. When she returned Cole's call, he confronted her again: "Has there been an assay or hasn't there been an assay?"

When she assured him there hadn't, Cole suggested the company get a lab to test some samples to deal with the matter one way or the other. Viola said there was no reason to do an assay until the hole was finished. Sensing he was uncomfortable with this decision, she asked him if he wanted to resign from the board.

"I don't know," he said.

Later that day, Cole dictated a resignation letter. But he didn't submit it. He had several reasons for sticking around. As far as he knew, the MacMillans weren't doing anything illegal or unethical, and he still had confidence in them despite the difference of opinion on the need for an assay. His departure might generate bad publicity that would affect the share price, hurting some shareholders and weakening the position of the MacMillans, who were already worried about losing control of the company. And, as he later admitted, "I didn't wish to alienate a client who might be on the verge of finding another Texas Gulf."

□

On Bay Street, the oft-repeated question was, "What have you heard?" As customers swamped brokerage houses with requests for information, research departments responded with a barrage of memos and wires to salesmen and branches. An interoffice wire from Len Bednardz of James Richardson & Sons on July 6 read: "Indirect reports indicate that a mineralized section was encountered from 410 feet 585 feet in the latest hole." The next day, J.W. Dennis of Davidson & Company sent this: "I understand from reliable sources that heavy buying came from Noranda and Timmins. This buying represents very good mining people, who have access to information, and I am quite sure there will be a good section of good grade ore in the first hole." On July 9, a J.H. Crang & Company wire said: "We hear rumour WINDFALL have 70 to 90 feet of 2% copper; 7% zinc."

Less formally, other stories spread from person to person. Some contained more truth than others. Various versions of the basic gossip that the Windfall drillers had hit ore, sometimes with mineral values, sometimes without, made the rounds. One story had it that Viola was keeping rich core in her Cadillac and guarding it carefully. According to another, after she first looked inside a core box, she hugged the drill foreman and did a little jig. Still another contended that someone walked onto the property, only to find a guard with a shotgun sitting on a case of beer, but after paying a twenty-dollar bribe, the snoop was able to take a sludge sample. In addition, rumours began to circulate that Texas Gulf or Noranda, or some other company or group of shareholders, was trying to get control of Windfall.

The MacMillans weren't even saying anything to friends. Art Barnt had known Viola and George for two decades. He spoke to her frequently because she had several accounts with Tom & Barnt, and he'd been busy trading for her since Monday. But even he couldn't get anything from her other than they'd stopped drilling because of the helicopters. He ran one rumour by her, and she responded, "It can't be." Another time he asked if there was any truth to some gossip, and she said, "You know better. I have told you there were no assays." Even when the MacMillans went out for dinner with Barnt and his wife and sister-in-law on Wednesday, they revealed nothing.

All of this made it impossible for reporters to get reliable information, and the papers resorted to printing rumours, identifying them as such. Initially, they just mentioned mineralization and refrained from citing specific numbers. That began to change after the *Stock Market News and Comment* came out on Thursday. Written by Alan Percival, the weekly newsletter had 1,500 subscribers who paid thirty-five dollars a year. The July 9 issue noted that investing in Windfall was a gamble, but "rumours around Bay Street suggest that there are some 80-odd feet of core which will assay 2.3 per cent copper plus 8 per cent in zinc plus silver values. Some gossip says that drilling was stopped while still in ore." This was based on nothing more than what Percival had heard from several people. He did try to get confirmation, but no one he talked to could say for sure what was in the core. And the MacMillans did not return his calls.

Whether the newsletter had anything to do with it or not, Thursday ended up being the busiest trading day for Windfall, with more than 1.9 million shares bought and sold before the stock closed at $2.55. As much as Viola MacMillan professed her reluctance to give up stock, she needed to pay the bank to get back the shares that were serving as collateral for her loan. She'd unloaded no stock on Wednesday when the price dropped. On Thursday, she sold 380,200 shares. Again, she attributed it to requests from brokers to provide them with stock to support the market. But Breckenridge, McDonald wasn't asking for stock; instead, at her request, the firm opened an account for Airquests and sold 70,700 Windfall shares.

Meanwhile, Claude Taylor was working on his weekly piece for the *Herald Tribune*, which he would submit the next day. When it ran on July 13, with a "Windfall Stirs Investors, New Canadian Bonanza?" headline, it stated the couple had "pulled a major base metal drill core north and east of the multi-million-dollar discovery of Texas Gulf Sulphur near Timmins, Ontario." The article cited the same copper and zinc values as Percival's newsletter. The rumours were starting to seem more and more like fact.

One person attempting to find out what was really in the core was in Kingston. On Thursday, Willis Ambrose examined the samples he'd carried back from Toronto. Under a microscope, he could see no tetrahedrite, which ruled out any copper or zinc and made any silver highly unlikely, though only an assay would confirm that. And only an assay would determine if any gold was present. The MacMillans knew that, but they hadn't asked Ambrose to do one.

□

Jim Scott lucked into a meeting with Viola and George late Thursday evening. The city's newspaper printers had walked off the job earlier that day because the International Typographical Union's Local 91 had failed to reach an agreement on automation with the *Globe*, the *Daily Star* and the *Telegram* despite nearly two years of contract negotiations. While Scott waited to see if the next day's papers would ever come off the presses, he and a couple of colleagues decided to go for a drink. They crossed York

Street to the Sentry Box, a bar in the Lord Simcoe Hotel that, aside from being handy for *Globe* employees, was a favourite of mining promoters. Around eleven o'clock, Viola and George MacMillan and a woman Scott didn't know walked into the crowded, noisy and smoky room. As soon as they sat down, the journalist headed over to their table, said hello and met Louise Campbell. A former model, she was married to John Campbell, a lawyer who'd become the director of the Ontario Securities Commission in November 1963.

Viola had first met John when she was lining up panellists for a financial symposium at the 1964 PDA convention. After the convention, a social relationship developed between the MacMillans and the Campbells. On Thursday, John called Viola and asked if she'd meet him at the Royal York at five o'clock. Hearing so many Windfall rumours, he wanted to find out what was going on. She gave him an account of what had happened since she'd gone up to Timmins, and though she didn't reveal much beyond what he already knew, his impression was that the drillers had hit mineralization. Eventually, they decided to call their spouses and invite them to dinner at Julie's Restaurant and Tavern on Jarvis Street. Located in a restored Victorian mansion that had once been the home of industrialist Hart Massey, Julie's had been a popular spot since opening in January. Louise Campbell was an investor in the stylish restaurant. But so was a prominent financier, which had led to an embarrassing *Daily Star* article suggesting her stake represented a conflict of interest for her husband.

The menu options, an example of the state of fine dining in the city at the time, included French onion soup, chopped chicken liver, salmon, tenderloin tips, tournedos Rossini and Caesar salad. As they ate, the MacMillans appeared extremely optimistic about Windfall, and at one point, George asked Louise if she'd like to make a lot of money. "Certainly," she replied. He suggested Windfall could go to $5.

George and John discussed the ethics of a company president selling stock at a time of intense speculation. George said he had 308,000 shares and wanted to sell 25,000 to pay off the loan he'd taken out to buy Windfall. Campbell didn't see anything wrong with that. After dinner, while the other three moved on to the Sentry Box, he went back to his office at the OSC to compose a letter for George. Not long after his dinner companions showed up at the Sentry Box, Campbell arrived with a draft of the letter. (The next day, after conferring with his lawyers, Campbell had his secretary type up the final version of the letter. "This will confirm our telephone conversation of today wherein I advised you that in my opinion under the circumstances you described to me," part of it read, "there would be no objection by this Commission to the sale by you of 25,000 shares of the capital stock of the above company owned by you, provided that such will take place on the Toronto Stock Exchange.")

At the Sentry Box, Campbell listened as Scott prodded the MacMillans with many of the questions he'd asked Viola earlier that evening. The *Globe* man asked if the core showed 3 percent copper mineralization over ninety feet, and Viola responded, "Where did you hear that?"

"It is a pretty general rumour on the street," said Scott.

Several times, he asked if he could see the core, but he couldn't get the MacMillans to agree to it or even say where it was. Viola did most of the talking. When the journalist asked George a question, the Windfall president looked at his wife and let her answer. But she was evasive, saying little and often changing the subject. None of this surprised Scott. Having interviewed the MacMillans many times since the late 1930s, he found they rarely gave satisfactory answers to his questions.

After almost half an hour of getting nowhere with them, Scott had to return to the newsroom. As he was leaving the table, he received some free advice from George: "If you want to be poor all your life, don't buy Windfall."

Then, appearing to be scolding her husband for being indiscreet, Viola said, "Oh, George."

CHAPTER FOURTEEN

PENDING SUSPENSION

A t mid-morning on Friday, July 10, Viola called Howard Graham, the president of the Toronto Stock Exchange. The two knew each other, and she had a couple of requests. First, she was following up on Tom Cole's letter about the release from escrow of the 225,000 shares from her sale of the claims to Windfall. Second, she wanted his approval for the company to sell shares into the market directly from its treasury. Although the directors had approved the sale of up to 400,000 shares, she asked Graham for permission to sell half that number. She planned to price them at $3. Making more shares available would help maintain an orderly market while giving the company money to pursue its exploration and drilling plans. To the first request, Graham said it was up to the Filing Statement Committee. To the second, he told her that this was against TSE policies; treasury sales required an underwriting. But he agreed to call a special meeting of the committee.

Because all the members worked within five minutes of the exchange, he was able to gather them later that morning. Given the lengthy and sometimes antagonistic back-and-forth over MacMillan's sale of the Prosser and Wark claims to Windfall, there was some exasperation in the room over her desire for special treatment. But it didn't really matter because her requests had no chance anyway. TSE regulations called for stock to stay in escrow a minimum of six months, and the committee decided that insufficient work had been completed on the property to justify the release of shares, let alone early release. Nor did it see any reason to break the established rules on treasury sales.

That wasn't enough for Graham, who had no interest in putting up with any funny business from MacMillan. She'd never been intimidated by men, even powerful ones such as politicians. In fact, she was pretty good at intimidating them, especially as her stature in the industry grew. One prospector erroneously explained MacMillan's Queen Bee moniker to the *Globe and Mail* by saying, "She's always buzzing about and boy, can she sting." But Graham wasn't going to allow her to push him around. President of the TSE since 1961, he was the first outsider in the role; before him, exchange presidents always came from member firms. And he arrived with a no-nonsense background. After enlisting at seventeen, he fought in the First World War, then practised law in Trenton and served as the town's mayor. In the Second World War, he commanded a regiment, and then stayed with the army, rising to chief of the general staff in 1955. He was used to people doing things his way.

Once the Filing Statement Committee finished quashing MacMillan's requests, Graham and TSE chairman Marshall Stearns called a meeting of the board of governors. The only issue on the agenda was Windfall. The exchange was alarmed by the unexpected and largely unexplained jump in the share price, the unusually high trading volume and the unchecked rumours. On Friday morning, after a delay of half an hour due to difficulties matching buy and sell orders, the stock had another jump opening, then climbed higher in heavy buying and selling.

Tuesday's press release had been, in Graham's words, "rather non-committal and not very informative," and the three days since had been enough time to complete an assay. The governors decided Windfall needed to issue a statement that was acceptable to the TSE. Failure to do so would mean the stock would not open for trading on Monday. And since the MacMillans had become so hard to reach, the board decided each of the company's directors should receive a wire warning of its plans to suspend the stock unless the exchange received the information it sought.

Graham finally reached MacMillan at around one thirty in the afternoon. "Well, General, there will be a statement in your hands this afternoon," she told him. "Mr. Cole will see that you have got a statement." The problem for the MacMillans was they didn't have much to offer. They'd told no one—not even Cole or Willis Ambrose—about the assay on the first two samples, and they weren't about to publicize the results now. That left progress on the core shack as the only new information they were willing to offer. Viola phoned Edgar Bradley. The drilling contractor told her that people in Timmins kept pestering him for the scoop on Windfall. Outside of town, snoopers continued to disturb the crew by hovering over the drill site in helicopters or walking in through the bush. MacMillan asked how the core shack was coming along.

After Bradley hung up, he wired George. "Diamond drill core building about half completed. Expect to be finished by next Monday night. Stop. Your bunkhouse should be finished by next Wednesday," the telegram read. "Our men having trouble to move lumber in on account of road. Stop. We are having trouble to keep snoopers trying to get information of the property. Stop. We will be ready to continue drilling as soon as the camps are finished. Stop. Weather very hot." Viola, who had dictated the telegram to Bradley during their call, hoped it would help satisfy the TSE.

MacMillan and Cole spoke frequently during this time, and some of their conversations suggested she was struggling to deal with the pressure. She claimed that all the shares she'd sold since July 7 had been to slow the rise in the stock price. The brokers had been clamouring for stock, and she felt forced into selling shares despite her fear of losing control of the company. She complained about Moss, Lawson, though Cole was well aware that the underwriter had an obligation to try to maintain an orderly market while shares were in primary distribution. She also wanted an investigation into the TSE and the brokers.

The stock was going up based on no information, and MacMillan felt helpless to do anything about it. "What am I going to do? This is terrible," she said. "I can't do anything right."

"You are making money," Cole said. "Why do you worry?" But he knew she was more interested in developing her own mine than in making more money. She even said that she wouldn't mind if the exchange suspended the stock because it would help her keep control of Windfall.

That was increasingly a possibility. By three thirty, when the market closed on Friday afternoon, Graham still hadn't received Cole's statement. Just as he had warned he would do, he sent a telegram to the Windfall directors: "The Governors of the Toronto Stock Exchange because of exceptional activity in the stock of Windfall must insist that your company make an up-to-date statement to be delivered to the president of the exchange 234 Bay Street Toronto not later than 9:15A.M. local time Monday July 13." If the company failed to do so, the TSE would suspend trading in Windfall stock. Graham also issued a press release about the exchange's request for more information, but without mentioning the threat to suspend the stock. Though it was the only move available when the exchange wanted to sanction a company, a suspension would be a drastic step, one that could have serious consequences not just for Windfall, but for its shareholders. The TSE had no way of disciplining the former without also punishing the latter.

CN Telegraph phoned Cole at four thirty and read him the telegram. He knew it was coming, and by that time, he had Bradley's wire and was already working on a letter to the TSE. "You have seen the press release of July 7. No further drilling has been done, and the President advises that core samples of the completed portion of the first hole have not yet been sent for assay. Any rumours to contrary are unfounded," it said. "Facilities for dealing with core have been lacking, and the unexpected interest has made a suitable core shack essential." It went on to quote Bradley's telegram. Cole's office mailed the letter late Friday afternoon, with the expectation Graham would receive it Monday morning. Then the lawyer went up to his cottage.

Later, while Marjorie Humphrey was eating dinner, the telegraph office called and read her Graham's wire. Alarmed, she phoned Viola, who said, "We will have a meeting Monday morning, but don't worry about it."

Having learned about the telegram, John Campbell called Viola and arranged to drop by her home. Although the Ontario Securities Commission and the exchange maintained a collegial working relationship, the two organizations had separate roles. The exchange was responsible for listed companies; the commission was responsible for licensing sales-men and overseeing the brokerage industry, as well as the acceptance of prospectuses for companies not listed on the TSE. The overlap was a bit murky, but the only power the OSC had over the latter was the ability to withdraw recognition of the exchange. Still, in Campbell's mind, the commission was the senior organization and was to "keep a paternal eye on the Toronto Stock Exchange." That meant the TSE had an obligation to inform the OSC when it was threatening to suspend a company as high profile as Windfall. He was annoyed that Graham hadn't done so.

Campbell, who had practiced law in the Red Lake mining district for three years earlier in his career, also believed the exchange was treating the company unfairly and had failed to use any diplomacy with the MacMillans. He worried that forcing Windfall to divulge the results from the drill hole would set a bad precedent. Brokers might see it as an invitation to start rumours, so the exchange would insist other companies reveal their drill results. Suspending the stock also seemed unwise, hurting only the public. While a suspended company's shares couldn't trade on the TSE, they would still be available on the over-the-counter market. That could lead to chaos since there would be no controls or even a sense of the trading volumes. Strictly speaking, none of this was the business of the director of the OSC, but Campbell wanted to arrange a meeting between the MacMillans and the exchange brass.

When he arrived at 303 Oriole Parkway early Friday evening, Viola and George were getting dressed for a seven o'clock wedding. The three of them sat in the den, and Campbell asked how they planned to respond to the TSE. They said the letter Cole had written, which they didn't have yet, would add little to what the company had already revealed. "It was, as I suspected, more or less telling the Toronto Stock Exchange to go to hell," he later recounted. "It was none of their business." He didn't have a big problem with that. He also got the impression that the MacMillans weren't worried about a suspension, perhaps because Viola had told him weeks earlier that she had tried to get the stock delisted, but the exchange wouldn't allow it. Given that the couple was pressed for time, Campbell kept his visit short and arranged to visit them at their farm the next day. Viola and George made it to the church just in time.

After leaving the Sentry Box on Thursday, July 9, the MacMillans and the Campbells climbed into Viola's Cadillac. Louise and John sat in the back seat with the spare tire. John assumed there were core boxes in the trunk, especially after he heard the big thud of something heavy when the car went over a bump. The two couples went to the Campbells' apartment in Rosedale for a nightcap, the evening stretching past one in the morning. At one point, John went to mix drinks while the other three sat on the porch, and George again said Windfall could go to five dollars. Viola said if it was a good hole, the stock could go to twenty-five dollars. But Louise Campbell was skeptical. Once the MacMillans left, she expressed her doubts to John. He disagreed, pointing out that mining types were enthusiastic because they were optimists by nature, adding, "Why would these people, with all their money and wanting a good reputation, why would they do such a thing like this?"

Louise later put it down to women's intuition, but she'd already been burned once on the stock. Back in April, Viola had suggested she buy Windfall. The problem was the wife of the director of the OSC wasn't supposed to be in the market. When John took the job, he'd asked Louise to sell all her stock and not do any securities trading. But she held on to her portfolio until the controversy flared over her involvement in Julie's Restaurant and Tavern. Then she sold everything, taking a considerable loss. Wanting to take advantage of Viola's tip without John knowing about it, she acted on a broker's advice and set up a numbered account on April 20. She purchased 2,500 shares of Windfall at eighty cents, as well as shares in two other companies she'd heard about. After the stock fell, she had no choice but to admit what she'd done and ask John, "Do the best you can to get the situation cleared up." He unloaded the Windfall shares at fifty-nine cents and sixty cents.

Now she was ready to try a different tack. The morning after dinner at Julie's, drinks at the Sentry Box and more drinks at her place, Louise called Harry Richardson at Tom & Barnt. She opened an account for V.L. Sherwood, which was the name of a boat her father had owned, though she told the broker it was her maiden name. She sold 2,000 shares of

Windfall. The stock was trading at $3.25. On paper, she'd made $6,355 on the transaction. The problem was she didn't have any Windfall shares to sell. She was engaging in a risky investment strategy called short selling that involves borrowing a stock and selling it when the market is high and then repaying the borrower by buying it after the price has dropped. The danger is the stock doesn't go down, and the short seller must meet the market price to pay back the borrower.

Louise was not a sophisticated investor; in fact, she was, by her own admission, "one of those people who get a tip from the hairdresser." As the price rose that day, she began to panic. She bought one hundred shares at $3.35 through her bank. That would be little help if the stock continued to go up, but it was all she could afford. That night, after Windfall had closed at four dollars, she told her husband what she'd done. John was furious and told her there was nothing he could do to help her this time.

On Saturday morning, Campbell visited George Gardiner at his farm in the Caledon Hills, northwest of Toronto, and not far from his own country place near Orangeville. The president of the Gardiner, Watson brokerage had preceded Marshall Stearns as chairman of the TSE board of governors. Campbell had known him since they were at the University of Toronto together, and he had great respect for him. The two men went for a walk down by the pond, and the OSC director explained what was going on between Windfall and the exchange. He believed the TSE was being unfair in threatening a suspension. When Gardiner asked why he'd come to see him instead of Stearns, Campbell said he thought the current chairman, who was also a senior partner with T.A. Richardson, was biased because some of his firm's clients were shorting the stock. So, Gardiner suggested talking to Howard Graham.

Then John and Louise Campbell drove to the MacMillans' farm, arriving late morning. While Louise walked around the property with George, John met with Viola in the living room. He asked her to write a statement about her difficulties with the exchange. In six pages of point-form notes, written in pencil, she detailed what had happened on Friday.

The Campbells ended up staying the day at the farm. In the late afternoon, George drove to Toronto to get a copy of Cole's letter and gave it to John when he returned. Campbell didn't think it would satisfy the exchange, and once he was home, he began working the phones. The OSC reported to Arthur Wishart, the province's attorney general, but he was at his cottage and unreachable. So were Jack Kimber, the OSC chairman, and Forbes McFarland, the province's mining commissioner and the second member of the OSC (the commission had three members, but one position was vacant. Finally, Campbell reached George Wardrope, who he'd met only once. The mines minister was at home in Port Arthur but would be flying back to Toronto on Sunday and agreed to meet at his hotel.

Other people arrived, and eventually Viola went into the kitchen to prepare some steaks for dinner. Louise followed her in and said, "Viola, will you help me out? I am short on Windfall." But someone walked in the room, squelching the conversation. Campbell pulled out her cigarette package, opened it and tore the flap off. She wrote "V.L. Sherwood" on it and handed it to Viola. MacMillan didn't know what it meant, and the Campbells left before Louise could explain.

□

Graham was at home in Oakville when Campbell phoned and said he wanted to meet to talk about Windfall. The TSE president didn't see what there was to discuss. As far as the exchange was concerned, the matter was simple: Windfall must produce an acceptable statement or face suspension. But the OSC director persisted, and Graham relented. "All right," he said, "come out about ten o'clock and I will be here."

When Campbell arrived Sunday morning, he was worked up about the possible suspension. He read Viola's notes to Graham. He also pulled a carbon copy of Cole's letter from his pocket and handed it over. "You will be getting this tomorrow morning," he said. "Is that going to be satisfactory?"

"No, I don't think it will," Graham said after reading it. "But it is up to the board." Neither the message nor the messenger impressed him. He said the company needed to deny the rumours, but when Campbell asked which ones, he said, "Just deny the rumours."

"Do you wish them to deny the rumour about Viola having hugged the foreman of the drilling crew?"

"No, they know the rumours as well as I do."

"Well, if you tell me the specific rumours you would like them to deny, I would be glad to go back to them and try to get them to do it."

Campbell argued that it wasn't the company's responsibility to confirm or deny rumours that it didn't start. Graham held firm that the public had a right to know if there was any truth to all the stories going around. Campbell said Wardrope was concerned about a possible suspension of the stock and suggested that such a move could lead to the MacMillans losing control and Windfall, and a potential mine, falling into foreign hands. Even as they disagreed, the two men remained calm and professional as they chatted over coffee in the study. But they were getting nowhere. Finally, after this had gone on for an hour, a clearly unsatisfied Campbell left, saying, "I will have to speak to my minister about this."

On Sunday afternoon, Campbell met with the MacMillans at the Constellation Hotel out near the airport. The couple had decamped there to escape constantly ringing telephones. They'd received 176 calls on Saturday. Campbell tried to convince them to "put a little more warmth in the reply" to the exchange and that releasing more information, or at least denying some of the rumours, would be in the best interests of their shareholders. George was coming around to the wisdom of that idea, but even though he was the company's president, and Viola wasn't even an officer, she was clearly making the decisions.

As Campbell was leaving to go meet Wardrope, Viola walked him to the elevator. She continued to carp about the TSE, insisting she didn't owe the exchange anything. Campbell was getting frustrated. He'd been working hard to help Windfall and getting nowhere. "For God's sake, Viola, you have got to be a little bit reasonable about this thing because, after all, I am working against my wife's best interests in this damn thing," he said, explaining that Louise was short 2,000 shares of Windfall. MacMillan said she could fix that. For many years, her secretary would deliver share certificates to her safe deposit box at the bank, but now that she had to do it herself, she rarely got around to it. They went back to the room, and she pulled three 1,000 share certificates out of her purse and handed them over. Campbell said, "You had better make it five." Viola gave him two more. "She doesn't want to buy it and she will give it back to you in a few days," he said before leaving with $20,000 worth of Windfall shares in his pocket.

Later that evening, John gave the certificates to Louise. "Look, this is the absolute end as far as you are concerned," he said. "Give these to Harry and I don't want to hear any more about your trading in the market. This is it."

◻

When Wardrope made it to Toronto on Sunday evening, Campbell was waiting for him in the lobby of the Royal York. The OSC director said he was worried about the exchange's threats to suspend Windfall. He asked if the mines minister would meet with the MacMillans, who, he claimed, were trying to understand what information the TSE wanted from them. Since Wardrope was good friends with Graham, maybe he could help straighten things out. Campbell didn't mention the growing tension between him and the TSE president. Wardrope agreed to meet with the MacMillans. Then, thinking someone who knew more about the situation than he did ought to be there, he tried to bolster the invitation list. That's when he learned that Wishart and McFarland were at their cottages. His deputy minister was at a conference in Nova Scotia, but Brady Lee, the mine assessor and comptroller of the Department of Mines, agreed to come.

The Texas Gulf discovery had spurred an exploration boom in the Porcupine and had generated excitement in an industry that had been sluggish. Which was good. But, for the minister, a new Canadian-owned producer would be even better, boosting Timmins, the provincial economy and the country's mining business. Maybe it would lead to even more mines in the region. He was also pleased with the involvement of the MacMillans. He'd attended receptions at their home during Prospectors and Developers Association conventions, and he considered them reputable people with a commendable record of success. Worried that a suspension of the stock would be a "black eye" for the mining industry, he was happy to help improve relations between the company and the exchange.

When Lee made it to the hotel room, Wardrope, Campbell and the MacMillans were in the midst of a conversation. Viola was doing most of the talking, and it was mostly about how unfairly the TSE was treating her. Lee asked about the source of the rumours, and George, who'd already complained about snoopers, said he didn't know, but maybe someone grabbed a sludge sample and assayed it. When Lee asked how the core looked, George just shrugged his shoulders. This did not fill the bureaucrat with confidence.

The MacMillans tried to bully Wardrope a bit, asking if he was running the mining industry in the province? Or was the TSE? Did he want them to continue trying to find mines or not? They also raised the spectre of Windfall falling into American hands. The mines minister handled the situation smoothly, buttering Viola up in an effort to get everyone co-operating. After reading the letter Cole had written on Friday and learning that Graham had already deemed it inadequate, Wardrope sat at the desk with Campbell, and the two drafted a new letter by hand. The mines minister phoned the TSE president to ask what additional information the exchange needed. Graham wanted to know if there were any assays and, if so, what did they show? If not, why not? During the call, Wardrope took notes on the letter he and Campbell had been working on. After he hung up, he handed the piece of paper to George, who put it in his pocket and said, "Well, we will leave and get this letter amended." If they hadn't before, the MacMillans should now have had a good idea of what the exchange wanted. But George later said about the meeting, "As far as I was concerned, nothing was accomplished."

After Campbell and the MacMillans went back to the Constellation to polish the letter, Viola made it clear that she wanted Tom Cole to look at it before it went to the exchange. Meanwhile, Wardrope phoned Graham again. It was around eleven o'clock on a Sunday night, and the TSE president was already in bed. The mines minister asked if they were going to be able to straighten out the Windfall problem. "Well, I don't know. To me, it seems quite a simple problem," said Graham. "They just make a statement and set the record right."

"Well, I hope that it will be worked out, because it would be too bad if control of this company gets away into the States."

"Well, George, I hope it will be straightened out, too. It should be."

CHAPTER FIFTEEN

UNEASY PEACE

When Howard Graham arrived at his office at eight thirty on Monday, he learned that Campbell had already called to say a new statement would soon be coming from Windfall. He also found the letter Cole had sent Friday afternoon in his morning mail. Marshall Stearns and William Somerville, the executive vice-president of the exchange, were in his office, and he showed the letter to them. They all agreed it was inadequate. If a satisfactory letter didn't arrive before the nine-fifteen deadline, they had a hard decision to make. A suspension was not something they would do lightly, because it would almost certainly cause the stock price to crash, or in market parlance, "fall out of bed." Somerville was not in favour of allowing the stock to open; Stearns agreed it didn't deserve to open but worried that some people might see their definition of satisfactory as arbitrary. As they discussed the matter, Wardrope called Graham and said the new statement would be arriving at around ten thirty. The exchange bosses inferred that Windfall would be providing a proper update.

When Graham called Campbell back, he learned that the letter wouldn't arrive until after Cole returned from a dental appointment. "Well, I appreciate the interest you are taking in this company," Graham said. The OSC director became angry and said he didn't appreciate the insinuation.

Apologizing, the exchange president said he hadn't meant to insinuate anything. Furious, Campbell said he didn't want anything more to do with Graham and hung up without saying goodbye.

Reluctantly, the TSE executives decided to hold off on suspending the stock. Instead, they issued a floor bulletin at nine forty-five, making it clear that there had been no further drilling on the Windfall site, and the company had not assayed any of the existing core but would make a statement later that day. If people bought the stock knowing all this, that was up to them. At least they knew the risk. Or should.

Given how his phone call with Campbell had ended, Graham decided to play a little piano, not wanting the heads of the TSE and OSC to be at what he called loggerheads. He sent his counterpart a letter thanking him for his help and saying that while Friday's letter was "hardly as complete as we think necessary," based on Campbell's assurances that a new statement was on its way, the exchange had held off suspending the stock. Then the TSE brain trust waited even as Windfall's share price rose on heavy trading. But nothing arrived that morning.

Doris Drewe was also frustrated. She was spending her summer at the cottage, and though she was a Windfall director, she hadn't been paying much attention to what was going on with the company. But Viola had asked her to attend a directors meeting in the offices of Roberts, Archibald, Seagram & Cole on Monday morning. Drewe, Ron Mills and Marjorie Humphrey arrived at nine o'clock, as requested. They'd all come in from out of town: Drewe from Novar, Mills from Tottenham and Humphrey from Troy, where she now lived with her new husband. Only Cole wasn't there yet. And he wasn't seeing a dentist. He'd been at the cottage his family rented. Since it didn't have a phone, he was unaware of what had transpired over the weekend or that the MacMillans had called a directors meeting. Even still, he'd normally be in the office earlier than this, but fog and rain had made the drive back to the city a slow and miserable one. That left the directors stewing in the waiting room.

Once the lawyer finally showed up at eleven o'clock, he met with George to go over a draft of the letter to Graham. Since the challenge was the lack of new information to work with, he needed to find the right wording. Hoping to ensure the letter would be satisfactory, he had two phone calls with Campbell and two with Somerville. The former told Cole that he'd helped George with the draft of the letter, telling the lawyer, "I roughed something out on paper."

The other directors grew increasingly annoyed as the wait stretched on until noon. After they finally filed into Cole's office, George read the letter, which would appear over Cole's signature. The only significant change from Friday's version was the addition of two sentences: "No further drilling has been done and the President advises that core samples of the completed portion of the first hole have not yet been sent for assay. Any rumours to the contrary are unfounded." This wasn't new information, just a statement of what had been implied in the previous letter. Though it did seem to contradict the July 7 press release that had stated, "The core is being sampled," none of the directors mentioned it. The board approved the letter, and the meeting was over in five minutes.

The only thing the directors learned during the session was that George planned to continue drilling as soon as the core shack was complete. They didn't know the building was already finished and the carpenter and the drill crew, still waiting to restart their rig, had begun work on a camp for the MacMillans to sleep in when they were on site. And the board still didn't know about the assays of two samples or about Ambrose's visit to Toronto to examine the core.

Shortly after noon, MacMillan phoned Lawson. He'd learned that her calls were never short, usually lasting half an hour, even at the end of the day when he was trying to leave the office. Today's conversation went on for nearly two hours. Although he didn't press her on all the sales she'd made through other firms, despite her underwriting agreement with Moss, Lawson, she talked about how he hadn't been around on July 6 and claimed she was panic-stricken and unable to reach his floor traders. Mostly, though, he listened to a litany of complaints, which he recorded in his notes as "Usual criticism of the TSE." She was demanding the attorney general and the OSC launch an investigation into Windfall trading. She was also upset that the exchange wouldn't let her sell shares from the Windfall treasury. When he asked if she'd sat down with an underwriter to figure out a way to do it within the rules, he found "it was like talking to a brick wall."

At two fifteen, Cole's new letter made it to the TSE. When Graham read it, he was frustrated. Even if Windfall had done nothing about getting the core assayed, as he had hoped, the company could have at least offered some information based on a visual examination and said when assay results would be available. Nor had it dealt with any specific rumours by, for example, stating that it had or had not received offers from Texas Gulf, Noranda or any other suitor. And if the exchange president had hoped the stock might cool on its own, he was disappointed. More than one million shares in Windfall had changed hands, and the price briefly had reached a new high of $4.75, though it ended the day at $1 below that.

While he was far from placated by Cole's letter, Graham issued a press release after the market closed that quoted all of it except the opening paragraph. Later, the TSE president told *Toronto Daily Star* financial reporter Alistair Dow, "We hope they will do what any good company should do—keep shareholders informed of any developments." In his story, Dow described the situation between Windfall and the exchange as an "uneasy peace."

□

Jack Kimber was a quiet but amiable pipe-smoking lawyer. He'd left private practice in 1947 to become master of the Supreme Court of Ontario, a position that made him a troubleshooter for the justices. In 1962, he added OSC vice-president to his responsibilities, which meant a lot of mad dashes across Queen Street from the commission's offices to Osgoode Hall and back. After he became chairman, he set about beefing up the organization. Hiring John Campbell to fill the new position of director and handle administrative duties allowed Kimber to concentrate on policy.

While at his cottage the previous week, he hadn't followed Windfall beyond what he read in the newspapers. When he returned to the office on Tuesday, July 14, Campbell filled him in. Along with leading Kimber to believe the MacMillans had just entered what appeared to be rich ore before pausing the drill, he contended that the exchange was treating Windfall unfairly and worried that suspending the stock would be good for professional traders but bad for individual investors. The chairman was uncomfortable with what he heard about the animosity between Graham and Campbell; he didn't want the TSE and the OSC working at cross-purposes. He was also worried about relations between the exchange and Windfall being so sour, and Campbell suggested getting everyone in a room. When Kimber called Graham, the exchange president said he'd be delighted to attend a meeting that afternoon and was sure Stearns and Somerville would be, too. Even though Viola wasn't a Windfall official, Kimber wanted both MacMillans there. She was also pleased by the invitation and was hoping it would be a chance to sort things out. She'd been feeling a lot of pressure from the TSE and didn't have a lot of respect for the mining knowledge of the people there. Maybe Kimber and the OSC would be easier to deal with.

In the meantime, MacMillan spent a lot of time on the telephone, as usual. She finally called Willis Ambrose back. The geologist had left messages with the MacMillans' answering service on Friday and Saturday. Although Kingston was a long way from either Bay Street or Timmins, some rumours travelled that far, and he'd been reading the *Globe and Mail*. He wanted to give his clients the results of his closer look at the samples but didn't hear back from them until Viola reached him at home Tuesday morning. He told her there was no tetrahedrite and there were no commercial amounts of chalcopyrite and sphalerite. In other words, he'd seen nothing of value in the samples. Her response was puzzling. "I am glad to hear it," she said. "I will let George know."

She may have told George, but neither of them said anything about it to Cole, though they spoke to him several times that morning. They were concerned about the trading in Windfall shares, which seemed out of control. The lawyer also received an unexpected call from Wardrope, who said he was happy to see the MacMillans active in Timmins and that he hoped the Windfall property would be a success. "Let's hope so," said Cole. "Let's hope it's a good one."

At four thirty that afternoon, the MacMillans and Cole filed into the boardroom in the OSC's office at Queen and University. Also in attendance were Kimber, McFarland, consulting geologist Hans Froberg and Graham, Stearns and Somerville from the TSE. Campbell, who as director was essentially the commission's CEO, wasn't in the room. Kimber didn't invite him to the meeting because of all his contact with the MacMillans over the previous few days and because of his quarrel with Graham. Campbell still wanted the TSE president to apologize for implying he had a financial interest in Windfall and did not consider his conciliatory letter sufficient. What no one knew was that Campbell, hoping to make up his wife's losses, had begun shorting the stock.

Kimber opened the meeting with some introductory remarks. "This is an explosive situation," he said. "Forget about the past. What are we going to do in the future?" Ignoring this, Viola and the exchange officials rehashed their past dealings. She claimed, implausibly, that she'd been eager to talk, but the TSE people had been hard to reach. Graham said he didn't see any problem; all Windfall had to do was issue a statement about what the core showed. MacMillan, who did most of the talking during the meeting, argued that she and George should not have to release assay results or any other information because the public respected their long history in the business and had confidence that they knew what they were doing. That gave Stearns the impression she believed she deserved special treatment.

Graham said Windfall was acting in a way that encouraged rumours. Any reasonable company would issue a clear statement, and it was ridiculous that the MacMillans refused to do so. Viola argued that Windfall wasn't responsible for all the action on the market, and since the company hadn't started the rumours, it shouldn't be responsible for denying them. Veering off topic, she complained that the TSE was acting in a way that protected brokers at the expense of companies and the public. She accused brokers of heavily trading Windfall from firm accounts, also known as house accounts, including doing a lot of undeclared short selling. In some cases, brokerages provided floor traders with, say, $10,000 so they could buy and sell stock. The floor trader and the firm split the profit. Viola didn't come right out and say this at the meeting, but it was hard not to see that if the brokers were shorting the stock, they'd benefit if the TSE suspended it. She hoped the OSC would investigate. Her comments didn't surprise Graham, who'd long known about her hostility toward the brokerage fraternity. Somerville, who hadn't forgotten how combative Viola had been during the negotiations over selling the claims to Windfall, didn't take her complaints too seriously either. After all, promoters regularly griped about short sellers. Besides, if there was that much short selling, the stock would be going down, not up. The mood in the room was tense and the mistrust between the two sides was obvious.

MacMillan, showing her anxiety over losing control of the company, contended that the stock she'd sold the previous week had been to maintain an orderly market, and it had diluted her position. Not for the first time, she said the worst thing she had ever done was put the claims into Windfall instead of a private company. One threat was Ned Bragagnolo. He'd called her that morning to say that he was part of a group with a substantial block of shares that was looking for more information. Although he professed to support her, she suspected his group might try to get a director position or even control. The other threat was that a mining giant would move in. But when she said Texas Gulf and Noranda had been large buyers of Windfall stock, Cole spoke up. "Viola, you don't know that," he said. "Don't say things like that. You don't know that."

When McFarland asked why the MacMillans hadn't published any assay results, George said they hadn't finished drilling the hole and weren't planning on doing any assays until it was complete. He argued it could be misleading to release results from only part of a hole. It was a fair point: if Windfall had said it had found no commercial minerals and then continued drilling and hit an ore body, investors would have suspected that the company was manipulating the market. The MacMillans evaded all questions about the core and certainly didn't say anything about the two samples that the Toronto lab had assayed. Nor did they admit that Ambrose had examined samples under a microscope in his lab and found nothing of value, or even that the geologist had seen the core. There was a copy of the previous week's *Northern Miner* in the room, and Kimber asked why it quoted Windfall's press release that said, "The core is being sampled." George denied that information had been part of the company's July 7 announcement and claimed it was typical of the paper to add things like that. No one had a copy of the press release to confirm that the statement was an exact quote.

Viola said it wasn't fair to single out Windfall when other companies didn't have to report assay results so early. It was true that waiting until drillers had finished a hole before doing assays was standard procedure. And even announcing results after just one hole would be unusual. Viola

asked if every operator in the Timmins area would be required to immediately publicize the results of every drill hole. Kimber and McFarland
said no, but that because of all the rumours, Windfall needed to make a
statement. "If we release the results, it would set the camp on fire," said
Viola. Neighbouring properties would become more expensive, and that
would be bad for the company's shareholders. The MacMillans wanted
to buy the property to the north of Windfall's Prosser claims, but the
primary owner was in Europe and unreachable. Revealing assay results
could push the price up, and they might not be able to afford it. She also
told Kimber that if he forced them to put out results now, it would be a
stone around his neck for the rest of his life. Annoyed, he said the stone
wouldn't be around his neck, it would be around hers.

"What happens if the results are negative?" McFarland asked.

She admitted that was a possibility. But, of course, just as one good
hole did not make a mine, one bad hole did not make a property worthless.
Although the TSE and OSC representatives believed no assay results
were available and that the core was still in Toronto, several of them had
the impression the last part of the core was promising. Certainly, the
MacMillans appeared confident. In fact, Viola said, "Everybody knows we
hit it," and "Everybody knows we are in the same structure as the Texas
Gulf Company and that we are going to have a mine." Not all around
the table shared that optimism. Froberg, for one, was skeptical, though he
didn't say so at the meeting. And after forty years in mining, McFarland
tended to be pessimistic about anybody having anything until a property
had been thoroughly drilled, but he also believed that optimism was an
essential ingredient for success in mineral exploration.

At one point, Viola asked if Kimber and McFarland would step out into
the hall with her. She wanted to speak to them without the TSE officials,
particularly Stearns, around. Outside the room, she again complained about
heavy trading by brokers. Much of her ire was aimed at T.A. Richardson.
She explained that before the market opened on July 6, Stearns's firm
had called her and told her about the high demand for Windfall shares
and requested she provide stock so it could fill the orders. She'd turned
over 100,000 shares, but, she claimed, the brokerage house held onto the

shares until it could sell them for a higher price. Kimber pointed out that this was a separate issue from what they were discussing in the meeting.

"You are complaining about the wrong people," she said. "You are pressuring us; you should be pressuring the exchange."

"Well, you agree to give out the information as soon as it is available," he offered, "and I will investigate this complaint then."

Grudgingly, she consented. When they returned to the conference room, Kimber said he wanted to come up with a statement that everyone would be happy with. He believed it needed to do two things: confirm the rumours of any completed assays were false and indicate when the public could expect authentic information. With the secretarial staff gone for the day, he wrote a draft by hand, and they discussed it. Viola contended that another release with nothing new to say would make things worse. She lost the argument, with the only consolation being that the OSC was putting it out, so it could take the blame if the result was more exuberance in Windfall trading. Kimber suggested a ten-day deadline for Windfall to release a report, which the TSE men thought was far too long. But Viola argued strenuously against any deadline. George backed her up, pointing out that the drillers could always run into problems that might cause delays. But he committed to resume drilling as soon as the core shack was finished, probably on the weekend. Not realizing the core shack was already built, Kimber relented. Graham had already left the meeting, but Stearns and Somerville remained. They were disappointed, though there was nothing they could do about it, as the OSC seemed to have stepped in and taken charge. Once he had a rough draft, Kimber said he would finalize it later.

Then he changed the subject. "Now, there have been some allegations made about the brokerage profession, and I think there should be an investigation."

"I would welcome this very much," Stearns said, who'd felt Viola had been looking at him when she'd complained about brokers earlier in the meeting. As a senior partner of T.A. Richardson, he wanted to clear his firm's name and his own. By the time the meeting finally ended after seven o'clock, calling the peace between the two sides uneasy seemed generous.

The next morning, Kimber read a revised version of the letter to Somerville over the phone. The latter man was eager to ensure that it was clear that this was not a joint statement from the commission and the exchange. He also stressed the importance of releasing it before the market opened. But Kimber had sent it to Cole and wanted to wait until the lawyer had a look. That afternoon, after the market closed, the statement went out on OSC letterhead. Noting the meeting that had taken place the day before, it said, "At this discussion it was established, to the satisfaction of those present, that no assays of drill cores taken from the property have been made to date." It went on to say, "When this drilling has been completed, the cores will be assayed and the results announced forthwith. This work will take some time."

Now it was Graham's turn to be unhappy. For one thing, he did not know of another case where the OSC had stepped into the TSE's turf like this. And when he read the commission's statement, he saw it had failed to address the exchange's concerns about rumours, provide any information gleaned from a visual examination of the core or promise that assay results would be coming soon. The release continued to keep the public in the dark about developments on the Windfall claims. Worse, because George had said that once the core shack was up, the core would be under lock and key, Kimber had inserted this sentence: "To lessen the possibility of rumours during the period of this work all cores will be under guard." Why would a company need security for core that was worthless?

CHAPTER SIXTEEN

CRAZY BUYERS

Although Noranda had balked at the asking price for the Prosser claims in April, the mining giant continued to follow developments with the property. In late June, MacMillan called Ralph Woolverton, Noranda's eastern supervisor, to ask if the company wanted to buy some other claims she had. He passed, then added: "I thought you might be calling to offer us some Windfall ground."

"Oh, no, I'm saving that for myself," she said, "but I can give you a piece of the underwriting."

After making sure she was serious, Woolverton said he'd get back to her. Although company executives discussed it, they came to no decision until all the rumours and stock market activity rekindled their curiosity. On July 10, Archibald Bell, the manager of Noranda Exploration, wrote Viola to say, "The members of Noranda will be very interested in financial participation if there was a mine in the making, and we would appreciate any information and consideration you can give us."

By the following Wednesday, the day after the meeting in the OSC boardroom, MacMillan had not replied. But she and George were on their way to Timmins, leaving Toronto at three o'clock in the morning and taking turns sleeping and driving. When they reached Englehart, they stopped, and George called Cole to suggest that he invite Froberg, the

OSC's consulting geologist, or even the resident geologist for the Porcupine, to come by the Windfall office in town and look at the core. The lawyer conveyed the offer to Kimber, who said it wasn't necessary because he was comfortable relying on the integrity and honesty of the MacMillans.

Later, Greg Reynolds of the *Daily Press* found Viola in a busy restaurant and interrupted a business meeting she was having with three men he didn't know. She made it clear she wasn't in the mood to answer questions. "Just leave us alone and let us get on with mining," she said. "All we want to do is find a mine." Undeterred, he pressed her for information. She wouldn't comment on the rumours about the first drill hole results but did say drilling would begin again soon.

That evening, Woolverton was in the lobby of the Empire Hotel with several other mining men when he saw the couple come in. George immediately climbed the stairs while Viola headed for the elevators. Woolverton went over and asked if she'd received Bell's letter. She had but appeared distracted by other concerns. Because it took a long time before she realized the elevator was out of order and she'd have to climb the stairs, Woolverton managed to have a lengthy conversation with her. According to MacMillan, some TSE members, who'd been caught in short positions on Windfall, were blaming her and forcing her to sell them stock. She told Woolverton that she believed Texas Gulf had been a heavy buyer of Windfall since back when it was at sixty-two cents, and she didn't want the company to fall into American hands.

MacMillan was far more reserved when it came to discussing the core. She claimed it remained unsplit and unassayed and was under lock and key in the basement of the hotel. This wasn't true. On Saturday, George had dropped by Ron Mills's farm and asked him to drive four core boxes to Windfall's Timmins office. The two men moved them from Viola's Cadillac to Mills's car. Then George gave him a key to the back door of the office. Mills, who understood that George thought the core would be more secure there, left at one o'clock and arrived in Timmins eight hours later. He carried the boxes down to the basement, then he drove back to Tottenham. George hired a watchman to provide security.

When Woolverton asked what was in the core, Viola said, "I can't tell until I get it assayed."

"Have you got a mine?" the Noranda man pressed.

"I can't tell that with one drill hole."

During this time, the MacMillans usually spoke with Cole several times a day. The lawyer passed on a request from Kimber to Viola: did she have any suggestions for where to start an investigation into the trading by brokerage houses to help him cut to the heart of the matter? She said she would give it some thought but that it would be easier when she returned to Toronto and could look at the exchange's trading sheets.

Edgar Bradley was one of the few people to get any information from Viola that day. The drill crew had just finished helping the carpenter build the bunkhouse and now had nothing to do but wait for the MacMillans to say they wanted to resume drilling. While driving the couple to the Windfall site, Bradley asked when that would be. "In a day or two," Viola said. "We will let you know."

When he mentioned the frenzy over the stock, she said, "People are crazy to buy that stock when we don't know what we've got."

□

Many investors saw Windfall as a chance to make some money by placing a bet, either long or short, on the stock. But all the market activity upset Texas Gulf's Walter Holyk. The possibility that the MacMillans might have something haunted him. Of all the claims his company had to lose due to a staking error, why did it have to be those four in Prosser Township? If that ground held an ore body, he'd have to live with his regret over the mistake.

Based on his company's airborne electromagnetic survey, followed by ground geophysics, he believed the conductor the MacMillans were drilling extended into Texas Gulf property. Holyk, who'd earned a promotion from chief geologist to exploration manager in May, decided to check it out. Viola and George learned of this when they came out of the cookery and saw helicopters delivering a drill rig to the edge of some Texas Gulf claims, about 600 metres from Windfall's hole.

Holyk was working from his home in Oakville on Thursday. He called the Timmins office to speak to David Lowry, who was now Texas Gulf's lead exploration man in the region. Viola, who just happened to be visiting Lowry at the time, asked to speak to Holyk. Although they'd met several years earlier, they didn't know each other well. During a conversation that lasted fifteen or twenty minutes, she did most of the talking but divulged nothing about what she was finding on her claims. Instead, she talked about the crazy situation on the market and how the stock price kept going up, even though she and George hadn't released any information. She also complained about the TSE, short sellers and what the "boys on Bay Street" were doing to her. Holyk thought she seemed shaken by the exchange's request for the company to issue a statement. It was, she argued, a dangerous precedent that could inhibit people's ability to look after their own business affairs without being forced to reveal sensitive information. Mostly, though, MacMillan wanted to know about the Texas Gulf drill, asking several times during the call why it was so close to her property. Although she didn't come right out and admit it, she certainly gave Holyk the impression that she was unhappy about it. She said he wouldn't get the necessary information from one drill hole and warned that the TSE might ask the company to release the results. But she was unable to dissuade him from continuing with his plans.

News of Texas Gulf's new drill hole sent the price of Windfall shares higher, while George moved the core that had been sitting in the office basement to the core shack and finally gave the drillers word to continue the hole. But they quickly ran into delays. First, there was difficulty getting the rig started, and then a problem with the pump, which required a trip to Rouyn for a new one.

□

Before Graham Ackerley had returned to the *Northern Miner* offices in Toronto on July 14, he'd been trying to do as much actual reporting in Timmins as possible. When he flew over the Windfall site in a helicopter, he spied plenty of activity, with the core shack and camp buildings going up, but the drill was idle. In town, he spoke to sources who'd collected and sampled sludge, though the results had not indicated anything worthwhile. He also heard a lot of unusable rumour. His efforts to speak to any company official remained fruitless.

All this might have increased his doubts, except much of what he did know made him optimistic about Windfall's prospects. There was the proximity to the Texas Gulf find and the expectation that the Porcupine would see more strikes. The MacMillans had quickly raised money for exploration work, and the stock price remained aloft. The airborne geophysics showed anomalies, and the couple claimed their geophysical surveys on the ground did, too. Viola told him the core shack would be big enough to hold 10,000 feet of core, which suggested she expected to do a lot of drilling. Two geologists thought the geological structure that held the big find might extend to the MacMillans' ground. Someone from Texas Gulf showed Ackerley good assay results, claiming they were for Windfall. And the American company moved a drill to the boundary of its property. At a more official level, the letter Tom Cole sent Howard Graham added to the sense that everything was legit. And the OSC had met with the MacMillans and not taken any action against them or the company, which suggested the commission was happy with what it heard.

Still, much of this evidence was circumstantial or inconclusive. Since John Carrington, the editor of the *Northern Miner*, was on holiday, senior assistant editor Maurice "Mort" Brown, who'd worked as a mining engineer before joining the paper, was responsible for making the final editorial decisions. The previous week, he'd pulled a map showing Prosser and surrounding townships because the Windfall press release hadn't included any assay results. He knew that Carrington was a stickler for assays. As Ackerley and Brown discussed what to do now, the reporter suggested seeking guidance from George Wardrope. Like the mines minister, Brown was from Port Arthur, and the two had known each other a long time.

"My spies tell me you saw the MacMillans over the weekend," he said when he made the call Wednesday morning. He explained that no one at the paper had been able to get in touch with Windfall officials, and he was trying to figure out how heavily to cover the potential discovery.

"You're not quoting me?" asked Wardrope. Assured it was off the record, he gave Brown the impression that it was an important situation and the paper wouldn't be making a mistake in giving the story some prominence.

Competitive pressure also influenced the decisions. This was a huge story, the biggest since Brown had joined the paper. Everyone in mining and the markets was talking about it, and many journalists were chasing it. Although the *Northern Miner* needed to be careful, it couldn't risk getting scooped by the *Financial Post* or the dailies. The July 16 edition gave Windfall lots of play, all of it written by Ackerley, without much in the way of skepticism. The front-page story, headlined "Major Situation in the Making for Windfall?", did not mention any mineral content—unlike the *Post*, which cited a rumour and then debunked it—and made it clear that what was in the hole was unknown. But it was otherwise optimistic, pointing out that visual examination of core was enough for mining people to identify ore and going on about the electromagnetic anomalies and geological structure. A page-two article—with a photo of George and Viola and the headline "Have the Mining MacMillans Scored Again?"—was even less cautious. Praising the couple for their professionalism, their instincts and their careers, it stated, "The names 'Porcupine' and 'MacMillan' are, in many ways, practically synonymous." An enthusiastic editorial was even more fawning. "Although the full significance of it is not known as this is being written, the fact remains that Windfall Oils and Mines have apparently come up with a promising base metal discovery in the new area north of Timmins," it said. "For this, congratulations are due to the mining MacMillans—vivacious and colourful Viola, quiet and competent George."

Stock markets had been using ticker tape to transmit share prices since the late nineteenth century. Abbreviated company names and their current prices would go out from the trading floor over telegraph lines to stock tickers, machines that printed out the results on a thin ribbon of paper. This allowed the investment industry to follow the trading. A series of new technologies, including the telephone, radio and television, helped customers follow the action without visiting the brokerage house or waiting until the papers came out. Computer technology loomed, but ticker tape was still around in 1964. And people who worked in the business, despite being eager rumourmongers, still liked to say, "The tape tells the story."

Unfortunately, reporters require more than stock prices to write their stories. They need to separate the facts from the fictions and, whenever possible, get on-the-record statements from company officials. That made things tough for Ackerley and the other journalists covering Windfall, which was WDM on the ticker tape. The *Northern Miner* reporter was accustomed to being in regular contact with Viola MacMillan. But since talking to her on July 7, he hadn't been able to get her, or anyone else from the company, to return his calls. It was frustrating because it meant he had to cover the story with only rumour and secondary sources. And even the MacMillans' friends didn't know anything.

As acting editor, Mort Brown wanted to see what was going on in Timmins for himself. On Saturday, the same day drilling finally restarted at the Windfall site, he headed up there with Ackerley. The two journalists had also arranged a Sunday visit to the Canadian Jamieson site, another Timmins-area property that was generating interest. The company's drillers had pulled some good core, and Ned Bragagnolo, the proud vice-president and a major shareholder, wanted to show it off. In the morning, Ackerley heard that the MacMillans were eating breakfast in the dining room at the Empire Hotel. He walked over from the Bon Air to see if he could get them to talk. He found George in the lobby. The two men shook hands, and MacMillan promised that the *Northern Miner* would get the drilling results first, though he didn't expect any for at least ten days. He wanted to complete more holes before sending any core to be assayed. When Viola joined them, she seemed wound up, talking a lot and making flippant remarks like, "Oops! Now I'm saying too much!" and "I should have my tongue cut off!"

Bragagnolo had also invited the MacMillans to come out to his drill site because he knew of their interest in the property before he acquired it. Everyone climbed into the station wagon, with George at the wheel. They drove over to the Bon Air to pick up Brown and Ackerley, who'd gone back to grab his boots. Outside the motel, the MacMillans saw Eric

Cradock, who'd been president of Windfall before they'd bought it. They invited him along.

During the next two hours, in the car and at the site, George wore what Ackerley later described as an "impressive smile." He talked little and wouldn't say anything about Windfall except to repeat that the assay results were at least ten days away. Viola talked almost nonstop and didn't seem herself. She wouldn't answer questions and said more than once that she wanted to make a mine and wished people would leave her alone. Her biggest regret was selling the claims to Windfall instead of putting them into a company she'd formed called Lucky Texas. "Why should I bail out the old Windfall shareholders?" she said in front of Cradock. To Brown, this suggested that the Prosser property was so promising that she wished she had it all to herself. MacMillan also ranted about how badly the TSE, especially Howard Graham, had treated her and said she found Campbell and Kimber of the OSC much better to deal with. Ackerley later said, "It was one of the weirdest conversations I have had in my life."

When Brown and George walked back to the car together, the *Northern Miner* editor said, "One more specific question, George, and I will leave you alone."

"Shoot."

"Has Consolidated Golden Arrow Mines any Windfall stock?"

Golden Arrow was the other public company that Viola planned to use to develop properties. Viola was president; George was vice-president. Moss, Lawson's first underwriting for the MacMillans was for Golden Arrow shortly after Viola had regained control of it. After the Texas Gulf discovery, Viola wanted to buy some claims for both companies and was still interested in acquiring something for Golden Arrow if the right deal came along. Brown had asked about it because if the MacMillans were buying or selling shares in Windfall through another of their companies, it might offer a clue about the value of the Prosser claims.

"No," said George, "but it has $350,000 that it didn't have a few weeks ago."

Surprised, Brown wondered what that meant. Maybe the property wasn't good after all. Or maybe the MacMillans had sold the shares to themselves. Or maybe they had sold to keep the market down because they'd been short selling, which was one of the rumours going around. Or maybe they'd done it in anticipation of doing another round of underwriting. He tried to pursue the subject. "Well, how many shares did the company own and what did you get for them?"

"I told you too much now. I don't think Viola would want that. No more questions."

The *Northern Miner* journalists weren't the only ones seeking information that day. Bragagnolo had hoped that by showing the MacMillans his core, they'd reveal something about theirs. But he got nothing. Still, everyone was in good spirits, and some of the men began serenading Viola with a parody of "On Top of Old Smokey," changing the lyrics to be about Windfall and Prosser. She responded by suggesting they read "If—," a poem by Rudyard Kipling, saying it captured where she was in her career.

After they returned to Timmins, Bragagnolo had a drink with Ackerley, Brown and Craddock in a room at the Bon Air. They talked about what they'd heard and seen and tried to make sense of what, if anything, it said about Windfall's prospects. They all believed the MacMillans probably had something valuable. The men also discussed the Kipling poem. Viola had referred to the third stanza, though when they looked at it, they wondered if she meant the fourth, which begins, "If you can talk with crowds and keep your virtue / Or walk with Kings—nor lose the common touch."

But given that she'd long believed that no one could be a "crybaby" and be a successful prospector, maybe she did mean the third stanza after all:

> If you can make one heap of all your winnings
> And risk it on one turn of pitch-and-toss,
> And lose, and start again at your beginnings
> And never breathe a word about your loss;
> If you can force your heart and nerve and sinew
> To serve your turn long after they are gone,
> And so hold on when there is nothing in you
> Except the Will which says to them: "Hold on!"

Whatever point she was trying to make, it was lost on the men.

CHAPTER SEVENTEEN

SHEER NONSENSE

G reg Reynolds spent the late afternoon of May 16, 1964, in front of a television with Viola MacMillan and a few others in the Empire Hotel's suite 538. The occasion was the Preakness Stakes. Two weeks earlier, Northern Dancer had thrilled the nation by winning the Kentucky Derby in record time. If the Canadian colt won the Preakness, he'd be two-thirds of the way to horse racing's Triple Crown. After Northern Dancer had finished more than two lengths ahead and the cheers had died down, the *Daily Press* reporter had a chance to ask MacMillan what she planned to do with Windfall. She said she was going to burn the short sellers so badly that they would stay away from the company.

Short sellers are a problem for stock promoters because if enough investors short a stock, the price will go down. MacMillan hated them and thought they were destroying the mining business. She wanted the TSE to ban short selling. Since that wasn't likely to happen, she was going to deal with them herself. To do this, she wanted to keep the stock trading between fifty-five and sixty-five cents until drilling started. Then she planned to make the price jump enough to squeeze the short sellers, forcing them back into the market to cover their position. Once the stock hit one dollar, they'd be hurt so badly, she wouldn't have to worry about them again. As usual, Reynolds found MacMillan knowledgeable and confident; he didn't think it was an idle threat. Two months later, MacMillan was still angry about the short sellers, but punishing them would have to wait. She now had a bigger problem: maintaining control of the company.

When Mort Brown and Graham Ackerley first arrived in Timmins, they ran into Ken Darke before they'd even checked into the Bon Air. The geologist was no longer with Texas Gulf. After informing his bosses that he'd traded shares on insider information, he had taken a two-week leave of absence, starting in late April. He left the company for good at the end of June. One reason: he wanted to be in town to look after his investments instead of out in the bush. But he continued to live in the Bon Air as he started his own consulting firm. After Ackerley introduced him to Brown, the conversation soon turned to Windfall. Darke said he was part of a group that had 600,000 shares. Given that he knew as much about the area's geology as anyone, this news seemed to be evidence that the Windfall claims held something valuable.

But it wasn't that simple. On Monday, July 6, after returning to Timmins in the chopper with a tiny piece of core and the sludge sample he'd picked up at the Windfall site, Ned Bragagnolo showed the chip of core to Darke. The geologist said it was graphitic with some pyrite but no visible copper. He wasn't surprised. While he'd originally wanted the Prosser claims for Texas Gulf, he had considered them part of a group of third-priority claims. And despite all the rumours, he doubted the property held an ore body. In fact, he started off shorting the stock. On Tuesday, July 7, Conwest's Pat Heenan heard back from the lab in Kirkland Lake. The sludge sample he'd collected at the site contained nothing to suggest commercial values. He told his colleagues and no one else, but word spread. Neither Bragagnolo's chip nor Heenan's sludge was definitive, of course, and Darke well knew the tricks Texas Gulf had used to hide its first good hole, including leaving worthless core on the site. Still, by noon on Thursday, he was short 25,000 shares. In the afternoon, though, he started to worry about his exposure. Based on a conversation with garage owner Roy Powley, who had talked to George MacMillan and said the drillers had pulled core with mineralization that looked good, Darke changed his position. He ended the day long 20,000 shares. Then, after speaking to drill contractor Edgar Bradley, he kept buying. Soon, spurred by little more than second-hand accounts and speculation, he owned 100,000 shares.

After meeting at the Bon Air, Darke, Brown and Ackerley went out for lunch. Bragagnolo joined them. He'd also been skeptical when the stock price first went up, and Darke's assessment of the core chip convinced him to sell 10,000 Windfall shares short. But as the stock continued to rise, Bragagnolo thought the MacMillans must have something. Otherwise, he told Greg Reynolds, the couple would soon be going to jail. He went long 25,000 shares.

Over lunch, Bragagnolo and Darke told the *Northern Miner* men that their group, which also included John Larche, Fred Rousseau and Don McKinnon, might even have more shares than the MacMillans. Brown got the impression the men were thinking about trying to get control of Windfall. He wasn't imagining it. The men often hung around the Doherty, Roadhouse branch, and they began to wonder if they might have enough Windfall stock for control. Bragagnolo thought MacMillan was too clever to lose her company, especially if it had something good, but the others weren't so sure.

As the share price continued to defy common sense, with the price now above four dollars, the speculation started to seem like certainty. In a *New York Herald Tribune* piece that ran July 20, Taylor referred to the value of the core as "rumoured and no doubt factual." This was not exactly rigorous journalism. Although he never had any confirmation, he believed the gossip he heard had credence because people were citing the copper value down to a tenth of a percent. "Now, if it had been one per cent or two per cent, I don't think people would have placed the same faith in this," he said later. "But when you get down to the decimal point you feel they come from some source."

The gang of shareholders that hung out in the Doherty, Roadhouse office didn't trust "some source"—they wanted information from *the* source. They elected Bragagnolo to walk over to the Windfall office to see what he could find out from MacMillan. She gave him a cup of coffee and not much else. When he asked about the core, she wouldn't tell him anything; he asked if he should hang on to his stock, and she wouldn't give him any advice. He told her that he was part of a group with enough shares for control. "Well, I don't know how you figure that out," she said. "I don't know, they must have an awful lot of stock because we have an awful lot of stock, and I don't know how you can have control."

Afterward, Bragagnolo reported back to his friends that MacMillan didn't seem at all worried about them. In fact, his visit had rattled her. She phoned Tom Cole and vented about a possible conspiracy by the Timmins group to call a meeting and take control of Windfall. The lawyer knew she and George had always held control of any business they were involved in. Ideally, they wanted absolute control, or at least 50 percent of the shares, but at a minimum, they needed effective control, which in a widely held company might be as little as 25 or 30 percent. If the Prosser claims were to yield a mine, she wanted it to be hers, not one she just had a piece of. She and George and their companies owned a little over one million of the 3.8 million shares, a position that was more precarious than she'd like.

Not knowing if Bragagnolo was right that she wasn't worried or if it was just a good act, Darke wasn't satisfied. Believing it was "sheer nonsense that this drill had been unreported so long" and the company had allowed so many rumours to spread, he decided to start some of his own. He asked several brokers he had accounts with if they had any clients with large blocks of Windfall stock and, if so, to pass along word that there was a group in Timmins looking to snatch control. Rather than being serious about a takeover, he just wanted to force the company to release some information.

The one bit of good news for MacMillan was that Bragagnolo remained unsure if he wanted to join forces with the others or back her instead. As it turned out, he sold the last of his shares that day. In two weeks of trading the stock, during which he'd been in both short and long positions, he'd made $65,599. But other threats, including from Darke, still loomed, and Viola MacMillan was feeling the pressure.

MacMillan arrived late to the mining industry dinner at the McIntyre Community Building in Schumacher on Tuesday, July 21. She came in with Timmins mayor Leo Del Villano. Although she appeared to have been drinking, she agreed to address the room when prompted. As much as she was tight-lipped about what was in the core, she was enthusiastically outspoken on other matters. Windfall had closed at $4.75 that afternoon, after briefly hitting a new high of $5.70, but she had lots to complain about, and her fiery and emotional speech lasted half an hour and earned her a standing ovation from the roughly fifty people in attendance. She attacked short sellers; the TSE; government regulations; the underwriting system, which forced mining companies to sell stock to brokers at a fixed price while the brokers could charge whatever the public would pay; and unscrupulous promoters. She also argued that mining areas, especially the Porcupine, should hold seats on the TSE or be allowed to create their own exchanges.

MacMillan had asked that her comments be off the record, but Reynolds and the news director from the local TV station took notes. Seeing that, she asked them to stop, and they did—at least until she said something else noteworthy. Afterward, they wanted her to hold a press conference so they could get her comments on the record. She refused, but they cornered her and convinced her to talk for a bit. After all, so many people had heard the speech that nothing she said was going to stay secret for long. This time, her remarks were less incendiary, but she did say, "If Toronto can have an exchange, then the Porcupine can have one. It never needed one as badly as it needs one now." The headline in the *Daily Press* the next day was, "Porcupine Needs Own Exchange: Mrs. MacMillan."

Reynolds also managed to get a few minutes alone with her to ask about Windfall. She confirmed that the drillers had started again and were setting up another rig to begin a second hole but was less helpful when he tried to find out what the core from the first hole showed. In the past few months, he'd learned what many other reporters already knew: that as much as she was willing to talk, getting a candid answer out of MacMillan could often be difficult. She could be evasive. She could be combative. And she could be elliptical. After telling Reynolds that the core from the first hole had not been split or assayed yet, she said, "Babies not yet born will benefit from our experience this week."

Uncomfortable spending too much time away from the office, MacMillan returned to Toronto the next day. Driving down by herself, she stopped at Drewe's cottage around seven o'clock in the evening. On her two previous visits that month, MacMillan had seemed excited about Windfall, but now her former secretary noticed how edgy and upset she was. She complained about how brokers were short selling the stock, but she was talking so quickly it was hard to take everything in.

"Well, why don't you get the drill core assayed?" asked Drewe. MacMillan ignored the question and kept talking.

Later, Drewe asked, "Why don't you stop the rumours that are going around?"

"I didn't start the rumours," MacMillan said. "Let the people who started them stop them."

That wasn't going to happen. Takeover speculation flared. "Rumours swept the Street that Noranda Mines had been buying large gobs of Windfall, had acquired control, etcetera, etcetera. Although refraining from making any official comment on the rumours, The Northern Miner got the impression from talking to Noranda officials that the stories were rather far-fetched," the industry bible noted in its July 23 edition. That didn't mean the mining giant had no interest in Windfall; the day before, Noranda chairman John Bradfield had written MacMillan to say, "We would be glad to help with the financing when that becomes appropriate, thereby keeping control in Canada." She'd also received letters from other companies, including the subsidiary of a British one a week earlier and an American one back in June.

On Thursday, MacMillan dropped by Cole's office, and, later, the two had a long phone conversation. The lawyer noted how tired she was. The last couple of weeks had clearly been a strain on her. "She seems to worry more about the stock she might have retained or the money she might have made rather than be happy with the stock that she has," he wrote in a memo afterward. "The stock is extremely valuable, and she is already some dollars in pocket on the transaction." Another concern for her was that the money she'd made, all in one year, was going to push her into a higher tax bracket.

She was also, as always, upset about the short sellers. Around lunchtime, she'd gone over to the TSE to pick up a report on short positions and gone in to see Howard Graham. As they noshed on cheese and crackers in his office, she complained bitterly about the stock she had to give up and that she couldn't sell from the treasury after the underwriting. She also took the opportunity to give him instructions on how he should run the TSE and told him there should be a new exchange run by people who knew something about mining.

Even as MacMillan continued to whinge, the OSC hadn't forgotten her request for an investigation into Windfall trading. On Friday, Cole called Kimber to say he was going to be away for a few weeks. The OSC chairman said the commission was still waiting for information from MacMillan before getting started. In a letter to his client, the lawyer said the OSC wanted "pointers from her as to what to look for and where to look," and that, while Kimber appreciated the pressures she'd been under, he hoped she could get something to him on Monday because the investigation is "likely to be more successful if made while everything is 'hot'" and because any further delay might leave the commission open to criticism.

Then Cole picked up a camping trailer and headed out on a three-week tour of the Maritimes with his family. He wasn't fleeing his controversial clients; the trip had been planned since December. But he did send George a new letter of resignation as a director "to take effect upon acceptance." Cole urged Viola to go on the board now, something he'd been advising her to do for months. In addition, he believed the company needed to revamp its board by replacing the loyal friends with directors who had mining experience.

Before leaving the office, he'd written a memo for one of his partners, Roger Archibald, updating him on Windfall and requesting that he advise the company during Cole's absence. "With any luck," he added, "you will be away before anything comes of this."

□

The day after the Windfall drillers had restarted their rig on July 18, Willis Ambrose was at his cottage. A messenger showed up and said the MacMillans wanted to talk to him. Ambrose found a phone and called

George, who asked him to come to Timmins. When the geologist made it to the Porcupine a few days later, the two men spotted the next two holes, logged core and split some of it to prepare samples for assaying. Ambrose went home on Thursday, July 23.

The next day, Texas Gulf's Walter Holyk dropped by the site and chatted with George, each man trying to glean some useful information from the other. After Holyk left, George looked at the most recent core and told the drillers the first hole was complete. They'd gone 863 feet. After packing twenty-seven canvas sample sacks into his station wagon, he drove to Swastika Laboratories. Almost all the core with him was from above 570 feet; only one sample bag was from after the crew restarted on July 18. By the time George made it to the lab, it was five o'clock and the staff had gone home, but Douglas Kerr-Lawson, the president of the company, was still there, watering the back lawn. He helped unload the samples.

At the meeting with OSC and TSE officials on July 14, the MacMillans had agreed to publish the assay results promptly. For a client in a hurry, the lab could complete assays on twenty-seven samples in a day, but Kerr-Lawson sensed no urgency. George didn't request a rush job and asked that the lab mail the assay results to Windfall's Toronto office. He didn't want any calls, and no one was to give the results out over the phone. The reason, he later claimed, was that he had a distinctive voice that was easily imitated.

On Saturday morning, the lab staff prepared the samples for assay. First, they crushed the rock to about the size of rice. Then they took about a pound of those grains and reduced it to a powder similar to flour. That's what the lab would assay on Monday and Tuesday. Knowing about all the market activity and the swirling rumours, Kerr-Lawson told his employees in the crushing room that if anyone asked about the Windfall samples, they were to "act dumb."

Back in Timmins, Texas Gulf abandoned the hole near the border of the Windfall property at 515 feet. The drillers had made it through to the other side of the graphite conductor and pulled only negligible copper mineralization. Having seen nothing promising, the company didn't even bother to split and assay the core before removing the drill rig.

CHAPTER EIGHTEEN

UNWELCOME RESULTS

A man walked into the Western Union telegraph office in New York City on Monday, July 27, and wired twelve newspapers in Canada. He gave the Hilton Hotel as his address and paid cash. All the messages contained assay results: "For immediate release Windfall Mines Lot 9, Concession 1, drill core, high grade 8 percent copper and 14 percent zinc per ton. Further reports when I return Toronto." They were signed "George MacMillan President Windfall Mines." At about the same time, a woman who was about 24, had "party-blonde" hair and wore a print dress entered a nearby Western Union office on Forty-Second Street. She filed two telegrams with similar wording to the man's, though hers were from Assay Laboratories and included personal messages.

When one addressed to "Bradley Brothers Limited, Windfall Mines Limited" arrived at the drilling contractor's office in Timmins, Edgar Bradley wasn't sure who it was for. Then, seeing the New York address, he assumed it was for the MacMillans and didn't open it. Instead, he asked one of his employees to give it to George.

The other was addressed to Tom Cole and ended with "Congradulations [sic] on great strike—Regards to Marjorie Oliver." Since the Windfall lawyer was on vacation, it landed on the desk of Roger Archibald at one twenty-five that afternoon. Busy with his own clients' files, he glanced at it and put it aside. A minute or two later, it dawned on him that something wasn't right. It was, he thought, a most curious telegram. He'd never heard of Assay Laboratories, and Cole had mentioned nothing about a New York lab in his memo about Windfall. Something had come up sooner than either lawyer had expected.

Surely, it was a ruse. He called CP Telegraphs to ask for a trace, then tried to reach Viola MacMillan, who was out of town. But before he could continue his search, he received a message that Alistair Dow, the *Toronto Daily Star* financial reporter, had called. When one of the telegrams signed by MacMillan showed up in his newsroom, he was immediately suspicious. All the unsubstantiated rumours about Windfall meant he was wary of everything he read or heard about the company. Adding to his skepticism was the crude composition of the telegram, and after everyone had been waiting so long for assay results, it seemed strange that they would come from New York. When he called the Windfall office and asked to speak to the MacMillans, the woman who answered the phone said, "I will get them to call you."

Dow suspected he was getting the same brush-off he'd often received from the company. "This is important," he said. "We've just received a telegram purportedly from Mr. MacMillan, and I want to know if he is in New York."

Sounding unnerved, she replied, "I am almost sure he is not in New York, but I will get someone to call you back right away."

When Archibald returned the call, Dow read him the telegram he'd received. The lawyer now realized the wires were a coordinated effort. He told the reporter, "This is a complete hoax."

An amateur one at that. Assay results came in percentages or ounces per ton; "8 percent copper and 14 percent zinc per ton" made no sense. George MacMillan would never have written that. Although Archibald hadn't worked on the Windfall file before, he had three decades of experience with mining companies. Convinced the telegrams were more than a prank, he tried to alert the OSC, but Jack Kimber was away, and John Campbell was at lunch. After another effort to get information from the telegraph office, he spoke to Viola and informed her of the multiple wires. She said George was at the drill site and asked Archibald to let the other directors know. A third call to CP Telegraphs paid off in a conversation with a senior agent, and the lawyer asked him to take the matter seriously.

At two thirty, Archibald walked down Bay Street to the TSE, where he found Howard Graham, who already knew about the telegrams because Dow was with him. All three men agreed the wires were a scam. Since Archibald didn't have the authority to put out a public statement, he suggested Graham might want to make an announcement to stop the spread of false rumours. Then, in conversation with Dow, Archibald argued that it would be wrong to publish something known to be bogus. The reporter disagreed, saying that as long the *Star* made it clear the telegram was false, it was newsworthy. He also pointed out that his paper wasn't the only one to receive the wires. Sure enough, when Archibald returned to his office, he took calls from several other reporters.

Before the market closed, Graham put out a statement saying the telegrams were not authentic. But that was not enough to ease Archibald's mind. In between fielding calls, he wrote and delivered a letter to CP Telegraphs registering his dissatisfaction with the company's inability to find out who'd sent the telegrams and to raise the issue of legal liability in the event of any damages. Finally, unable to get anywhere with CP Telegraphs, he called Western Union Telegraph System in New York and spoke to a supervisor, who later called back with some details but no names. By now, Archibald was certain this was a criminal matter. Shortly before six o'clock, after conferring with Viola again, he called the Toronto detachment of the Royal Canadian Mounted Police. But the Mounties never would get their man and woman, so the identities and motivations of the telegram senders would remain just more to speculate about. One thing was certain: if the goal of the wires was to generate a spike in the share price, it failed. No one was fooled and the stock closed the day lower.

□

Strachan Bongard* was a stockbroker with Bongard & Company, which his grandfather had started and his uncle and father now led. Like the

---

* The author's now-late uncle.

rest of Bay Street, the brokerage house couldn't ignore the excitement over what was going on near Timmins. Late morning on July 6, the firm's A.G. Vance messaged all branches: "Stories we hear say Windfall has up to 185 feet of massive sulphides. Understand some of this core at least was brought to Toronto this weekend. I would say the strength of the stock indicates that visually the core must look promising."

Although Viola MacMillan was nearly three decades older than he was, Bongard knew her, not just because of the business he was in but because his office was on the sixth floor of 25 Adelaide Street West, the same building as her penthouse apartment and where she had an office before selling ViolaMac. Someone he knew even better was Cuthbert "Cuffy" Dixon, a senior partner with Doherty, Roadhouse, who was almost a generation older than Bongard and much better connected in the mining world. He was from Cobalt and had started out working underground in Kirkland Lake's Wright-Hargraves gold mine. Before MacMillan had purchased her twelve claims from Larche, Rousseau and McKinnon, he'd bought claims in Wark Township from them on behalf of Hunch Mines. One of the reasons he was such a successful broker was that a lot of his clients were in the industry, and they often gave him tips. Despite the difference in their ages and backgrounds, he and Bongard saw each other often, in part because they were both serious curlers. They inevitably also talked shop, and one day in late July, Dixon surprised Bongard by revealing that he'd started shorting Windfall.

Dixon's best industry connection was his old friend, Vernon Oille, a mining engineer with Noranda Exploration. They spoke most days, often more than once. Oille usually worked in Quebec and the eastern United States, but after the Texas Gulf discovery, his bosses sent him to Timmins to coordinate the company's exploration and acquisition program in the region and to keep tabs on what other miners were doing. So forwarding rumours to the head office in Toronto was part of his job. Late on July 5, his fieldman, Mel Rennick, told him the word was the Windfall drillers had intersected sulphide mineralization. When Oille started working the phones the next morning, he discovered that what he had heard wasn't exactly exclusive information. He spoke to Noranda geologist Richard Edwards, saw Frank Spencer at Bradley Brothers and called three brokers:

T.A. Richardson's William Robertson; Albert Applegath at J.W. Nicholson & Company; and Dixon. All but Applegath and Dixon had heard basically the same story.

Like many other mining people, Oille was intrigued by the geology of the Windfall site and the anomaly that airborne surveys had picked up. He already owned 5,000 shares in the company, which he'd bought when drilling began, but now he wanted more. Before the market opened, he made three orders of 10,000 shares each with Applegath, Robertson and Dixon. After initiating Oille's trade, Dixon called as many of his regular clients as he could to tell them about the rumour and take orders from those who were interested. He also bought for himself as well as his wife and daughter.

Over the next couple of days, Dixon bought and sold shares in the company, but on Thursday, July 9, he heard upbeat rumours about the core from three sources. The stories varied a bit, depending on who was telling them, but for the first time they included mineral values. According to a friend who knew someone in the office of George Wardrope, the mines department believed the MacMillans had hit ninety feet of mineralization with 2.04 percent copper, 7 percent zinc and silver values to come. Another version had it that the assay indicated sixty feet of 1.5 percent copper, 8 percent zinc and unknown silver. That one came from Ned Bragagnolo. And Oille had heard eighty-eight feet, 2.33 percent copper, 7 percent zinc. Dixon bought 12,000 shares but sold 2,000 later that day.

After that, he traded in and out of the market, but as the month wore on, his skepticism grew. For one thing, the MacMillans wouldn't release any assay results or make any statement about the core. They weren't even talking about what they had privately. Although he'd met them, Dixon didn't know them well enough to call them up himself, so, at one point, he asked Murdock Mosher to contact Viola to find out what he could. But she remained tight-lipped, even to good friends. Later, Dixon's unsettled feeling grew after he read in the July 23 issue of the *Northern Miner* that the MacMillans had sold all the Windfall stock held by Consolidated Golden Arrow.

Then, around the time Dixon started hearing rumours that the first hole was a dud, Oille told him about the setup of the drill rig on the third hole. Typically, a mining company will try to get a sense of the dimensions of a potential ore body by drilling the second hole at sixty degrees in the opposite direction of the first one and then a third hole at sixty degrees behind the first. But when Rennick flew over the site in a helicopter, he saw that Windfall wasn't doing that. The first hole had been from south to north and the second one was parallel to it, one hundred feet to the east. And the third hole was from north to south (to save a little money, George had asked the crew to simply turn the first rig around and drill in the opposite direction). Hearing this, Dixon was baffled. "Vern," he said, "this is no way to drill an ore body."

Oille agreed it wasn't the way he'd do it and said he'd ask Rennick to take a helicopter and check out the site again. Having had the initial reports confirmed, Dixon advised his clients to get out of Windfall; oddly, the one who maintained his position was Oille, even though he'd also been in and out of the market in the past three weeks. Convinced the MacMillans had nothing, Dixon didn't just sell his shares; he bet the stock would go down. He sold 500 shares short on July 28, another 3,000 the next day and 4,500 more the day after that. Although Bongard now knew from Dixon that the Windfall core was probably worthless, he'd promised his friend that he wouldn't do anything with the information.

Others, even people close to the MacMillans, were also shorting the stock. Instead of clearing up his wife's short position after borrowing 5,000 Windfall shares from Viola at the Constellation Hotel on July 12, John Campbell sold 1,000 shares through her V.L. Sherwood account on July 13. The next day, his broker, Harry Richardson, went to the Campbells' apartment to pick up the certificates for the 5,000 shares. John asked him to keep them in the box, if possible—in other words, if Richardson had to deliver shares, he should try to use other certificates so Campbell could give MacMillan back the same ones she'd given him. On July 15, he sold 2,500 more Windfall. The next week, on July 22, he sold 2,000 shares and another 3,000 the following day; these trades were from accounts under different names, one of which was fictitious, and he did not declare them as short sales.

During this time, Viola spoke to Campbell frequently. He kept asking when the assays were coming, but she always had an excuse: the core shack wasn't finished, the pump had broken down, Texas Gulf had started drilling and so on. Although Campbell shared the MacMillans' optimism for the property in the long term, because of the geological structure, he continued to short the stock, convinced the rumours going around were false. Viola had told him they hadn't assayed the core, and even if they had, getting the high values people were bandying about on a first hole seemed so unlikely; after all, Texas Gulf had drilled sixty-five holes before its big strike. Even if an assay was encouraging, it wouldn't be as spectacular as the gossip suggested. He figured the stock should be trading around $2.50. But with each short sale, he increased his exposure, and he'd be in big financial trouble if the share price stayed aloft. By the third week of July, his doubts about the first-hole results grew because Viola seemed to be hedging on that hole and talking more about the second and third ones. Still, even if his bet paid off, the OSC director was risking his job and his reputation.

□

The MacMillans expected the assay results to arrive in the evening mail on Wednesday, July 29, but they wanted to hold off on releasing the information until after the market closed on Friday. That, they argued, would give everyone a chance to digest the numbers properly over the August long weekend. Neither the TSE nor the OSC liked that idea at all. The results would have to come out on Thursday. Viola called Willis Ambrose in Kingston and asked him to come to Toronto to discuss the findings and what they should do next. The geologist arrived Wednesday evening and checked into the Royal York. MacMillan also spoke to Archibald and told him George would be coming in from Timmins. But later he called the lawyer to say he couldn't get on the late flight and would return in the morning. The evening mail included an envelope from Swastika Labs, but it remained unopened. The next day, it went to the offices of Roberts, Archibald, Seagram & Cole.

At George's request, Archibald arranged a directors meeting for noon on Thursday in his office and set an agenda. George flew in from Timmins, where the drill crew was working on the second and third holes. He made it to the law firm's offices by late morning. With the help of George and Archibald, Ambrose wrote most of a press release. They would wait until they'd opened the results before finishing it. Then Ambrose borrowed a slide rule from one of Archibald's colleagues so he could make calculations once he saw the numbers.

During the meeting, the directors handled other business, including a report on the fake telegrams. Then they debated when to release the results and agreed that after the market closed would be best. The mood was tense. No one knew if the assay would provide good news or bad. George was unhappy about having to release the results, promising or not, from a single hole because he believed it would be too easy for the public to misinterpret the numbers. He feared he'd be damned either way. Around two o'clock, after Ambrose had come in and given the directors a geology report, the meeting adjourned. Now hungry, Archibald and the directors went out for lunch. Ambrose and MacMillan stayed behind with a couple of sandwiches to open the envelope, correlate the results with the drill log and determine what it all meant.

While there were good arguments for not releasing results in the middle of the trading day, as it gave an advantage to people who were closer to the market, the waiting allowed misinformation to continue to spread. And new rumours were pushing the price of Windfall stock up again. When Claude Taylor dropped by the offices of Davidson & Company, he ran into Graham Ackerley. The *Northern Miner* reporter said he'd heard that MacMillan was at the Royal York, gave Taylor a room number and suggested he call her to see what he could find out. But the switchboard said there was no such room number. Taylor had another idea. He called back and asked for Willis Ambrose. The switchboard put him through, and MacMillan answered. When she asked how he'd found her, he put it down to the ingenuity of an old newspaperman. That did not cheer her up. She said she was having a tough time and wished people would leave her alone so she could develop a mine.

"When do you think you will make an announcement?" Taylor asked.

"Oh, I am sorry, I have to go," she replied.

Shortly before three o'clock, T.A. Richardson's William Robertson called Vern Oille and told him a "top dog" in his firm's Toronto office heard that the official assay results were on their way and would show 120 feet of 3.5 percent copper and 8 percent zinc. The stock closed at $4.15.

By then, Ambrose and MacMillan had opened the envelope and read the lab report. The geologist wouldn't need the slide rule, after all. The mineral values were negligible.

Once the directors reassembled, Ambrose tabled the results and explained what they meant. As they discussed the press release, each director suggested changes, and the document went through several drafts before everyone was satisfied. The meeting adjourned at five ten. When George, Ambrose and Archibald delivered the news to Jack Kimber, the OSC chairman asked, "Does this kill the property?" By no means, replied Ambrose, adding that the core showed "very interesting" copper traces.

The press release went out for wide distribution at six thirty. The last lines read: "Assay results were received July 30th. Copper mineralization was encountered throughout, but no commercial assays were obtained. Drilling is continuing."

When he saw it, Robertson called Oille back and told his client to forget what he'd said four hours earlier. He then read him the press release. The Noranda engineer still held 10,000 shares. Although one bad hole didn't mean much, it was still an unwelcome development for Oille and all the other investors who were long.

While stockbrokers made or received uncomfortable phone calls, havoc reigned in newsrooms as journalists struggled to get more information before their deadlines. When a reporter told Howard Graham the assays showed no commercial values, the TSE president said, "Go on!" But the sources everyone sought were Viola and George. At the *Globe and Mail*, Jim Scott was scrambling when a friend called and asked, "What's all this about the Windfall assays?"

After telling him about the press release, Scott explained that he couldn't talk because he was trying to find the MacMillans. "I can tell you where they are," said the friend, who was at the Royal York. "They are eating in the Venetian Café right now."

Scott immediately popped over to the mural-adorned restaurant that the hotel billed as "a little bit of Venice." He found the couple at a large table with Ambrose, Marjorie Humphrey, Doris Drewe, Ron Mills and an old prospector named Bill "Hard Rock" Smith. They were not a cheerful lot, and having been found by a journalist didn't help. Scott asked Ambrose if he hadn't gleaned a good sense of the value of the core from his visual examination of it. "I knew there was nothing to get excited about as far as copper was concerned," the geologist said, "but we could not tell about silver and gold."

For their part, the MacMillans were unhappy about the whole situation. "You know, George could have made an awful lot of money out of this," Viola said, as if she hadn't just made a killing on the market in the last month. Slamming the TSE for not letting Windfall sell more shares to raise money and for insisting the company release assay results, she said, "Imagine them trying to tell a mining company what to do."

CHAPTER NINETEEN

WIDESPREAD FALLOUT

B efore leaving on the road trip in the Maritimes with his family and forgetting about work for a bit, Tom Cole had one last thought about Windfall: "Let's hope the hole is as good as some people think it is." He didn't pay attention to the news on his vacation until August 8, when he saw a three-day-old copy of the *Globe and Mail* in Halifax. A front-page headline declared, "Robarts Orders Probe of Windfall's Affairs." Cole was horrified. The lawyer had missed a lot while away, and the fake telegrams from New York were just the beginning.

On Tuesday, July 28, the day after the telegrams, at the request of Jack Kimber, Ontario Attorney General Arthur Wishart directed the OSC to investigate the trading of Bunker Hill Extension Mines, Glenn Uranium Mines and Windfall. The first two companies had been part of the Timmins frenzy in April. "It would be interesting to know whether someone was manipulating it," Wishart said. "I don't say Windfall has done anything wrong, but I think it would be worthwhile to know what stock was sold and who was purchasing it." For some reason, the attorney general didn't make that statement, or even make the investigation public, until the stock fell out of bed on Friday. After closing at $4.15 on Thursday, Windfall opened at eighty cents following a thirty-five-minute delay, and only because brokers stepped in to buy shares since so few of their customers wanted them. The stock ended the week at $1.04 as nearly 1.4 million shares changed hands.

The big winner was Viola MacMillan. For all her talk of losing control, and her increasingly erratic behaviour, she'd directed trading in fifty-two accounts, some of which she'd opened in July. Twenty-four were with Tom & Barnt; nine with Moss, Lawson; eight with Ross, Knowles & Company; five with Breckenridge, McDonald; five with T.A. Richardson; and one with J.H. Crang & Company. They weren't all hers; one was George's and several belonged to their companies as well as their friends, neighbours and employees. When she sold 169,000 shares through T.A. Richardson on July 6, the only account she had with the brokerage house was in the name of Vianor Malartic Mines. A day or two later, she went to the firm's office and opened ones for V.R. MacMillan, MacMillan Prospecting and Development, Airquests and Consolidated Golden Arrow. Then she indicated which should be credited with each of Monday's transactions. The most profitable trades went to her personal account or an account of a wholly owned company; the less profitable ones went to the Vianor or Golden Arrow accounts. The MacMillans had only a controlling interest in those two companies. Viola made similar moves at Breckenridge, McDonald at the end of the week. She also demonstrated a keen ability to buy during lulls in the share price, propping up the stock in the process, and sell at new highs.

On July 30, four MacMillan companies—Airquests, MacMillan Prospecting and Development, Vianor and Consolidated Golden Arrow— were in short positions for tax purposes. But her other companies were long, and she had lots of shares in Windfall. Early in August, acting on legal advice, she flattened her accounts so none of her companies was short.

Between July 1 and August 10, MacMillan purchased 900,000 shares through the underwriting and another 39,941 through the exchange. During that time, she sold 795,100 shares from companies she and George controlled or from personal accounts. That included George's only transaction, a sale of 1,000 shares made by Viola on July 6. In addition, she sold 158,000 Windfall shares from Golden Arrow at an average of $2.24, putting nearly $355,000 into that public company's coffers. All this activity generated a profit of $1.46 million. Since she completed the vast majority of her sales between July 6 and July 9, she could have admitted that the first hole wasn't promising much earlier without jeopardizing her windfall.

July had also been a profitable month for a few other investors. Cuffy Dixon made $60,000 buying, selling and, finally, shorting the stock. Although his friend Vern Oille didn't sell his shares after learning about the drill setup, he'd been in and out of Windfall three times, so he ended up with a profit of about $20,000. John Campbell proved to be a savvier market player than his wife, earning more than $29,000 with his short sales. Others, many of them small investors, lost a total of $2.7 million. Not all of them were rubes. Ken Darke, who really should have known better, lost $128,000 on Windfall, even though Bragagnolo had told him, "You have a good profit, get out of there." Of course, earlier in the year, Darke had made $300,000 selling claims as part of his partnership with Bragagnolo and John Angus. Noranda geologist Richard Edwards bought 20,000 Windfall shares in April, just after MacMillan acquired the claims. He believed the property's geology was a favourable environment for a base metals deposit, and he considered the MacMillans "top-drawer" managers. He purchased another 5,500 shares on July 6 and bought and sold heavily over the following days, at one point holding 51,200 shares. He lost $60,000.

Although reporters knew that investing heavily in the stock market would get them in trouble with their bosses, most newspapers had few, if any, rules against their journalists owning stocks they covered. Many reporters did buy and sell Windfall in July. Ackerley lost money after buying on Viola's tip and then selling before the stock took off, but his colleague Mort Brown made over $4,000, though he'd lost more than that on other Timmins-area penny stocks. Greg Reynolds of the *Daily Press* didn't trade Windfall shares, but his mother made a little money on the stock on his recommendation. And the *Globe*'s Jim Scott bought 500 shares, a hundred at a time, at prices ranging from $3.40 on July 10 to $4.90 on July 20. He still held them when the stock crashed.

Most of the losers weren't connected to mining, the investment business or journalism. They just liked to take their chances on penny stocks, and the result was a lot of public anger and more than a sneaking suspicion that the game was rigged. Many people blamed the TSE and the OSC, while the two organizations blamed each other. "Even by the notoriously loose standards prevailing in the Toronto stock market, the case of Windfall Oils and Mines Ltd. sets some sort of a mark for official laxity," began a *Toronto Daily Star* editorial. Acknowledging that the buyers knew that they were speculating but did so under the assumption that proper regulations were in place, it declared: "Yet, far too often, an Ontario investor is justified in feeling like a lamb waiting to be shorn." The afternoon paper even called out Premier John Robarts for being "inexcusably tolerant of the OSC's slackness and inefficiency in the face of one stock scandal after another." Of course, the *Star* was a Liberal paper, so it would jump at any chance to attack the Tories. But even the *Globe and Mail* agreed. "The Ontario government should act at once, by legislation, if necessary, to tighten policing of the share market," the paper urged. "We cannot afford another scandal."

The front-page headlines, outraged editorials and furious shareholders threatened to turn "the Windfall fiasco," as the *Globe* called it, into a political liability for the government. Robarts responded by appointing Arthur Kelly, a Court of Appeal justice, to head the Royal Commission to Investigate Trading in the Shares of Windfall Oils and Mines Limited. The mandate included looking into the role of the Toronto Stock Exchange and the Ontario Securities Commission.

□

A barroom musician quit his gig at the Larder Lake Hotel in October 1964 and hitchhiked out of town. The twenty-nine-year-old ended up in Timmins, where he stepped out of the rain-snow mix and into the empty ladies' and escorts' room of the Maple Leaf Hotel on Balsam Street. Although he was a nickel short of the cost of a beer, the bartender agreed to cover him if he'd take out his guitar and play. Soon, Tom Connors and his foot-thumping performances of country songs, including ones he wrote about the places he went and the people he met, were packing the bar six nights a week. That led to regular live appearances on CKGB, the radio station Roy Thomson had started in the '30s, and he began to cut 45 rpm records there. His second single, "The Birth of the New Dragon Mine," about the Texas Gulf discovery, quickly became a popular anthem in town. (New Dragon was originally to be the mine's name, and many years later, he re-recorded the song as "The Birth of the Texas Gulf Mine.") Connors would go on to add Stompin' to his name, influence generations of musicians and become a national icon. But in March 1965, he was still making his name during a fourteen-month residency at a local dive.

A different crowd gathered a few blocks away on Algonquin Avenue for the royal commission hearings. Viola and George MacMillan ate breakfast with their lawyer, Joseph Sedgwick, in the Empire Hotel, then crossed the street to the courtroom of the brick-and-sandstone town hall. Despite the mania that had overwhelmed the Porcupine the year before, most residents—even many who'd lost money—weren't that excited about going over the past, so the local brokerage houses usually attracted larger crowds. Even when the MacMillans testified in Timmins, fewer than fifty people were in the audience. Viola attended some of the sessions, but George sat in on most of them. He'd often take advantage of recesses to ask journalists, "Well, how do you think it went today?"

Before the hearings began, a team of investigators had spent months researching and interviewing. Commission counsel Patrick Hartt and his assistant, James Karfalis, also had the transcripts from the OSC's inquiry, which had examined dozens of witnesses under oath from August to October 1964. The royal commission invited 800 people who'd owned Windfall stock to fill out a questionnaire, and nearly 80 percent of them did. And, in a first, an IBM computer—or, as everyone called it, "electronic data processing equipment"—had analyzed more than 26,000 stock market transactions. For the most part, Justice Kelly maintained great patience during the sessions, though he occasionally became exasperated, particularly with Sedgwick.

Fittingly, the first witness was Ken Darke, who appeared March 1 and 2. Many of those who followed him during the Timmins sessions helped Kelly and the lawyers get a good grounding in geology as well as mining terminology and techniques. The night before Fenton Scott testified, he attended a meeting of the Porcupine Geological Discussion Group, an informal club that convened about ten times a year for dinner and a presentation by a member. At this meeting, the group had a chance to examine core from the Windfall property. The geologists were deeply unimpressed, making comments such as "obviously barren" and "not worth a hoot." It was no different than what most of them had encountered, much to their disappointment, many times on the job. "This core is very common," Scott told the commission. "This type of material is found all over Eastern Canada." Drillers had pulled it for him at least fifty times in his career, and none of the sites came to anything. Just the sight of that rock was discouraging. He'd prefer to see as little of it as possible. In the case of the Windfall core, there was no indication of copper or zinc. Silver was so rare in this type of rock that Scott had never seen it and didn't even know anyone who had. And while iron sulphides can contain gold, in the Porcupine region that was true only when quartz was present, and there was no quartz in the sample. Still, he admitted that he'd have sent it to be assayed, but only to be absolutely sure there wasn't anything he'd later regret walking away from; in fact, if the assay found economically viable mineral values, he'd be so surprised that he'd doubt the validity of the results. Scott's testimony did nothing to explain George MacMillan's initial enthusiasm for the Windfall core. Just the opposite.

The commission spent a lot of time trying to find out where the rumours about good core started and how they spread, with only limited success. Most of the witnesses, especially those connected to Bradley Brothers, weren't much help. A lot of them were unable to recall saying and doing things that would be hard to forget. Later, in his report, Kelly would acknowledge that remembering events long after the fact was difficult, but write, "Nevertheless, the high incidence of amnesia displayed amongst those who were examined concerning this period was beyond what would ordinarily have been expected." Still, the evidence suggested that the original rumour of mineralization in the core travelled from Timmins to Noranda to Bay Street.

One of the MacMillans' fiercest critics also had a chance to have his say. Ralph Allerston had written the commission in October 1964, requesting to testify. Although he was a Windfall shareholder, his bigger concern was as a full-time prospector and past president of the Porcupine Prospectors Association. "I resent the damage to the Timmins area and the industry including particularly those in exploration work," he wrote. "The damage in my opinion is directly due to the dereliction of duty on the part of the directors, the MacMillans, and perhaps Dr. Ambrose, the consultant for Windfall." He worried that the scandal would hurt prospectors and small developers by making it harder to raise money, leaving exploration in the hands of large corporations such as Inco, Falconbridge and Noranda. His fear was that everyone in mining would have to go work for one of the big companies or be out of the business. Allerston testified that Windfall "paid quite a fabulous consideration, in my opinion, for twelve discontiguous and unpatented mining claims without any known showings of mineral or outcrop," and he doubted there were other competitive bids for the land. Once the "violent stock gyrations" began, the MacMillans should have been more candid about the core, and he didn't understand the long pause in drilling, noting that he could have put a core shack on that property in a day and a half if he was building one, or in just four hours if he was driving one in. He was also disturbed by the delay in sending core to be assayed and to get the results back, which should have taken no more than two days.

Although he'd disagreed with Viola about changes to the Mining Act at a past Prospectors and Developers Association convention, he otherwise denied a previous antagonistic relationship with her. That had clearly changed. "I feel badly, quite resentful, of the fact that the name MacMillan has been synonymous with the Prospectors and Developers Association, the Dominion body," Allerston said, adding, "I shall not belong to the Association if Mrs. MacMillan is there." He wasn't alone. The furor over MacMillan's role in the scandal meant she could not stay on as president. In her January 1965 resignation letter, she wrote, "As you know, criticism has been directed at me by a few members of the Association, criticism which unfortunately I am not in a position to answer at this time." With her departure, the organization cancelled its convention. The official explanation was the Canadian Institute of Mining and Metallurgy was also hosting its annual meeting in Toronto in March. But everyone knew that if MacMillan had stayed on as president, the PDA convention would have gone ahead no matter what. The collateral damage from the cancellation included Toronto tourism, because the event was worth $200,000 to the city, and especially the Royal York Hotel, which annually enjoyed full rooms and rollicking business in its bars and restaurants during the four days of dealmaking and partying.

Whatever role personal animosity played in Allerston's testimony, most of his criticisms were well-founded. But it was silly when he complained about MacMillan calling the Prosser and Wark Townships claims the Lucky Texas Group. He said that was "window dressing" designed to confuse unsophisticated shareholders into thinking there was some connection to the Texas Gulf property and justify the high cost of the acquisition. Perhaps it was, but surely it was a standard marketing ploy, and she was, after all, a mining promoter, even if she hated the term.

Certainly, the *Globe and Mail* was enthusiastic about Allerston's appearance. "The well-spoken prospector, perhaps the most articulate witness yet to appear before the Kelly commission never raised his voice above ordinary conversation during the eighty minutes he occupied the witness stand," the paper reported. "An impassive-faced George MacMillan sat in a front-row seat and heard Mr. Allerston lay the blame for the Windfall affair at his door."

After eleven sessions in Timmins, the commission moved to Toronto, and a parade of officials, brokers, journalists, investors and many others testified. When the MacMillans appeared again in mid-May, Sedgwick unwittingly revealed the attitude toward women at the time. Before examining Viola, he asked her to speak up because there were no microphones, and the commissioner, the press and everyone else wanted to hear her. "Then," he added, "as the little girl has to take it down, please don't speak too fast."

MacMillan did have a lot to say, and she did talk too fast, though her memory was highly selective. She maintained that she had never liked the name Windfall and insisted that she'd asked the producers of *To Tell the Truth* not to refer to the company when introducing her. She denied knowing the core was worthless and, predictably, complained about the TSE, including for not consulting her as the underwriter when the stock took off. She regretted lending shares to Campbell, but otherwise insisted she'd done nothing wrong. George was able to talk at length about his career and successes and his approach to seeking a mine, but he claimed not to remember much about what happened that summer and wasn't all that candid when he did. Still, it was clear that he deferred to his wife on most matters, and she'd been in charge during those twenty-five days in July.

□

Arthur Kelly hand-delivered a bound copy of his report to John Robarts in his room at the Westbury Hotel at eight forty-five in the morning of October 1, 1965. "Boy, is this impressive looking!" said the premier. Then, having spent more than a year looking into the scandal, including forty-four days of hearings, featuring 144 witnesses and 416 exhibits, and months of writing, the commissioner left for a vacation. The following week, after Robarts had given his approval, the province released 2,000 copies of the report. Once again, people were talking about Windfall, which was now trading around twenty-five cents. Upon reading the document, *Toronto Daily Star* financial editor Jack McArthur declared, "Judge Kelly writes with the shocked revulsion of a man who has stumbled suddenly into a snake-pit."

In his report, Kelly acknowledged that a combination of events had created the unusual market activity in July 1964, and it was "hardly conceivable" that they would all happen together again. But that didn't mean there wasn't a great deal to learn from what happened. He had little sympathy for the MacMillans, who had treated Windfall as a "personal venture" without regard for the shareholders or even the company directors. Accusing Viola of grooming the market in the months before drilling started with the heavy volume of buying and selling by companies the couple controlled and accounts she directed, he said the trades "warrant the scrutiny of the Crown Attorney."

Although there was no evidence the MacMillans had played any intentional role in starting or spreading the rumours, they certainly took advantage of them. When George halted drilling unnecessarily and didn't resume it for nearly two weeks, the couple used the stoppage to delay releasing any information that would have hurt Viola's chances of unloading shares at inflated prices. "It is impossible to believe," wrote Kelly, "that a person having the knowledge and experience of George

MacMillan could have made even a cursory examination of the drill core and continued to believe it contained copper and zinc in percentages to be considered commercial." Nor could the commissioner believe that George hadn't told Viola. That meant they both knew the core showed no promising ore but told no one. "Not only did they refrain from telling the truth," Kelly wrote, "but in such statements as were made, the facts which were stated and the manner in which they were framed were such as to be misleading and must have been calculated so to be." People were misled, he stated. Instead of being skeptical, they had taken the MacMillans' caginess as evidence that Windfall's core was valuable. The continued indulgence of the TSE and the OSC, including the latter's statement on July 15, gave more comfort to optimistic investors. Even if he did accept that the MacMillans had good reason to not make public what they knew about the core, their failure to inform Windfall's directors "offends every element of company law."

The scandal also damaged the reputations of the TSE and the OSC, at home and abroad, and Kelly had lots to say about both, especially the exchange. He noted that short sellers did not have a great effect on Windfall's share price, other than depressing it a bit on July 27 and 28, but that the TSE's requirement that all short sales be declared was regularly ignored. Although the exchange was supposed to be a self-governing body, Kelly found that it failed to keep up with the "ingenuity" of those who skirted the rules; adherence to the spirit of the rules seemed optional; and "there was a woeful lack of surveillance" to ensure compliance with the rules. Not all of this was the exchange's fault as, too often, people in the brokerage industry justified what they did by saying they'd always done it that way. Because Bay Streeters gave their own interests "all too high a priority," Kelly wasn't sure if they saw "the exchange as a public securities market or as a private gaming club maintained for their own benefit."

Rejecting the argument that the TSE had no right to demand information from Windfall while the company was still drilling its first hole, he criticized it for failing to act sooner and more forcefully in insisting the MacMillans release information. Although exchange officials had argued that, starting with the meeting on July 14, the OSC had taken over responsibility for Windfall, Kelly didn't buy it. Noting that the OSC's involvement was unusual, he concluded, "The full responsibility for the continued trading subsequent to 6th July was that of the Exchange."

When Howard Graham initially responded to the report in a press conference, he didn't seem too upset. But the next day, the TSE president issued a statement registering his indignation, including taking "the strongest possible exception" to Kelly's conclusion that the exchange had the sole responsibility to halt trading in Windfall. He claimed that the exchange would have suspended the stock if the OSC had stayed uninvolved.

Regardless of who was at fault, Kelly wanted changes. Lots of them. His recommendations concerned conflicts of interest at brokerages; buying and selling from house accounts by floor traders; the need for training in the industry; improving corporate disclosure; the TSE's right to demand information from companies that were the subject of rampant rumours; and much more. Along with stricter rules for those in the industry, splitting the roles of brokers and dealers would eliminate conflicts of interest when brokers acted for clients and their own trading interests. Speculative mining stocks should no longer be listed on the exchange, he argued; instead, they should trade on a separate market that would share resources with the TSE. Investors believed that listed companies met certain standards, but many mining stocks kept their listings even after they became shells. He also called for an end to the primary distribution of shares on the TSE, which was "incompatible with the true function of an exchange."

Finding a mismatch between what investors expected the OSC to do and what it actually did, Kelly said it should become an independent agency rather than operating under the control of the attorney general and called for legislation to define its "purpose, responsibilities and powers." Those should include authority over securities trading. He wanted all stock markets in Canada to operate under the same regulations. Even better, he believed, would be a national body to regulate all the country's exchanges.

Although an editorial in the *Toronto Daily Star* called the eagerly awaited document "one of the hardest-hitting reports in Ontario history," few on Bay Street found any surprises in it. But some did expect it to hurt their business for a while. "There are an awful lot of guys sitting around here doing nothing," one salesman said. "The speculative market is going to be pretty lean for about six months." He was underestimating how dramatic the reforms would be.

☐

Viola MacMillan called Robert Breckenridge before the market opened on July 10, 1964. She wanted to sell 200,000 shares of Consolidated Golden Arrow from MacMillan Prospecting and Development to her husband. Given it would be cheaper for her to do it privately, Breckenridge said, "Mrs. MacMillan, you know that I have to charge you full commission on each side of the transaction?"

"I know that," she said. "That makes no difference."

The sale went through at twenty-five cents a share. MacMillan also arranged to sell an additional 44,000 Golden Arrow shares from Airquests to accounts she created in the names of friends or employees, including Ron Mills and Doris Drewe. Eight of these purchased 3,000 shares; a ninth account, in the name of Lacy Sergent, a good friend of hers, bought 20,000. Breckenridge figured MacMillan was just doing favours for people she knew. And it was true that she often directed trading for friends' accounts, but this was a new level of coordination. The transactions seemed designed to give the impression of heavy market interest in the company. Wash trading, in other words. Trading in the stock jumped from only 850 shares the day before to 393,000. The burst in activity led to a rise in the price of the stock, and within an hour of the market opening, MacMillan sold 25,000 shares from various accounts at sixty cents. "The arrangement," noted Kelly, "can be looked at as nothing other than a skillfully managed piece of manipulation."

Five days after the royal commission report came out, the attorney general's office charged the MacMillans with wash trading, which carried a maximum sentence of five years. Only one person in Canada had ever been convicted of the offence. After mining promoter Albert Gould, the president of Cabanga Developments, had scammed the company out of $456,000, he went on trial for fraud in 1959. His sentence of six years in prison was the first time any Bay Streeter had received more than five years. The next spring, in a related case, he pled guilty to fraud and three counts of wash trading for transactions that cost a New York brokerage house $315,000. He received six years for the former and three years for the latter, with both to run concurrently with his previous sentence.

At the preliminary hearing for the MacMillans, which took place while the PDA held its 1966 convention after recovering from its long-time president's departure, the judge dismissed the charges against George and sent Viola to trial. A year later, she didn't testify in her defence, but her lawyer, Joseph Sedgwick, argued that she had made the trades through Breckenridge, McDonald instead of privately to ensure a fair price for the stock for tax purposes. He asked for a suspended sentence and a fine. The judge disagreed and, in March 1967, sentenced her to nine months in reformatory and fined her $10,000. Released on $15,000 bail, pending her appeal, she spent a couple of hours in Toronto's Don Jail, waiting for George to show up with the money. Ten months later, the Court of Appeal upheld the conviction and the sentence, although the judges reduced the latter to an indefinite one of "up to nine months" because she was a woman.

Many in the public, especially those who'd been burned on Windfall stock, were happy to see MacMillan get some comeuppance. Others believed she was a good person who'd made a mistake and that the government wanted to make an example of someone, and a woman who was the high-profile head of the PDA made for an ideal target. "Wash trading was routine in those days. Everybody was doing it," the *Northern Miner*'s Mort Brown later said. "I take a dim view of that sentence."

After an initial stay at the Mercer Reformatory on Toronto's King Street, MacMillan moved to the Ingleside Women's Guidance Centre in Brampton, Ontario. The *Toronto Telegram* described it as "motel-like" and said, "At Ingleside, which accommodates 24, inmates live in comfortable rooms. There is a television, record-players, radios, a good-sized library and parlor games." Given that the sixty-three-year-old was the oldest person to serve a sentence at the minimum-security prison, which was established for the rehabilitation of young women and girls, some critics saw the transfer as evidence of different rules for rich and poor.

During her incarceration, George visited regularly and wrote letters almost daily. He addressed them to "My Darling Wife" and signed them, "Your loving husband, George MacMillan." She usually signed her letters,

"All my love, Viola." At first, nights were the hardest part of being away from him. "I had my worst night so far last night—somehow I again had the feeling of not belonging to this life and when I went to bed—which I dread so much, that I could not stand the pain so I just cried and cried until about midnight," she wrote in one early letter. In another, she said, "I did not have a good night. I'm sorry the nervous system took over and after crying for hours I just could not sleep." But her minister brought her a copy of the New Testament, and she enjoyed reading it. She settled in as best she could. Soon, more and more of her letters were about business, including reminding George to extend claims, wondering if they should sell their shares in Kam-Kotia and requesting he bring proxies for her to sign for Windfall and Consolidated Golden Arrow. "Do you see any sign of them trying to take C.G.A. away from me?" she asked in one letter. "I want to find another mine—maybe [I] will have time yet in my life."

Years later, she rarely talked about her criminal past, but she did make one comment that glossed over how much she'd struggled in the beginning, while revealing how much she'd become part of what some people called polite society. "I think everybody should go to jail for one or two nights to realize what it's all about," she said, "because I was glad when it was time to go to bed to get away from the people, get away from some of the characters that were in there."

The press had relished the plight of a well-to-do woman, running headlines such as "Viola Bailed from Her Don Cell—and Goes Back to Her Luxury Home" and "Wealthy Viola Cleaning Jail Cells." (The *Daily Star* and the *Telegram* often referred to her by her first name in headlines, something they seldom, if ever, did with men.) But the papers soon had a better story. After just sixty-six days, MacMillan walked out a free woman.

The early parole thrust her into yet another controversy. Even before her release, word of the parole board's decision led to raucous sessions in the legislature. One MPP even suggested the millionaire had paid her way out. A legislative committee summoned the head of the parole board to explain the decision. Reform Institutions Minister Allan Grossman denied she'd received special treatment, but he later admitted that the early parole had embarrassed the government. Many angry citizens took the time to write the attorney general. "Can you in all honesty say she is not being given preferential treatment and consideration because of her (apparently ill-gotten) wealth?" read a typical letter to Wishart. "Would a penniless prisoner be given the same consideration?"

The public indignation didn't change anything. MacMillan was out, though she might soon have to go back in. Kelly had all but accused the couple of fraud in his report. The day it came out, the attorney general issued warrants for the MacMillans' arrest on two counts of fraud. Each charge carried a maximum penalty of ten years in prison. At the time, the couple was in Nevada, checking on Windfall's property there, but Sedgwick spoke to the press. "They were shocked and disturbed by the news," he said. "They have a feeling that they have done nothing wrong, and that a combination of events was responsible for what happened."

□

The Windfall scandal was not an elaborate scam, and the MacMillans didn't do anything as nefarious as salting samples. Instead, they took advantage of their enviable record as mine developers, of human greed and of the power of rumours to keep quiet and let investors believe what they wanted to believe. As much as Viola complained about the TSE, the exchange was too ineffectual to stop her. The fallout was widespread, and included damaged reputations, lost jobs and even criminal charges, because the royal commission hearings exposed a lot of broken rules during the fever that came over Timmins in 1964.

Kelly cleared some people. George Wardrope had received a rough ride from the press in the aftermath of the scandal, and rumours had spread that he'd made $100,000 on Windfall. The mines minister trusted the MacMillans too much, according to the report, but he never did anything unethical or profited from his involvement. In fact, he hadn't owned any shares in any company since going into politics. Kelly also praised Tom Cole for the way he kept the corporate records, noted that he never traded in Windfall shares and bemoaned that he "was deliberately kept in the dark."

John Campbell did not fare so well. In fact, other than the MacMillans, his fall was the most stunning. On August 25, less than a month after the stock crashed, Wishart suspended him as the director of the OSC, pending an investigation into his possible conflict of interest. Initially, Campbell denied doing anything "illegal, immoral or unethical." A few days later, the attorney general amended the OSC inquiry's mandate to include a look at the trading of John and Louise Campbell. During his lengthy testimony to the commission in early September, Campbell admitted to financial problems and that as July wore on, he was drinking too much and his marriage was in trouble. "I just wasn't thinking straight," he said. "Let's face it." On September 24, he resigned. In the royal commission report, Kelly said that Campbell, as the OSC director, should not have interfered in a matter that should have been between the company and the TSE and called his dealing in Windfall stock and borrowing shares from MacMillan "the most shocking incident revealed before the Commission." Campbell went on trial for breach of trust in 1966 but was acquitted. After the Ontario Court of Appeal ordered a new trial, he was acquitted again in September 1968.

A couple of brokers found themselves in trouble for their actions, even if they weren't directly connected to Windfall. John Angus had received shares in Bunker Hill Extension Mines as payment for claims during his partnership with Bragagnolo and Darke. The TSE allowed partners of member firms to do this, but not employees. In an affidavit to the exchange, Angus denied receiving the shares. T.A. Richardson fired him as manager of its Timmins branch, and he had to fight charges of making a false statutory declaration. In 1967, after his acquittal, the Court of Appeal dismissed the Crown's appeal. Another broker served as a higher-profile target for the attorney general. Robert Breckenridge went on trial for two counts of wash trading in 1969 for his handling of MacMillan's Consolidated Golden Arrow manoeuvres. He was acquitted and the Crown's appeal failed.

The royal commission also attracted the attention of the Securities and Exchange Commission. Officials from the US regulatory agency were among the observers in attendance at Kelly's hearings. The *Telegram* reported that chief investigative counsel, Edward Jaegerman, was "interested in 'anyone from anywhere' who has capitalized on inside information to make a profit in trading in shares of Texas Gulf." After an eleven-month investigation, the SEC charged the mining giant and thirteen current or former officers, directors and staff, including Walter Holyk and Ken Darke. The contention was that the company's first press release in April 1964 was misleading, and the accused employees had bought shares before the public disclosure of the Kidd Township discovery. After the US Court of Appeals for the Second Circuit ruled that Texas Gulf was guilty of issuing a deceptive press release, the Supreme Court declined to review the case. Several people received fines based on their profits. Holyk had to pay US$35,000 plus interest. Darke was on the hook for US$90,000 plus interest; more than half of that was for what the people he'd tipped off about the stock had made. The case, which became a landmark of American securities law, changed the rules on corporate disclosure and expanded the meaning of insider trading.

□

Rubbernecking drivers slowed to a crawl and pedestrians stopped and gawked as the MacMillans walked three blocks along King Street at nine thirty in the morning on October 15, 1965. After a month in Nevada, Viola and George looked tanned but not exactly relaxed; after all, they were on their way to police headquarters. They were part of a procession that included a lawyer, two cops and a cluster of photographers and reporters. They'd turned themselves in on fraud charges at their lawyer's office but still had to be photographed and fingerprinted. Then, in magistrate's court inside Toronto's Old City Hall, a judge set bail at $5,000 each. After paying with one hundred crisp hundred-dollar bills, the MacMillans were free to go.

Three years later, in November 1968, the couple went on trial for defrauding the public in the promotion and sale of Windfall shares and fraudulently affecting the price of the stock. The couple's formidable legal team featured Sedgwick, John J. Robinette and Kelso Roberts. Robinette was one the most prominent lawyers in the country; Roberts was a former attorney general of the province. Viola had known him since the early '30s, when she hired him to fight for prospector Art Wilson and his friends who'd been stiffed by Buffalo moneymen.

On the last day of the trial in February 1969, Viola wore a burgundy suit and a stylish mauve hat as she listened to Judge Harry Dreyman read his thirteen-page decision. Much more forgiving toward the MacMillans than Kelly had been, he found that they were not responsible for the high share price in July 1964, that the company's press releases contained nothing that wasn't factual and that the delay in sending samples for assay was reasonable and not an attempt to deceive anyone. Then Dreyman asked the defendants to stand up. "I must find you not guilty on both counts," he said. "You are discharged."

"I just can't believe it," Viola exclaimed and smiled at George. "I just can't believe it." Then she kissed Roberts. Afterward, the Crown said there would be no appeal. "We're glad it's over," said the woman at the centre of the Windfall affair. "We always felt we were not guilty." Then they disappeared for a bit.

A few months later, Viola threw a party for the first time since the scandal erupted. She invited twenty friends to their place in the country to surprise George on his seventieth birthday. The next day, 250 bargain hunters and the simply curious showed up when the couple auctioned off two of her five ponies, as well as furniture, farming equipment and "old junk" from one of their five barns. Viola offered a tour of the property and even grabbed an axe to smash a rock from the Kam-Kotia mine, producing splinters for souvenir seekers.

Life was returning to something close to normal for the MacMillans. They were pursuing their mining interests and had an exploration crew working some claims up north. Although they planned to avoid the limelight, Viola talked to the press at the auction. She admitted that the worst part of their "five years of hell" was that "we stayed away from people and I just love people."

Viola MacMillan had been the protagonist in an infamous scandal, reluctantly resigned from a job she loved, served time, nearly been incarcerated again and suffered scorn throughout. The experience, which for the rest of her life would remain too painful to talk about, did little to diminish her self-confidence. "There are so many great Canadians and I consider myself one of them," she said. "I'm a great developer." Under the circumstances, a little humility might have been wise, but she wasn't wrong.

EPILOGUE

V iola MacMillan appeared to have it all: friends, admirers, money, success, respect and even, through her long-time leadership of the Prospectors and Developers Association, influence. By any measure, she'd fashioned an exceptional career for herself. Accomplishing it all as a woman at that time and in that industry made it even more extraordinary. And then, at age sixty-one, she'd jeopardized her good standing in July 1964. Arthur Kelly's royal commission succeeded in revealing much about the messy business of financing mining companies in the province and how the scandal happened. But one question left unanswered was why did she do it?

The easy answer is money. She certainly didn't need it, though history is full of rich people who've acted unethically or illegally in the pursuit of more wealth. Although she steadfastly maintained that all she wanted to do was find a mine, throughout the twenty-five days of the scandal, she'd operated just like the unscrupulous promoters she so often disparaged. Still, MacMillan's motivation was likely more complicated than simple avarice. After so many years, and significant success, in the industry, she'd developed a considerable ego. That contributed to her stubbornness, especially toward the Toronto Stock Exchange, and her attitude that she knew more about the business than anyone else. Most of all, she couldn't resist the excitement of a mining boom and she suffered from the prospector's obsession with the big strike. So, it's not hard to believe that some of her decisions stemmed from an inability to give up her dream of a major discovery.

Still, she finally had to admit the claims she'd bought that April night in the Empire Hotel did not hold what she was looking for. Windfall Oils and Mines ended its drilling program in November 1964. Despite drilling eleven holes on the three groups of claims, producing over 8,000 feet of core, the company never found an ore body. Nor did any other miner in the Porcupine. Except Texas Gulf, of course. The great Timmins boom of 1964 resulted in just one find, but it was big. The Kidd Creek Mine, which opened in 1966 and remains in operation today under different ownership, proved to be one of the largest base metals deposits in the world.

Although Arthur Kelly's hope for a national body to regulate all of Canada's stock exchanges has yet to happen, the royal commission had lasting consequences for the TSE and the OSC. Both institutions had already started making changes before the report came out, and more followed based on Kelly's recommendations. Soon, speculative mining companies and shady mining promoters headed west to the Vancouver Stock Exchange. Two of the emigres were Murray Pezim and Earl Glick. They'd been active during the April 1964 frenzy that followed the Texas Gulf announcement, but they were burned on Windfall. "She was so respected," Pezim said of MacMillan. "But she out-and-out lied to us. The day before it dropped, Earl and I dropped a fortune—$450,000—that was a big loss. She phoned and told us how great it was and then—a sad thing." The pair moved to Vancouver the next year, and by the 1980s, Pezim was one of the highest-profile promoters on the VSE, which became known as the "Scam Capital of the World."

Rather than rob the TSE of its energy, the departure of the junior mining business helped the exchange mature into a larger, more sophisticated operation. While the new rules may have taken the fun out of the game for some in the investment business, they were necessary to increase trust. Today, Toronto remains the world's pre-eminent hub of mining finance, and while the exchange, which now uses TSX as its short form, is only the eighth largest in the world by market capitalization, it has the most mining, oil and gas companies listed on it.

MacMillan stayed involved in the mining business, though she kept a much lower profile. Eventually, her reputation went through a rehabilitation. After George died in 1978, the *Northern Miner* looked back at the MacMillans' career but refused to put the blame for the Windfall debacle on the couple. "It was undoubtedly the atmosphere that existed at that time that fomented the ill-fated balloon," the paper argued. "The matter got out of hand simply because the stock market, the public, and, yes, indeed, the mining people wanted it!"

That same year, MacMillan received a pardon on the wash trading conviction. (She talked about it as if it meant she was innocent; it didn't. The government was suspending her record.) In 1985, the PDA honoured her by introducing the Viola R. MacMillan Award to recognize people or organizations "demonstrating strong leadership in management and financing for the exploration and development of mineral resources." When the industry created the Canadian Mining Hall of Fame in 1989, Mort Brown, by then the top editor at the *Northern Miner*, served as the chairman. He wanted to induct MacMillan into the hall's inaugural class of members, but one of the sponsors balked, citing "the Windfall fiasco." Since Brown had the power to decide who would grace the head table at the ceremonial dinner at the Royal York in January 1990, he invited MacMillan. Before introducing the honoured guests, he asked the audience members to withhold their applause until he'd finished, but when he came to the only woman at the table, the crowd ignored his request and gave her a thunderous ovation. "They applauded Viola because they loved her," Brown said later. When he inducted her into the hall in 1991, she was the first woman to receive the honour.

Even royal commission counsel Patrick Hartt ended up a MacMillan friend and fan. The commission's mandate had been broader than just Windfall, and he regretted not paying enough attention to the freewheeling havoc that ruled the stock market. "All of the penny stocks were going wild and there were bucket shops up and down Bay Street," he said nearly three decades later when he was serving as a judge on the Ontario Court of Justice. "I unfortunately concentrated on Windfall and didn't put it, I don't think, into a proper context at all so that Viola was highlighted and the full weight came down on Viola."

Epilogue

Not everyone in the mining industry, or the public, was so willing to forgive her. In 1989, she pledged to donate $1.25 million to the Canadian Museum of Nature, one quarter of the purchase price for the Pinch Collection of 16,000 rare geological specimens. When the museum responded by naming a wing after her, it generated snark and outrage about honouring a convicted criminal. Some people were also unhappy when, in 1993, on the day she turned ninety, MacMillan travelled to Ottawa and paid a visit to Rideau Hall, where she received the Order of Canada from Governor General Ray Hnatyshyn. She still hadn't stopped making deals. Mining giant Falconbridge had recently bought some claims she'd held since staking them in 1939. And she was excited about a Golden Shaft property; maybe it represented one last chance at another mine. But she didn't live long enough to find out. A few months later, on August 26, she had a heart attack and collapsed, later dying in Women's College Hospital in Toronto. She'd been on her way to the bank.

ACKNOWLEDGEMENTS

When I first had the idea for this book, I emailed my uncle Strachan Bongard, who'd worked on Bay Street, and asked, "Do you remember the 1964 Windfall scandal?"

"Sure," he wrote back, "I remember Viola quite well. Have one really good story." The 91-year-old invited me for lunch at his place, where I learned that his office had been in the Knight Building, the same as MacMillan's. Then he told me how Cuffy Dixon had come to short Windfall, a secret he'd kept at his friend's request (though, as it turned out, Dixon later told the Ontario Securities Commission inquiry). "You have to write this book," my uncle urged. Unfortunately, neither he nor my mother, his sister, lived long enough to see it published.

No one would have seen it if I hadn't received a lot of help since that lunch. I was fortunate to receive grants from the Ontario Arts Council and the Access Copyright Foundation's Marian Hebb Research Program. Those made it possible for me to visit a number of archives, where many people helped me. I am particularly grateful to Laura Smyk and Mylène Philippe-Gagnon at the Canadian Museum of Nature archives in Gatineau, Quebec; Karina Douglas-Takayesu at the Timmins Public Library; Kaitlyn Dubeau at the Timmins Museum; Kelly Gallagher at the Museum of Northern History in Kirkland Lake; and the great staff at Archives of

Acknowledgements

Ontario, Toronto Reference Library, City of Toronto Archives, Library and Archives Canada and the Teck Centennial Public Library in Kirkland Lake. Thanks also to John Michael McGrath for research help when my deadline loomed. Several other people assisted me with various bits of valuable knowledge. Along with geologist David Graham, they include Tabitha Fritz, Peter Greyson at the Cobalt Mining Museum, David Hayes, Jim Houston, Chris McCormack, Kevin Reeves, Rick Taylor and Karen Watt.

I'd like to extend a special thanks to the wise and talented friends who accepted the unenviable mission of reading the first draft: Ruby Andrew, Matthew Church, Chris Goldie, Tom Meredith and Ian Pearson.

Once again, the folks at ECW Press were great to work with. Art director Jessica Albert gave me another beautiful cover. Samantha is a diligent and enthusiastic proofreader. Victoria Cozza expertly shepherded the book through production. And Michael Holmes is as enthusiastic and accommodating an editor as any writer could hope for and always provides good advice. Special thanks to my longtime friend, mentor and colleague Lynn Cunningham, who handled the line and copy editing and made this book far more readable.

Finally, thanks to Carmen, who has offered love, support and tolerance for more years than she'd like to admit.

TIM FALCONER
TORONTO
SEPTEMBER 2024

SELECTED BIBLIOGRAPHY

Abel, Kerry. *Changing Places: History, Community, and Identity in Northeastern Ontario.* Montreal & Kingston: McGill-Queen's University Press, 2006.

Angus, Charlie. *Cobalt: Cradle of the Demon Metals, Birth of Mining Superpower.* Toronto: House of Anansi, 2022.

———. *Mirrors of Stone: Fragments from the Porcupine Frontier.* Toronto: Between the Lines, 2001.

Armstrong, Christopher. *Blue Skies and Boiler Rooms: Buying and Selling Securities in Canada, 1870-1940.* Toronto: University of Toronto Press, 1997.

———. *Moose Pastures and Mergers: The Ontario Securities Commission and the Regulation of Share Markets in Canada, 1940-1980.* Toronto: University of Toronto Press, 2001.

Baldwin, Douglas O. *Cobalt: Canada's Forgotten Silver Boom Town.* Charlottetown: Indigo, 2016.

Barnes, Michael. *Gold Camp Pioneer: Roza Brown of Kirkland Lake.* Cobalt, Ont.: Highway Book Shop, 1973.

———. *Looking Back: Cobalt, Ontario.* St. Catharines, Ont.: Looking Back, 2004.

———. *Fortunes in the Ground: Cobalt, Porcupine and Kirkland Lake.* Toronto: Boston Mills, 1986.

———. *Great Northern Characters.* Burnstown, Ont.: General Store Publishing House, 1995.

———. *The Scholarly Prospector: Don McKinnon.* Renfrew, Ont.: General Store Publishing House, 2006.

———. *Timmins: The Porcupine Country.* Erin, Ont.: Boston Mills, 1991.

Selected Bibliography

Bothwell, Robert, and William Kilbourn. *C.D. Howe: A Biography.* Toronto: McClelland and Stewart, 1979.

Bothwell, Robert. *Eldorado: Canada's National Uranium Company.* Toronto: University of Toronto Press, 1984.

Bourrie, Mark. *Flim Flam: Canada's Greatest Frauds, Scams, and Con Artists.* Toronto: Hounslow, 1998.

Braddon, Russell. *Roy Thomson of Fleet Street.* Toronto: Collins, 1965.

Conners, Stompin' Tom. *Stompin' Tom: Before the Fame.* Toronto: Penguin Books, 1996.

Croft, Roger. *Swindle! A Decade of Canadian Stock Frauds.* Toronto: Gage Publishing, 1975.

Cruise, David, and Alison Griffiths. *Fleecing the Lamb: The Inside Story of the Vancouver Stock Exchange.* Vancouver: Douglas & McIntyre, 1987.

Deneault, Alain, and William Sacher. *Imperial Canada Inc.: Legal Haven of Choice for the World's Mining Industries.* Vancouver: Talonbooks, 2012.

Falconer, Tim. *Klondikers: Dawson City's Stanley Cup Challenge and How a Nation Fell in Love with Hockey.* Toronto: ECW, 2021.

Fetherling, George. *The Gold Crusades: A Social History of Gold Rushes, 1849-1929*, rev.ed. Toronto, University of Toronto Press, 1997. (First published 1988 by MacMillan of Canada.)

———. *Gold Diggers of 1929: Canada and the Great Stock Market Crash.* Toronto: John Wiley & Sons, 2004.

Francis, Diane. *Bre-X: The Inside Story.* Toronto: Key Porter, 1997.

Fulford, Robert. *Accidental City: The Transformation of Toronto.* Toronto: Macfarlane, Walter & Ross, 1995.

Girdwood, Charles P., Lawrence F. Jones and George Lynn. *The Big Dome: Over Seventy Years of Gold Mining in Canada.* Toronto: Cybergraphics, 1983.

Gray, Charlotte. *Murdered Midas: A Millionaire, His Gold Mine, and a Strange Death on an Island Paradise.* Toronto: HarperCollins Canada, 2019.

Hanula, Monica, ed. *The Discoverers: A 50-Year History of the Prospectors and Developers Association, Some Famous Prospectors and Their Discoveries.* Toronto: Pitt, 1982.

Hind, Andrew and Maria Da Silva. *Muskoka Resorts: Then and Now.* Toronto: Dundurn, 2011.

Hoffman, Arnold. *Free Gold: The Story of Canadian Mining*, 2nd printing. New York: Associated Book Service, 1958.

Hutchinson, Brian. *Fools' Gold: The Making of a Global Market Fraud.* Toronto: Alfred A. Knopf Canada, 1998.

Joubin, Franc R., and D. McCormack Smyth. *Not for Gold Alone: The Memoirs of a Prospector.* Toronto: Deljay Publications, 1986.

Kelly, Arthur. *Report of the Royal Commission to Investigate Trading in the Shares of Windfall Oils and Mines Limited.* Toronto: Queen's Printer, 1965.

Kipling, Rudyard. *Rewards and Fairies.* Project Gutenberg, 1996.

Leacock, Stephen. *Sunshine Sketches of a Little Town.* Toronto: McClelland and Stewart, New Canadian Library ed., 1970.

LeBourdais, D.M. *Metals and Men: The Story of Canadian Mining.* Toronto: McClelland and Stewart, 1979.

Lonn, George. *Men and Mines: Short Biographies of Some Colorful Contemporary Figures Behind Canada's Mighty Mining Industry.* Toronto: Pitt, 1962.

MacMillan, Viola. *From the Ground Up: An Autobiography.* Toronto: ECW, 2001.

Morton, Suzanne. *At Odds: Gambling and Canadians, 1919–1969.* Toronto: University of Toronto Press, 2003.

Newman, Peter C. *Flame of Power: Intimate Profiles of Canada's Greatest Businessmen.* Toronto: Longmans, Green & Co., 1959.

Pain, S.A. *Three Miles of Gold: The Story of Kirkland Lake.* Toronto: Ryerson, 1960.

Patrick, Kenneth G. *Perpetual Jeopardy: The Texas Gulf Sulphur Affair: A Chronicle of Achievement and Misadventure.* Toronto: Collier-MacMillan Canada, 1972.

Pryke, Susan. *Windermere House: The Tradition Continues.* Erin, Ont.: Boston Mills, 1999.

Reeves, Kevin. *Let Me Call You Sweetheart.* MTR Production, 1992. https://www.youtube.com/watch?v=fMEESzso11A.

Rhindress, Charlie. *Stompin' Tom Connors: The Myth and the Man.* Halifax: Formac, 2019.

Roberts, Leslie. *Noranda.* Toronto: Clarke, Irwin, 1956.

Sandlos, John, and Arn Keeling. *Mining Country: A History of Canada's Mines and Miners.* Toronto: James Lorimer, 2021.

Shulman, Morton. *The Billion Dollar Windfall.* Toronto: McGraw-Hill, 1969.

Smith, Philip. *Harvest from the Rock: A History of Canadian Mining.* Toronto: Macmillan of Canada, 1986.

Tatley, Richard. *Windermere: The Jewel of Lake Rosseau.* Erin, Ont.: Boston Mills, 1999.

Thompson, William N. *The International Encyclopedia of Gambling,* 2 vols. Santa Barbara: ABC-CLIO, 2010.

Wells, Jennifer. *The Pez: The Manic Life of the Ultimate Promoter.* Toronto: Macfarlane, Walter & Ross, 1991.

Wilson, Maggie. *The Legend of Caroline Maben Flower: Lady Prospector of the Porcupine.* Cobalt, Ont.: White Mountain Publications, 2021.

Young, Scott. *Gordon Sinclair: A Life . . . and Then Some.* Toronto: Macmillan of Canada, 1987.

ENDNOTES

PROLOGUE

- "I, Viola MacMillan": *To Tell the Truth*, CBS, June 15, 1964, https://www.youtube.com/watch?v=LqpM-2-hxRE&list=PL39ftvD_GHaEXJCry46G3_qp2-e_hkBXj&index=66.
- Stenography was glamorous: MacMillan, *From the Ground Up*, 11.
- "cast off our shackles": *Maclean's*, July 20, 195.
- "how often I have wished": MacMillan, *From the Ground Up*, 154.

CHAPTER ONE

- Unsure she could afford Empire: Timmins *Daily Press* (hereafter *Daily Press*), Apr. 20, 1964.
- CIM meeting: *Globe and Mail*, Apr. 14, 1964.
- Fashion show, high tea: *The* (Montreal) *Gazette* (hereafter *Gazette*), Apr. 14, 1964.
- "may be the day": *Montreal Star*, Apr. 14, 1964.
- Unreleased assay results: Shulman, *The Billion Dollar Windfall*, 152-153.
- Ackerley: Ackerley testimony, Mar. 29, 1965, Royal Commission to Investigate Trading in the Shares of Windfall Oils and Mines Limited, RG 18-149, Archives of Ontario (hereafter Windfall commission); Ackerley's written reconstruction of events related to Windfall story (hereafter Ackerley memo), exhibit 134, Windfall commission; Ackerley testimony, Sept. 10, 1964, Ontario Securities Commission Inquiry, RG 18-149, Archives of Ontario (hereafter OSC inquiry).
- MacMillan in Timmins: MacMillan, *From the Ground Up*, 155–157.

- Larche: *Northern Ontario Business,* June 15, 2009; *Northern Ontario Business,* Nov. 21, 2012; Larche testimony, Mar. 3, 1965, Windfall commission; Larche testimony, Sept. 15, 1964, OSC inquiry.
- "most knowledgeable prospector": MacMillan, *From the Ground Up,* 156.
- Rousseau: Rousseau testimony, Mar. 3, 1965, Windfall commission.
- McKinnon: McKinnon testimony, Sept. 15, 1964, and Feb. 9, 1965, OSC inquiry; McKinnon testimony, Mar. 4, 1965, Windfall commission.
- Empire Hotel suite: *Maclean's,* June 6, 1964.
- Booze: Reynolds testimony, Oct. 13, 1964, OSC inquiry.
- "hot piece of ground": Larche testimony, Sept. 15, 1964, OSC inquiry.
- Press conference and party: Reynolds testimony, Mar. 3, 1965, Windfall commission.
- Negotiations: Rousseau testimony, Mar. 3, 1965, Windfall commission; Larche testimony, Mar. 3, 1965, Windfall commission; Larche testimony, Sept. 15, 1964, OSC inquiry; McKinnon testimony, Mar. 4, 1965, Windfall commission.
- Texas Gulf find: Holyk testimony, Mar. 1, 1965, Windfall commission; Holyk testimony, Apr. 26, 1965, Windfall commission; Holyk testimony Feb. 22, 1965, OSC inquiry; Darke testimony, Mar. 1, 1965, Windfall commission; Darke testimony, Apr. 23, 1965, Windfall commission; Patrick, *Perpetual Jeopardy,* 29–59; Shulman, *The Billion Dollar Windfall,* 1–29; Smith, *Harvest from the Rock,* 314–319; *New York Times,* Apr. 11, 1964; *Globe and Mail,* Apr. 13, 1964; *New York Times,* Apr. 17, 1964; *Financial Post* (hereafter *Post*), Apr. 18, 1964; *Globe and Mail,* Apr. 21, 1964; *Maclean's,* June 6, 1964.
- Clay belt: *Canadian Geographical Journal,* January 1975.
- Darke: Darke testimony, Mar. 1 and 2, 1965, Windfall commission; Darke testimony, Apr. 23, 1965, Windfall commission; Angus, *Mirrors of Stone,* 118–119; Shulman, *The Billion Dollar Windfall,* 2–11.
- Holyk: *The Discoverers,* 299–302; Holyk testimony, Mar. 1, 1965, Windfall commission.
- Improperly staked claims: Kelly, *Report of the Royal Commission to Investigate Trading in the Shares of Windfall Oils and Mines Limited* (hereafter Windfall commission report).
- Darke tried to buy the claims: Barnes, *The Scholarly Prospector,* 39.
- *Globe* story: *Globe and Mail,* Apr. 9, 1964.
- Errors in *New York Herald Tribune* story: Shulman, *The Billion Dollar Windfall,* 139.
- "work done to date": Shulman, *The Billion Dollar Windfall,* xii.
- "stiff headwind": Ackerley memo, exhibit 134, Windfall commission.
- Texas Gulf flew Wardrope to Toronto: Wardrope testimony, Apr. 13, 1965, Windfall commission.
- "trek 10 miles": *New York Times,* Apr. 17, 1964.
- Timmins frenzy: *Globe and Mail,* Apr. 17, 1964; *Ottawa Citizen* (hereafter *Citizen*), Apr. 17, 1964; *Globe and Mail,* Apr. 18, 1964; *Kingston Whig-Standard,* Apr. 18, 1964; *Globe and Mail,* Apr. 20, 1964; *Citizen,* Apr. 22, 1964; *Gazette,* May 23, 1964; *Citizen,* Apr. 24, 1964; *Maclean's,* June 6, 1964.
- "start moving": Reynolds testimony, Mar. 3, 1965, Windfall commission.

- High schoolers investing: *Citizen*, Apr. 22, 1964.
- Broadcasting from Doherty, Roadhouse: *Sudbury Star* website, Nov. 10, 2013.
- "virtual halt": *Citizen*, Apr. 17, 1964.
- "jewelry store" and "whirlybird staking rush": *Gazette*, May 23, 1964.
- Soft drink: *Globe and Mail*, Apr. 22, 1964.
- Within 80 kilometres: *Citizen*, Apr. 22, 1964.
- number of claims staked: Windfall commission report.
- Staking airport: Shulman, *The Billion Dollar Windfall*, 95.
- Inco: *Globe and Mail*, Apr. 21, 1964.
- Bragagnolo: Bragagnolo testimony, Mar. 2, 1965, Windfall commission; *Globe and Mail*, Apr. 18, 1964; *Edmonton Journal*, Apr. 18, 1964; *Nanaimo Daily News*, Apr. 20, 1964; *Citizen*, Apr. 22, 1964; *Gazette*, May 23, 1964; *Post*, June 6, 1964; *Maclean's*, June 6, 1964; *Toronto Daily Star*, Oct. 7, 1965.
- "mines killed my father": *Nanaimo Daily News*, Apr. 20, 1964.
- Partnership: Bragagnolo testimony, Mar. 2, 1965, Windfall commission; Angus testimony, Mar. 2, 1965, Windfall commission; Darke testimony, Mar. 1, 1965, Windfall commission; Windfall commission report.
- Bragagnolo's office: Shulman, *The Billion Dollar Windfall*, 24.
- Bragagnolo-Darke conversation: Bragagnolo testimony, Mar. 2, 1965, Windfall commission.
- TSE frenzy: *Globe and Mail*, Apr. 9, 1964; *Globe and Mail*, Apr. 17, 1964; *Globe and Mail*, Apr. 18, 1964; *Globe and Mail*, Apr. 20, 1964; *Globe and Mail*, Apr. 21, 1964; *Post*, Apr. 25, 1964.
- 1,700 shares: *Post*, Apr. 25, 1964.
- "unsophisticated investors": *Gazette*, May 23, 1964.
- "on the verge" and "all night": Reynolds testimony, Mar. 3, 1965, Windfall commission.
- "can't match": Rousseau testimony, Mar. 3, 1965, Windfall commission.
- "another experience like that night": Viola MacMillan testimony, Aug. 20, 1964, OSC inquiry.

CHAPTER TWO

- Windermere House: Tatley, *Windermere*, 29; Pryke, *Windermere House*, 22–25; Hind and Da Silva, *Muskoka Resorts*, 187–194; *Globe*, Aug. 9, 1901.
- "objectionable noise": Pryke, *Windermere House*, 25.
- MacMillan's childhood: MacMillan, *From the Ground Up*, 2–17; Reeves, *Let Me Call You Sweetheart*.
- One-room school: Tatley, *Windermere*, 32.
- "summer visitors": MacMillan, *From the Ground Up*, 11.
- Fife House: Tatley, *Windermere*, 29, 40.
- Windsor: "Windsor (Ont.)," *Canadian Encyclopedia*, https://www.thecanadian encyclopedia.ca/en/article/windsor-ont.
- MacMillan in Windsor: MacMillan, *From the Ground Up*, 18–29.

- John and Harriet Rodd: *Windsor Star*, Apr. 19, 1945; *Windsor Star*, June 16, 1920.
- George MacMillan: notes, Viola MacMillan fonds, CMNAC/1997-012, Canadian Museum of Nature Archives (hereafter MacMillan fonds); MacMillan, *From the Ground Up*, 72–76; George MacMillan testimony, Mar. 17, 1965, Windfall commission.
- "real hard time": MacMillan, *From the Ground Up*, 24.
- Joe Huggard: MacMillan, *From the Ground Up*, 4 and 13.
- "Black Jack" MacMillan: MacMillan, *From the Ground Up*, 32.
- "not the girl for him" and "her or me": Reeves, *Let Me Call You Sweetheart*.
- Visit to Coniagas mine: MacMillan, *From the Ground Up*, 27–28; Reeves, *Let Me Call You Sweetheart*.
- "bad luck": MacMillan, *From the Ground Up*, 27.
- Coniagas mine: Baldwin, *Cobalt*, 24.
- "glorious experiences" and "can handle her": MacMillan, *From the Ground Up*, 28.
- "got along all right": Reeves, *Let Me Call You Sweetheart*.
- "not that kind of girl": MacMillan, *From the Ground Up*, 29.
- First night: MacMillan, *From the Ground Up*, 32–45; *Saturday Night*, June 25, 1955; draft of 1955 *The Zontian* magazine article, MacMillan fonds; *Star Weekly*, May 3, 1941; Reeves, *Let Me Call You Sweetheart*.
- "find any gold" and "had a visitor": MacMillan, *From the Ground Up*, 33.
- "more than that": MacMillan, *From the Ground Up*, 37.
- Early prospecting experience: MacMillan, *From the Ground Up*, 32–45; "Having a Wonderful Time," *Saturday Night*, June 25, 1955; "Angel of the Sourdoughs," *Coronet*, June 1956; Reeves, *Let Me Call You Sweetheart*.
- Dishwashing dogs: *Chatelaine*, June 1945; MacMillan, *From the Ground Up*, 42.
- "my family": MacMillan, *From the Ground Up*, 42.
- "lived on it": *Chatelaine*, June 1945.

CHAPTER THREE

- Cobalt silver discovery: *Globe* (three stories), Oct. 3, 1908; *New York Times*, May 27, 1906; Baldwin, *Cobalt*, 8–36; Smith, *Harvest from the Rock*, 118–132; Hoffman, *Free Gold*, 102–105; Fetherling, *The Gold Crusades*, 165–173; Barnes, *Fortunes in the Ground*, 13–29; Windfall commission report, 123–126.
- Richardson's farm: *TVO Today*, tvo.org, Jan. 30, 2024.
- Indigenous silver trading: Angus, *Cobalt*, 12–13.
- forty-niner's advice: *Globe*, Oct. 3, 1908.
- La Rose first to stake claim: *Globe*, Oct. 3, 1908.
- "have a good thing" and "pull a gun": *Globe*, Oct. 3, 1908.
- straw boater hat: Baldwin, *Cobalt*, 20.
- "stove-lids and cannon-balls": Smith, *Harvest from the Rock*, 122.
- "text-book vein": *Globe*, Oct. 3, 1908.
- 4.5-kilogram nugget: *Globe*, Nov. 23, 1903.
- Trethewey: Baldwin, *Cobalt*, 22–23.

Endnotes

- "Cobalt Station, T&NO": *Globe*, Oct. 3, 1908.
- Cobalt's legacy: Baldwin, *Cobalt*, 1–5.
- Millionaires: *Maclean's*, Jan. 1909.
- La Rose in Montreal River: *Globe*, Oct. 3, 1908.
- Porcupine gold rush: Smith, *Harvest from the Rock*, 161–177; Girdwood, Jones and Lynn, *The Big Dome*, 18–29.
- "candle drippings": Girdwood, Jones and Lynn, *The Big Dome*, 26.
- "mother of gold": Pain, *Three Miles of Gold*.
- Benjamin Hollinger: *Dictionary of Canadian Biography*, http://www.biographi.ca/en /bio/hollinger_benjamin_14E.html.
- Sandy McIntyre: *Globe and Mail*, July 8, 1943; *Windsor Star*, July 8, 1943; Hoffman, *Free Gold*, 77–79.
- 200 men: *Cobalt Nugget*, Dec. 17, 1909.
- 2,000 claims: *Dictionary of Canadian Biography*, http://www.biographi.ca/en/bio /hollinger_benjamin_14E.html.
- Ferland transaction: *North Bay Nugget*, June 24, 1927.
- Weldon Young, former star with the Ottawa Hockey Club: Falconer, *Klondikers*.
- Weldon Young transaction: *Windsor Star*, July 8, 1943; Hoffman, *Free Gold*, 198.
- Jim Hughes transaction: Hoffman, *Free Gold*, 79.
- "lucky—for others": *North Bay Nugget*, June 24, 1927.
- "typical mining town": *Globe*, Mar. 25, 1911.
- Town of Timmins: Abel, *Changing Places*, 77–79; Barnes, *Timmins*, 37.
- Oakes backstory: *Murdered Midas*, 11–18.
- Oakes prospecting: *Murdered Midas*, 35–41; Pain, *Three Miles of Gold*, 13–27; Smith, *Harvest from the Rock*, 194–202; Barnes, *Fortunes in the Ground*, 173–181.
- Staking in winter of 1906–1907: *Post*, Feb. 21, 1914.
- Assessment work rules: *Twentieth Report of the Ontario Bureau of Mines, Parts I and II, 1911*, 277.
- "I'll show you": Pain, *Three Miles of Gold*, 17.
- Bill Wright: Hoffman, *Free Gold*, 94–95.
- Four dollars: Cobalt *Daily News*, July 13, 1912.
- Tough brothers: Hanula, *The Discoverers*, 288.
- "about four hours": Smith, *Harvest from the Rock*, 197.
- Oakes character: *Maclean's*, Sept. 1, 1950; Gray, *Murdered Midas*.
- Staking in Kirkland Lake: Cobalt *Daily News*, Apr. 9, 1912.
- 1,000 claims: Cobalt *Daily News*, July 13, 1912.
- "spent it on the drink": Hoffman, *Free Gold*, 79.

CHAPTER FOUR

- Move to London: MacMillan, *From the Ground Up*, 47–48.
- Going prospecting: *Post*, Aug. 13, 1938; *Maclean's*, July 20, 1957.
- "leaving for the north": *Weekend Magazine*, vol. 5, no. 34, 1955.

- "listen to a prospector": *Post*, Aug. 13, 1938.
- Mining in the 1930s: Smith, *Harvest from the Rock*, 251–255.
- Gold production: *Gold Mining in Ontario: Report of the Committee of Inquiry into the Economics of the Gold Mining Industry*, 1955.
- Caroline Mayben Flower: Wilson, *The Legend of Caroline Maben Flower*, Cobalt *Daily News*, Jan. 8, 1913; *Regina Leader-Post*, Jan. 23, 1911; *Globe*, Mar. 8, 1910.
- "the lady prospector": *Cobalt Nugget*, Jan. 8, 1913.
- "golden-haired heroine": *Regina Leader-Post*, Jan. 23, 1911.
- Mabel Fetterly: Mabel Fetterly file (including Carolyn O'Neil's interview notes), Museum of Northern History, Kirkland Lake; *Globe and Mail*, May 10, 1962; *The Northern News*, Oct. 30, 1947.
- Rosie Brown: Roza Brown file, Museum of Northern History; *Maclean's*, Dec. 2, 1964; *Northern Daily News*, July 10, 1969; Barnes, *Great Northern Characters*, 75–79; Gray, *Murdered Midas*, 48–50.
- "mind of its own": Gray, *Murdered Midas*, 49.
- "inexhaustible vocabulary": "The Rose of Kirkland Lake," publication and date unknown, Roza Brown file, Museum of Northern History.
- Lost council race: *Northern Daily News*, July 10, 1969.
- "expressing her mind": "Roza Brown Dies; Kirkland Pioneer," publication and date unknown, Roza Brown file, Museum of Northern History.
- "not entirely predictable": Joubin and Smyth, *Not for Gold Alone*, 117.
- Prospecting: *Maclean's*, Oct. 1, 1926; Joubin and Smyth, *Not for Gold Alone*, 117–123.
- claim-staking: *Three Miles of Gold*, 106–109; Windfall commission report.
- "tie-on" claims: Joubin and Smyth, *Not for Gold Alone*, 137.
- Mining Court case: MacMillan, *From the Ground Up*, 50–51.
- "rustling up the dough": Viola MacMillan testimony, May 13, 1965, Windfall commission.
- Oakes: Gray, *Murdered Midas*, 101, 147.
- population and mining workforce: Torlone, Joe G., "The Evolution of the City of Timmins: A Single-Industry Community" (master's thesis, Wilfred Laurier University, 1979).
- Hollinger Houses: Timminstoday.com, Apr. 7, 2019.
- Roy Thomson: Braddon, *Roy Thomson of Fleet Street*, 46–84; *Globe and Mail*, Aug. 5, 1976.
- Sense of humour and big laugh: MacMillan, *From the Ground Up*, 64.
- "mackinaw jacket": "Woman Has Part in Ramore Activity," *Mail and Empire*, date unknown, MacMillan fonds.
- Financially secure: *Star Weekly*, Oct. 7, 1950.
- "cubbyhole": MacMillan, *From the Ground Up*, 59.
- Golden Arrow: MacMillan, *From the Ground Up*, 63–64, 78; *Post*, Dec. 17, 1938.
- Jim Bartleman: Bartleman testimony, Mar. 4, 1965, Windfall commission; MacMillan, *From the Ground Up*, 90.
- Poulet-Vet deal: Reeves, *Let Me Call You Sweetheart*; MacMillan, *From the Ground Up*, 60–62 and 65–66.

Endnotes

- Horne's discovery: Roberts, *Noranda*, 15–32; Sandlos and Keeling, *Mining Country*, 101–102.
- "good geology": Sandlos and Keeling, *Mining Country*, 101.
- 200 kilometres: Roberts, *Noranda*, 55.
- Indigenous man with gold samples: George MacMillan testimony, Mar. 17, 1965, Windfall commission.
- James Murdoch and Noranda: Roberts, *Noranda*, 51–52; Sandlos and Keeling, *Mining Country*, 101–104.
- Quebec legislation: Sandlos and Keeling, *Mining Country*, 102.
- Timmins and Hollinger: Roberts, *Noranda*, 87–88; Sandlos and Keeling, *Mining Country*, 102.
- Town of Noranda: Sandlos and Keeling, *Mining Country*, 104; Roberts, *Noranda*, 125–126.
- Hallnor deal: *Post*, Dec. 11, 1937; MacMillan, *From the Ground Up*, 65–66, 77; Roberts, *Noranda*, 144–147.
- "If I had known": MacMillan, *From the Ground Up*, 65.
- "real thrill": *Star Weekly*, May 3, 1941.
- "Lombardo is tops," "favourite pastime" and "nothing I'd like better": *Star Weekly*, Aug. 27, 1938.
- "anything that looks good": *Post*, Aug. 13, 1938.

CHAPTER FIVE

- Reynolds breaks story: Reynolds testimony, Oct. 13, 1964, OSC inquiry.
- Windfall history: Cole testimony, Mar. 25, 1965, Windfall commission; George MacMillan testimony, Aug. 13, 1964, OSC inquiry; Patrick, *Perpetual Jeopardy*, 184; *Gazette*, Dec. 18, 1961.
- Viola visits Lawson: Lawson testimony, Apr. 22, 1965, Windfall commission.
- Underwriting agreement and negotiations: Windfall commission report; Cole testimony, Mar. 25, 1965, Windfall commission; Lawson testimony, Apr. 22, 1965, Windfall commission; Ketchen testimony, May 10, 1965, Windfall commission.
- Windfall buys claims: Windfall commission report; Shulman, *The Billion Dollar Windfall*, 39–40.
- Lucky Texas Group: Viola MacMillan testimony, May 13, 1965, Windfall commission.
- "our company": Windfall commission report.
- Doris Drewe background: recollection, MacMillan fonds; Drewe testimony, Sept. 22, 1964, OSC inquiry.
- Marjorie Oliver (Humphrey): Humphrey testimony, Sept. 23, 1964, OSC inquiry; Humphrey testimony, Mar. 24, 1965, Windfall commission.
- Fifty head of cattle: Lonn, *Men and Mines*, 53.
- Ronald Mills: Mills testimony, Mar. 24, 1965, Windfall commission.
- "quiet young man": Humphrey testimony, Mar. 24, 1965, Windfall commission.
- Directors' meeting: Humphrey testimony, Mar. 24, 1965, Windfall commission.

- "irons in the fire": Cole testimony, Mar. 25, 1965, Windfall commission.
- "change cars": Baldwin, *Cobalt*, 1.
- Curb market: Baldwin, *Cobalt*, 2; "'The New York Curb Market . . . Which Has No Organization Whatever': The Enclosure of New York's Last Outdoor Stock Market, 1900–1921," Gotham Center for New York History, Oct. 9, 2018; *New York Times*, Nov. 11, 1909.
- History of stock exchanges in Toronto and Montreal: Armstrong, *Blue Skies and Boiler Rooms*, 10–11; Ranald C. Michie, "The Canadian Securities Market, 1850–1914," *The Business History Review*, vol. 62, no. 1 (Spring 1988), 35–73; Deneault and Sacher, *Imperial Canada Inc.*, 97; "A Crash Course on Toronto's Black Tuesday," Jamie Bradburn's Tales of Toronto website, Jan. 17, 2018.
- 429 public companies, forty-four produced silver, seventeen paid dividends: Ranald C. Michie, "The Canadian Securities Market, 1850–1914," *The Business History Review*, vol. 62, no. 1 (Spring 1988), 35–73.
- Winnipeg Grain Exchange: Fethering, *Gold Diggers of 1929*, 51–63.
- Regulation: Armstrong, *Blue Skies and Boiler Rooms*, 5–7.
- *Post* series on SSME: Fetherling, *Gold Diggers of 1929*, 29–34.
- Boiler rooms: Armstrong, *Blue Skies and Boiler Rooms*, 7.
- Solloway: *Post*, Feb. 6, 1930; *Post*, Apr. 3, 1930.
- "most heavily fined men": *Toronto Daily Star*, July 8, 1931.
- TSE–SSME merger: *Post*, Nov. 25, 1933; Armstrong, *Moose Pastures and Mergers*, 7.
- Montreal Stock Exchange: Fetherling, *Gold Diggers of 1929*, 22–25.
- New TSE building: *Time*, Apr. 5, 1937.
- Royal Commission on Ontario Mining: Armstrong, *Moose Pastures and Mergers*, 36.
- Gordon Sinclair: Young, *Gordon Sinclair*, 80.
- "nine cases out of ten": Armstrong, *Moose Pastures and Mergers*, 158.
- Negotiations: Lawson testimony, Apr. 22, 1965, Windfall commission; Lawson testimony, Oct. 5, 1964, OSC inquiry.
- "deal is set" and "explained this": Lawson testimony, Apr. 22, 1965, Windfall commission.
- MacMillan believed she deserved something: Humphrey testimony, Mar. 24, 1965, Windfall commission.
- "can't tell me": Lawson testimony, Apr. 22, 1965, Windfall commission.
- Deal MacMillan accepted: Cole testimony, Mar. 25, 1965, Windfall commission.

CHAPTER SIX

- King Edward Hotel: Sally Gibson, *An Illustrated History of the King Edward Hotel*, report for Dundee Realty Corporation, date unknown; "The Palatial New Hotel," *Toronto Daily Star*, Mar. 14, 1903; Fetherling, *The Gold Crusades*, 171; Gray, *Murdered Midas*, 46.
- CIM meeting: *Montreal Star*, Mar. 3, 1904.
- "scores of crooks" and "'strong arm' salesmen": Armstrong, *Blue Skies and Boiler Rooms*, 39.

- Oakville farm: MacMillan, *From the Ground Up*, 68.
- Airquests: MacMillan, *From the Ground Up*, 69–70.
- California trip: MacMillan, *From the Ground Up*, 73–75; Reeves, *Let Me Call You Sweetheart*.
- "Canada needs us": Reeves, *Let Me Call You Sweetheart*.
- "sizeable fortune": *Post*, Aug. 13, 1938.
- Prospected across Canada: Hanula, *The Discoverers*, 252.
- Not a country estate: *Post*, Aug. 13, 1938.
- "How much": MacMillan, *From the Ground Up*, 69.
- Oriole Parkway house: MacMillan, *From the Ground Up*, 69, 113; *Magazine Digest*, Feb. 1946.
- Unable to have children: MacMillan, *From the Ground Up*, 63.
- Walter Segsworth: *Globe and Mail*, July 21, 1945; *Maclean's*, Oct. 1, 1926; Hanula, *The Discoverers*, 268–269.
- Engineers Act: *Globe*, Jan. 23, 1932; *Post*, Mar. 5, 1932.
- Association created: *Globe*, Mar. 1, 1932.
- Cockeram: *Montreal Star*, Dec. 30, 1950; Hoffman, *Free Gold*, 97.
- Meeting at King Edward: *Globe*, Mar. 2, 1932.
- Well over one hundred: 128 according to *Globe*, Mar. 2, 1932; 132 according to *Northern Miner*, Jan. 29, 2007.
- "hashing and chewing": Hanula, *The Discoverers*, 16.
- $168.45: *Northern Miner*, Jan. 29, 2007.
- Petition: *Globe*, Mar. 16, 1932.
- "old-timers": transcript of "Salute to the Girls," CFRB radio interview, MacMillan fonds.
- Murdock Mosher: Hanula, *The Discoverers*, 246–247; Baldwin, *Cobalt*, 36.
- "too soft" and "good president": MacMillan, *From the Ground Up*, 85.
- 1942 convention: *Northern Miner*, Jan. 29, 2007; Hanula, *The Discoverers*, 46; MacMillan, *From the Ground Up*, 87–89.
- "Wives have their rights": *Magazine Digest*, Feb. 1946.
- Cake: MacMillan, *From the Ground Up*, 89.
- Monture: *Queen's Alumni Review*, Aug. 26, 2013.
- Strategic metals: Joubin and Smyth, *Not for Gold Alone*, 110.
- Workshops: MacMillan, *From the Ground Up*, 93–95.
- Bateman: Bothwell, *Eldorado*, 100–101; Bothwell and Kilbourn, *C.D. Howe*, 135.
- War Metals Advisory Committee: *Toronto Daily Star*, June 19, 1942.
- "itching to rush": *Globe and Mail*, Jan. 12, 1944.
- George regularly received thanks: *Weekend Magazine*, vol. 5, no. 34, 1955.
- "75 per cent": *Star Weekly*, May 3, 1941.
- Puppet ruler: *Magazine Digest*, Feb. 1946.
- CIM barred her: MacMillan, *From the Ground Up*, 99–100.
- Emergency Gold Mining Assistance Act: "Summary Review of the Gold Mining Industry in Canada 1948," Dominion Bureau of Statistics, Department of Trade and Commerce.

- "Mining Day": Reeves, *Let Me Call You Sweetheart.*
- Mailing: Doris Drewe recollection, MacMillan fonds.
- Seventy-three members: Hanula, *The Discoverers*, 253.
- "fruit business": *Chatelaine*, June 1945.
- Fummerton and women in prospecting: transcript of "Salute to the Girls," CFRB radio interview, MacMillan fonds.
- "make it snappy": *Weekend Magazine*, vol. 5, no. 34, 1955.
- "keep them occupied and interested": MacMillan, *From the Ground Up*, 122.
- Office: *Chatelaine*, June 1945; *Magazine Digest*, Feb. 1946.
- 1,400 men, 360 women: *Northern Miner*, Jan. 29, 2007.
- "I'll be right over": *Magazine Digest*, Feb. 1946.
- Serenading MacMillan: *New York Times*, Sept. 1, 1964.
- "nothing more beautiful": *Star Weekly*, Oct. 19, 1963.
- 1964 convention and "Red tape, taxes and apathy": Hanula, *The Discovers*, 84.

CHAPTER SEVEN

- MacMillans showed map: Humphrey testimony, Sept. 23, 1964, OSC inquiry; Humphrey testimony, Mar. 24, 1965, Windfall commission.
- Fifty-fifty: Lawson testimony, Oct. 5, 1964, OSC inquiry.
- Forty drills: Armstrong, *Moose Pastures and Mergers*, 161.
- Szetu: Szetu testimony, Sept. 21, 1964, OSC inquiry.
- Ore-finding devices: Baldwin, *Cobalt*, 29; F. Gerali (2020), *Geophysics and Petroleum, the Early Years, 1900–1930*, Engineering and Technology History Wiki, https://ethw.org/Geophysics_and_Petroleum,_the_early_years,_1900-1930.
- Geophysics: Windfall commission report; Armstrong, *Moose Pastures and Mergers*, 156–157.
- "information you might want": George MacMillan testimony, Aug. 12, 1964, OSC inquiry.
- MacMillan aid $2,500: George MacMillan testimony, Mar. 17, 1965, Windfall commission.
- Willis Ambrose: "Memorial to John Willis Ambrose 1904–1974," Raymond A. Price, Queen's University; MacMillan, *From the Ground Up*, 102.
- Geophysics work on Windfall claims: Szetu testimony, Mar. 8, 1965, Windfall commission; Szetu testimony, Sept. 21, 1964, OSC inquiry; Hall testimony, Mar. 9, 1965, Windfall commission.
- "change our methods": Szetu testimony, Mar. 8, 1965, Windfall commission.
- Oliver wrote the show producers: Humphrey testimony, Mar. 25, 1965, Windfall commission.
- Shareholders meeting: Cole testimony, Mar. 25, 1965, Windfall commission; *Northern Miner*, July 2, 1964; Ackerley testimony, Mar. 29, 1965, Windfall commission; Ackerley memo, exhibit 134, Windfall commission.
- "very important people": Ackerley memo, exhibit 134, Windfall commission.

- MacMillan invited Kaplan to wedding: Kaplan testimony, Oct. 8, 1964, OSC inquiry.
- Windfall trading: Record of Windfall trading, exhibit 79, Windfall commission.
- New Texas Gulf estimates: *Gazette*, June 19, 1964.
- Viola congratulated Darke: Darke testimony, Mar. 1, 1965, Windfall commission.
- "a little silly": George MacMillan testimony, Mar. 17, 1965, Windfall commission.
- Texas Gulf spent $2 million: Windfall commission report.
- "200 miles" and "certainly would": George MacMillan testimony, Aug. 12, 1964, OSC inquiry.
- "D.H. No. 1": Windfall commission report.
- Drilling contract: exhibit 70, Windfall commission.
- Diamond core drilling: Boucher testimony, Mar. 8, 1965, Windfall commission; Boucher testimony, Mar. 9, 1965, Windfall commission; Vianney Lance testimony, Mar. 9, 1965, Windfall commission; *AZo Mining*, July 20, 2012.
- Appearance on *Graphic*: Reeves, *Let Me Call You Sweetheart*.
- "proud of me": Reeves, *Let Me Call You Sweetheart*.
- "hauled enough gravel": *Magazine Digest*, Feb. 1946.
- "Viola's show": *Star Weekly*, May 3, 1941.
- "white-haired and slow-speaking" and "George likes to hide": *Maclean's*, Apr. 15, 1953.
- "laid back" and "easygoing guy": MacMillan, *From the Ground Up*, 75.
- "longer chances": George MacMillan testimony, Mar. 17, 1965, Windfall commission.
- "can you separate": Humphrey testimony, Mar. 24, 1965, Windfall commission.
- "gotta have another mine": *Post*, June 13, 1964.

CHAPTER EIGHT

- "ten minutes away": MacMillan, *From the Ground Up*, 135.
- Apartment: *Maclean's*, July 20, 1957; *Saturday Night*, June 25, 1955; *New York Times*, Sept. 1, 1964.
- "not going to spend" and typical workday: *Weekend Magazine*, vol. 5, no. 34, 1955.
- "answers the telephone," *Saturday Night*, June 25, 1955.
- "happy in a tent": *Maclean's*, July 20, 1957.
- Victor Mine: MacMillan, *From the Ground Up*, 113–126; *CIM Magazine*, Aug. 2016; draft of 1955 *The Zontian* magazine article, MacMillan fonds; BC Ministry of Energy, Mines and Petroleum Resources MINFILE no. 082FNW204.
- Ambrose: Ambrose testimony, Mar. 16, 1965, Windfall commission.
- "ball rolling": MacMillan, *From the Ground Up*, 110.
- "hope you make a million": MacMillan, *From the Ground Up*, 117.
- "the main vein," "I'm so sorry" and "Now, Mrs. Mac": MacMillan, *From the Ground Up*, 124–125.
- "nearly dropped dead": "She Made Her Millions in Mines," *Weekend Magazine*, vol. 5, no. 34, 1955.

- Fruit ranch: *Star Weekly*, Oct. 7, 1950.
- Lake Cinch mine: Viola MacMillan testimony, May 13, 1965, Windfall commission; MacMillan, *From the Ground Up*, 139–140; *Post*, Jan. 15, 1955; *Globe and Mail*, Sept. 21, 1957; *Globe and Mail*, Sept. 23, 1957; *New York Times*, Sept. 24, 1957.
- "going to be disappointed": MacMillan, *From the Ground Up*, 139.
- 1955 visit to Lake Cinch: *Weekend Magazine*, vol. 5, no. 34, 1955.
- Gilbert LaBine: Newman, *Flame of Power*, 149–168; Bothwell, *Eldorado*, 16–23; *New York Times*, Jan. 5, 1956.
- Eldorado mine: Bothwell, *Eldorado*, 26–38, 68–77, 81.
- Howe meets British: Bothwell and Kilbourn, *C.D. Howe*, 168; Bothwell, *Eldorado*, 120–121.
- "haven't any regrets": Newman, *Flame of Power*, 165.
- Uranium boom: *Post*, Mar. 5, 1955.
- Uranium City: *Toronto Star*, Aug. 26, 2007.
- "particularly wanted": Viola MacMillan testimony, May 13, 1965, Windfall commission.
- ViolaMac's holdings: *Post*, Feb. 26, 1955; *Post*, Apr. 7, 1956.
- $2 billion: *Maclean's*, July 20, 1957.
- Flew more than 50,000 kilometres a year, president of a TSE-listed company: *Weekend Magazine*, vol. 5, no. 34, 1955.
- Lobbying in Washington: Bothwell, *Eldorado*, 392.
- More than $1.7 million: *Post*, Mar. 7, 1958.
- "dream of every prospector": *Globe and Mail*, Sept. 21, 1957.
- Kam-Kotia purchase: Viola MacMillan testimony, May 13, 1965, Windfall commission; MacMillan, *From the Ground Up*, 143–145.
- MacMillan–Jamieson conversation: MacMillan, *From the Ground Up*, 144.
- "fine copper ore": George MacMillan testimony, May 12, 1964, OSC inquiry.
- Eight drill holes: *Post*, July 25, 1959.
- Heart attack: MacMillan, *From the Ground Up*, 144–147.
- ViolaMac sale: *Gazette*, July 16, 1960; *Globe and Mail*, July 16, 1960.
- "old time's sake": MacMillan, *From the Ground Up*, 153.
- "have more time": *Toronto Daily Star*, July 18, 1960.
- "slow down a little bit": Viola MacMillan testimony, May 13, 1965, Windfall commission.
- Golden Arrow: Viola MacMillan testimony, Aug. 20, 1964, OSC inquiry.
- "against my doctor's orders": MacMillan, *From the Ground Up*, 154.

CHAPTER NINE

- July 3 weather: Environment Canada Historical Data website.
- Activities at drill site: Windfall commission report; Shulman, *The Billion Dollar Windfall*, 40–42.
- Sludge turned black: Turney testimony, Mar. 11, 1965, Windfall commission.

Endnotes

- Hand and knees: Armstrong, *Moose Pastures and Mergers*, 161.
- Geology of core: B.S.W. Buffam testimony, Apr. 2,1964, Windfall commission.
- MacMillan's impression of core: George MacMillan testimony, Aug. 13, 1964, OSC inquiry.
- "see brecciation": George MacMillan testimony, Mar. 17, 1965, Windfall commission.
- Liked to look at core again and again: George MacMillan testimony, May 18, 1965, Windfall commission.
- Large companies monitored drilling: Armstrong, *Moose Pastures and Mergers*, 161.
- Helicopters: Boucher testimony, Sept. 28, OSC inquiry; Rennick testimony, Mar. 10, 1965, Windfall commission; Oille testimony, Nov. 20, 1965, OSC inquiry; George MacMillan testimony, Mar. 17, 1965, Windfall commission.
- Drilling: Boucher testimony, Mar. 8, 1965, Windfall commission; Boucher testimony, Mar. 9, 1965, Windfall commission; Roger Dufresne testimony, Mar. 9, 1965, Windfall commission.
- Texas Gulf core shack: Darke testimony, Mar. 2, 1965, Windfall commission.
- MacMillan-Szetu phone conversation: Szetu testimony, Mar. 8, 1965, Windfall commission.
- MacMillan wanted acid: Guy Coté testimony, Apr. 22, 1965, Windfall commission.
- Timmins in 1964: *Canadian Weekly*, May 23, 1964; *Red Deer Advocate*, June 29, 1964.
- "rivers of beer": *Red Deer Advocate*, June 29, 1964.
- "splashing on their bellies": *Citizen*, Apr. 24, 1964.
- Rumours at Bon Air: Oille testimony, Nov. 20, 1965, OSC inquiry.
- Robertson on Sunday: Robertson testimony, Apr. 26, 1965, Windfall commission.
- Golf tournament: Armstrong, *Moose Pastures and Mergers*, 161.
- Spencer and Wilbert Bradley: Spencer testimony, Mar. 9 and 24, 1965, Windfall commission; Wilbert Bradley testimony, Mar. 9, Windfall commission.
- "good looking core": Spencer testimony, Mar. 24, 1965, Windfall commission.
- Drive to Timmins: Mills testimony, Mar. 24, 1965, Windfall commission.
- MacMillans meet Bradley: George MacMillan testimony, Mar. 17, 1965, Windfall commission.
- "You're the boss": Edgar Bradley testimony, Mar. 10, 1965, Windfall commission.
- "rhyolite breccia": Viola MacMillan testimony, May 13, 1965, Windfall commission.
- Car ride to Timmins: Dufresne testimony, Sept. 21, 1964, OSC inquiry; Dufresne testimony, Mar. 9, 1965, Windfall commission.
- "Don't lose my gold mine": Dufresne testimony, Sept. 21, 1964, OSC inquiry.

CHAPTER TEN

- "leading lady of mining," "lost a few dollars" and "named after you": *Toronto Telegram* (hereafter *Telegram*), date unknown.
- MacMillan was unhappy: Schlitt testimony, Apr. 23, 1965, Windfall commission.
- Europe trip: Phillip Smith timeline for MacMillan autobiography, MacMillan fonds.

- "unique group of entrepreneurs": Joubin and Smyth, *Not for Gold Alone*, 135.
- Stock promotion: Joubin and Smyth, *Not for Gold Alone*, 138–140; Armstrong, *Moose Pastures and Mergers*, 34–35.
- Hedley Amalgamated: Cruise and Griffiths, *Fleecing the Lamb*, 53–55; *Globe and Mail*, Apr. 9, 1937; *Globe and Mail*, May 10, 1937; *Globe and Mail*, July 24, 1937.
- "untruthful and misleading information": *Globe and Mail*, Apr. 9, 1937.
- "stock manipulation": *Daily Press*, Apr. 20, 1964.
- Lake Cinch opening: *Globe and Mail*, Sept. 21, 1957; *New York Times*, Sept. 24, 1957.
- "Tiny, vivacious, attractive": *New York Times*, Sept. 24, 1957.
- "Short, slim, dainty and pretty": "Woman Has Part in Ramore Activity," *Mail and Empire*, date unknown, MacMillan fonds.
- "schoolgirl-like dress" and "attractive young brunette": *Star Weekly*, May 3, 1941.
- "easy to look at": *Chatelaine*, June 1945.
- "dark-haired darling": *Time*, Aug. 14, 1964.
- "trim, very slight, attractive woman": *Post*, June 13, 1964.
- "Girl promoter" and "quartz from greywacke": *Post*, Aug. 13, 1938.
- Eleven kilometres, fifteen-kilogram pack: *Chatelaine*, June 1945.
- "just as a cook" and "if you know": *Sherbrooke Daily News*, Mar. 21, 1951.
- "at home in the northern bush": *Sherbrooke Daily News*, Sept. 9, 1957.
- "black hair and flashing blue eyes": *Magazine Digest*, Feb. 1946.
- "just ignore the fact": *Weekend Magazine*, vol. 5, no. 34, 1955.
- 3,720 Canadian women: *Star Weekly*, June 22, 1957.
- "in love with mining": *Saturday Night*, June 25, 1955.
- Bills in her name: MacMillan, *From the Ground Up*, 75.
- Couldn't register claims in Quebec: *Sherbrooke Daily News*, Sept. 9, 1957; Bourrie, *Film Flam*, 47–48.
- Letter from CIM: MacMillan, *From the Ground Up*, 100.
- "Prospectors are not tough," *New York Times*, Sept. 1, 1964.
- "see no reason": transcript of "Salute to the Girls," CFRB radio interview, MacMillan fonds.
- "made better friends with men": Reeves, *Let Me Call You Sweetheart*.
- Profanity: Barnes, *The Scholarly Prospector*, 43.
- "if men resented": MacMillan, *From the Ground Up*, 2.
- "they are talking shop": Lonn, *Men and Mines*, 53.

CHAPTER ELEVEN

- Stop at Drewe's cottage: Drewe testimony, Sept. 22, 1964, OSC inquiry; Drewe testimony, Mar. 30, 1967, Windfall commission.
- "have the core": Drewe testimony, Sept. 22, 1964, OSC inquiry.
- Ambrose: Ambrose testimony, Mar. 16, 1965, Windfall commission.
- Technical Service Laboratories: Nadia Rudnik testimony, Mar. 24, 1965, Windfall commission; Edwin Warren testimony, Mar. 24, 1965, Windfall commission.

- "men talking": Leacock, *Sunshine Sketches of a Little Town*, 26.
- Gambling laws: Morton, *At Odds*, 10–11.
- Irish Sweepstakes: Thompson, *The International Encyclopedia of Gambling*, vol. 2, 446–447; Morton, *At Odds*, 54.
- Customer lost $12,000: *Globe and Mail*, Sept. 2, 1965.
- Penny stocks: Joubin and Smyth, *Not for Gold Alone*, 138–139; Thompson, *The International Encyclopedia of Gambling*, vol. 1, 227–231; Morton, *At Odds*, 28–33.
- Share certificates for Christmas: *Time*, Apr. 5, 1937.
- "Strange as it may seem": *New York Times*, May 27, 1906.
- "gambling shoes": Spencer testimony, Mar. 9, 1965, Windfall commission.
- First day of trading: Spencer testimony, Mar. 9, 1965, Windfall commission; Jones testimony, Apr. 27, 1965, Windfall commission; Wilbert Bradley testimony, Dec. 9, 1964, OSC inquiry; Wilbert Bradley testimony, Mar. 9, 1965, Windfall commission; Edgar Bradley testimony, Sept. 17, 1964, OSC inquiry; Edgar Bradley testimony, Mar. 10, 1965, Windfall commission; Robertson testimony, Apr. 26, 1965, Windfall commission; *Globe and Mail*, July 7, 1964.
- "a real chance": Fenton Scott testimony, Mar. 11, 1965, Windfall commission.
- "good sidewalk publicity": Rennick testimony, Mar. 10, 1965, Windfall commission.
- "orders for 100,000": Wilbert Bradley testimony, Mar. 9, 1965, Windfall commission.
- "Why Windfall now?": Stearns testimony, Apr. 21, 1965, Windfall commission.
- Lecour and Field: Field testimony, Apr. 28, 1965, Windfall commission; George Hunter testimony, Apr. 9, 1965, Windfall commission; *Globe and Mail*, Oct. 8, 1965.
- Boucher didn't buy shares: Boucher testimony, Mar. 8, 1965, Windfall commission.
- Trading stats: Hugh Cleland testimony, Apr. 26, 1965, Windfall commission.
- Doherty, Roadhouse: Rousseau testimony, Mar. 3, 1965, Windfall commission; Larche testimony, Mar. 3, 1965, Windfall commission; Rousseau testimony, Sept. 15, 1964, OSC inquiry.
- "fell flat on my back": Larche testimony, Mar. 3, 1965, Windfall commission.
- McKinnon hears news on radio: McKinnon testimony, Mar. 4, 1965, Windfall commission; McKinnon testimony, Sept. 15, 1964, OSC inquiry.
- Rousseau–MacMillan conversation: Rousseau testimony, Mar. 3, 1965, Windfall commission.
- Lunch at Senator: Reynolds testimony, Mar. 3, 1965, Windfall commission; McKinnon testimony, Mar. 4, 1965, Windfall commission; McKinnon testimony, Sept. 15, 1964, and Feb. 9, 1965, OSC inquiry.
- "know darned well": Reynolds testimony, Oct. 13, 1964, OSC inquiry.
- Reynolds-Larche conversation: Reynolds testimony, Oct. 13, 1964, OSC inquiry.
- Reynolds's story: *Daily Press*, July 6, 1964.
- Bragagnolo takes chopper: Bragagnolo testimony, Mar. 2, 1965, Windfall commission.
- Heenan gets sludge sample: Hennan testimony, Mar. 11, 1965, Windfall commission.
- Swastika Laboratories: Kerr-Lawson testimony, May 3, 1965, Windfall commission.
- Bragagnolo shows sample to Darke: Bragagnolo, Sept. 25, 1964, OSC inquiry.

CHAPTER TWELVE

- Hunter calls MacMillan: Hunter testimony, Apr. 28, 1965, Windfall commission; Hunter testimony, Feb. 18 and 22, 1965, OSC inquiry.
- "orderly market": Hunter testimony, Apr. 28, 1965, Windfall commission.
- 150 phone calls: Viola MacMillan testimony, May 13, 1965, Windfall commission.
- "out of control": Viola MacMillan testimony, May 14, 1965, Windfall commission.
- Schlitt and Chisholm visit MacMillan: Schlitt testimony, Apr. 23, 1965, Windfall commission; Chisholm testimony, Apr. 23, 1965, Windfall commission.
- "That's good, eh?": Chisholm testimony, Apr. 23, 1965, Windfall commission.
- Lawson on Monday: Lawson testimony, Apr. 22, 1965, Windfall commission; Lawson testimony, Oct. 5, 1964, OSC inquiry.
- Direct line: Edward Hastie testimony, Apr. 27, 1965, Windfall commission.
- "Moss, Lawson boys fast": Viola MacMillan testimony, May 14, 1965, Windfall commission.
- "worst person": Watson testimony, Apr. 27, 1965, Windfall commission.
- "mastermind each trade": Lawson testimony, Oct. 5, 1964, OSC inquiry.
- "would not do that": Watson testimony, Apr. 27, 1965, Windfall commission.
- "what was going on": Lawson testimony, Apr. 22, 1965, Windfall commission.
- Breckenridge and MacMillan conversation and trading: Breckenridge testimony, Apr. 27, 1965, Windfall commission; Breckenridge testimony, Mar. 8 and 9, 1965, OSC inquiry.
- Assay results: Nadia Rudnik testimony, Mar. 24, 1965, Windfall commission; Edwin Warren testimony, Mar. 24, 1965, Windfall commission; Certificate of Analysis, exhibit 84, Windfall commission.
- "sent a couple of samples": Cole testimony, Mar. 26, 1965, Windfall commission.
- Closing price and trading stats: Hugh Cleland testimony, Apr. 26, 1965, Windfall commission; Kelly, Windfall commission report; record of Windfall trading, exhibit 79, Windfall commission; *Globe and Mail*, July 7, 1964.
- Humphrey visits Viola: Humphrey testimony, Mar. 24, 1965, Windfall commission.
- "some mineralization" and "very happy": Cochrane testimony, Mar. 30, 1965, Windfall commission; Cochrane testimony, Sept. 19, 1964, OSC inquiry.
- "much more than that" and "looks pretty good": Roberts testimony, Mar. 29 and 30, 1965, Windfall commission; Cochrane testimony, Sept. 17, 1964, OSC inquiry.
- Viola spoke to press: *Globe and Mail*, July 7, 1964.
- "in the bush": *Gazette*, July 7, 1964.
- Ambrose in Toronto: Ambrose testimony, Mar. 16, 1965, Windfall commission.
- Queen's Plate: *Toronto Daily Star*, June 22, 1964.
- Bragagnolo ran into George MacMillan: Bragagnolo testimony, Mar. 2, 1965, Windfall commission.
- CHUM charts: http://hitsofalldecades.com/chart_hits/index2.php?option=com_content&do_pdf=1&id=856.
- "Broker's Cocktail": *Time*, Apr. 5, 1937.

- "position to force her" and "more if you have to": Lawson testimony, Oct. 5, 1964, OSC inquiry.
- Call with Ketchen: Viola MacMillan testimony, May 13, 1965, Windfall commission.
- Bank loan: Philip Dodd testimony, Apr. 26, 1965, Windfall commission; Viola MacMillan testimony, May 13, 1965, Windfall commission.
- "terrifying experience": Viola MacMillan testimony, Aug. 20, 1964, OSC inquiry.

CHAPTER THIRTEEN

- James Scott: Scott testimony, Mar. 30, 1965, Windfall commission; Scott testimony, Sept. 16, 1964, OSC inquiry.
- Claude Taylor: Taylor testimony, Mar. 29, 1965, Windfall commission; Taylor testimony, Sept. 17, 1964, OSC inquiry.
- "Come on": Taylor testimony, Mar. 29, 1965, Windfall commission.
- "feels it is ore": Scott testimony, Sept. 16, 1964, OSC inquiry.
- "close to the company": *Globe and Mail*, July 7, 1964.
- MacMillan–Ackerley phone call: Ackerley testimony, Mar. 29, 1965, Windfall commission; Ackerley memo, exhibit 134, Windfall commission; Ackerley testimony, Sept. 10, 1964, OSC inquiry.
- "ought to have a meeting": Cole testimony, Mar. 26, 1965, Windfall commission.
- Directors' meeting: Cole testimony, Sept. 17 and 24, 1964, OSC inquiry; Cole testimony, Mar. 26, 1965, Windfall commission; Humphrey testimony, Sept. 23, 1964, OSC inquiry; Viola MacMillan, Aug. 20, 1964, OSC inquiry.
- press release: exhibit 85, Windfall commission.
- "on a target": Ackerley testimony, Mar. 29, 1965, Windfall commission.
- "graphitic shear zone": exhibit 85, Windfall commission.
- George wouldn't answer phone: George MacMillan testimony, Aug. 13, 1964, OSC inquiry.
- Cole: Cole testimony, Mar. 26, 1965, Windfall commission; Cole testimony, Sept. 17 and 24, 1964, OSC inquiry.
- Carpenter arrived: Edgar Bradley testimony, Mar. 10, 1965, Windfall commission.
- Pearce–Cole and Cole–Viola conversations: Cole testimony, Mar. 26, 1965, Windfall commission; Cole testimony, Sept. 17 and 24, 1964, OSC inquiry; Pearce testimony, Mar. 19, 1965, Windfall commission.
- "intrigues exploration people": exhibit 85, Windfall commission.
- Calls about rumours: Cole testimony, Sept. 17 and 24, 1964, OSC inquiry; Cole testimony, Mar. 26, 1965, Windfall commission.
- "I just don't get this," "Has there been an assay" and "I don't know": Cole testimony, Mar. 26, 1965, Windfall commission.
- Assay results: Certificate of Analysis, exhibit 84, Windfall commission.
- "I don't know" and "didn't wish to alienate": Cole testimony, Mar. 26, 1965, Windfall commission.
- Brokerage wires: rumours folder, Windfall commission.

- Rumours circulating: Graham testimony, Mar. 31, 1965, Windfall commission; John Campbell testimony, Apr. 15, 1965, Windfall commission.
- "can't be" and "you know better": Barnt testimony, Apr. 13, 1965, Windfall commission.
- "Stock Market News and Comment": exhibit 123, Windfall commission; Percival testimony, Mar. 30, 1965, Windfall commission.
- Viola sells shares: Viola MacMillan testimony, Aug. 20, 1964, OSC inquiry.
- Airquest account: Breckenridge testimony, Apr. 27, 1965, Windfall commission.
- "pulled a major": Taylor transcript, Mar. 30, 1965, Windfall commission.
- Ambrose examines core: Ambrose testimony, Mar. 16, 1965, Windfall commission.
- Scott goes to Sentry Box: Jim Scott testimony, Mar. 30, 1965, Windfall commission; Jim Scott testimony, Sept. 16, 1964, OSC inquiry.
- Meeting at Royal York: Viola MacMillan testimony, May 14, 1965, Windfall commission; John Campbell testimony, Apr. 15, 1965, Windfall commission; John Campbell testimony, Sept. 4 and 9, 1964, OSC inquiry.
- Louise Campbell was partner in Julie's: *Toronto Daily Star*, Feb. 13, 1964.
- Menu at Julie's: *Toronto Daily Star*, May 16, 1964.
- Dinner at Julie's: Louise Campbell testimony, Apr. 13, 1965, Windfall commission; John Campbell testimony, Apr. 15, 1965, Windfall commission.
- Campbell's letter: exhibit 205, Windfall commission; George MacMillan testimony, Aug. 13, 1964, OSC inquiry; John Campbell testimony, Apr. 15, 1965, Windfall commission; John Campbell testimony, Sept. 4 and 9, 1964, OSC inquiry.
- Scott talks to MacMillans: Scott testimony, Mar. 30, 1965, Windfall commission; Scott testimony, Sept. 16, 1964, OSC inquiry; Viola MacMillan testimony, May 14, 1965, Windfall commission; John Campbell testimony, Apr. 15, 1965, Windfall commission.

CHAPTER FOURTEEN

- MacMillan–Graham conversation: Graham testimony, Mar. 31, 1965, Windfall commission; Graham testimony, Sept. 14, 1964, OSC inquiry; Viola MacMillan testimony, May 14, 1965, Windfall commission.
- Howard Graham: *Canadian Encyclopedia*, https://www.thecanadianencyclopedia.ca/en/article/howard-graham.
- "always buzzing about": *Globe and Mail*, Oct. 8, 1965.
- Board of governors meeting: Graham testimony, Mar. 31, 1965, Windfall commission; Stearns testimony, Apr. 21, 1965, Windfall commission.
- "rather noncommittal" and "statement in your hands": Graham testimony, Mar. 31, 1965, Windfall commission.
- Bradley's telegram: exhibit 71, Windfall commission; Edgar Bradley testimony, Sept. 17, 1964, OSC inquiry.
- Cole: Cole testimony, Sept. 17 and 24, 1964, OSC inquiry.
- Cole–MacMillan conversation: Cole testimony, Mar. 26, Windfall commission.
- TSE telegram: exhibit 101, Windfall commission.
- "don't worry about it": Humphrey testimony, Sept. 23, 1964, OSC inquiry.

Endnotes

- "paternal eye": John Campbell testimony, Apr. 15, 1965, Windfall commission.
- John Campbell's age: *Toronto Daily Star*, Oct. 7, 1965.
- "go to hell": John Campbell testimony, Apr. 15, 1965, Windfall commission.
- Core in trunk: John Campbell testimony, Sept. 4 and 9, 1964, OSC inquiry.
- Drinks at Campbells': Louise Campbell testimony, Apr. 13, 1965, Windfall commission; John Campbell testimony, Sept. 4 and 9, 1964, OSC inquiry.
- "all their money": Louise Campbell testimony, Sept. 4, 1964, OSC inquiry.
- Louise Campbell trading: Louise Campbell testimony, Apr. 13, 1965, Windfall commission; Louise Campbell testimony, Sept. 4, 1964, OSC inquiry; Harry Richardson testimony, Apr. 20, 1965, Windfall commission; John Campbell testimony, Sept. 4 and 9, 1964, OSC inquiry.
- "best you can": Louise Campbell testimony, Apr. 13, 1965, Windfall commission.
- "tip from the hairdresser": Louise Campbell testimony, Sept. 4, 1964, OSC inquiry.
- Louise Campbell's age: *Toronto Daily Star*, Oct. 7, 1965.
- John Campbell on Saturday: John Campbell testimony, Apr. 15, 1965, Windfall commission; John Campbell testimony, Sept. 4 and 9, 1964, OSC inquiry.
- Campbell visits Gardiner: George Gardiner testimony, Apr. 20, 1965, Windfall commission.
- Viola writes statement: John Campbell testimony, Sept. 4 and 9, 1964, OSC inquiry; Viola MacMillan's handwritten notes, exhibit 206, Windfall commission.
- Louise Campbell approaches MacMillan: Viola MacMillan's testimony, May 14, 1965, Windfall commission; Louise Campbell testimony, Apr. 13, 1965, Windfall commission.
- "will you help me": Louise Campbell testimony, Apr. 13, 1965, Windfall commission.
- Campbell visits Graham: Graham testimony, Mar. 31, 1965, Windfall commission; Graham testimony, Sept. 14, 1964, OSC inquiry; John Campbell testimony, Apr. 15, 1965, Windfall commission; John Campbell testimony, Sept. 4 and 9, 1964, OSC inquiry.
- 176 phone calls: Dow testimony, Sept. 16, 1964, OSC inquiry.
- "a little more warmth" and "a little bit reasonable": John Campbell testimony, Apr. 15, 1965, Windfall commission.
- "doesn't want to buy it" and had shares in purse: Viola MacMillan testimony, May 14, 1965, Windfall commission.
- "this is the absolute end": Louise Campbell testimony, Apr. 13, 1965, Windfall commission.
- Campbell waited for Wardrope in lobby: John Campbell testimony, Sept. 4 and 9, 1964, OSC inquiry.
- Meeting in hotel room: Wardrope testimony, Apr. 13, 1965, Windfall commission; Lee testimony, Apr. 12, 1965, Windfall commission; John Campbell testimony, Apr. 15, 1965, Windfall commission; John Campbell testimony, Sept. 4 and 9, 1964, OSC inquiry; George MacMillan testimony, Aug. 14, 1964, OSC inquiry; Viola MacMillan testimony, Aug. 20, 1964, OSC inquiry.
- "black eye": John Campbell testimony, Sept. 4 and 9, 1964, OSC inquiry.

- "get this letter amended": Wardrope testimony, Apr. 13, 1965, Windfall commission.
- "nothing was accomplished": George MacMillan testimony, Aug. 14, 1964, OSC inquiry.
- Wardrope–Graham phone conversation: Wardrope testimony, Apr. 13, 1965, Windfall commission.

CHAPTER FIFTEEN

- Monday morning at TSE: Graham testimony, Mar. 31, 1965, Windfall commission; Marshall Stearns testimony, Apr. 21, 1965, Windfall commission.
- Graham–Campbell phone conversation: Graham testimony, Mar. 31, 1965, Windfall commission; Graham testimony, Sept. 14, 1964, OSC inquiry.
- "appreciate the interest" and "loggerheads": Graham testimony, Mar. 31, 1965, Windfall commission.
- "hardly as complete": exhibit 155, Windfall commission.
- Drewe goes to meeting: Drewe testimony, Sept. 22, 1964, OSC inquiry; Drewe testimony, Mar. 30, 1967, Windfall commission.
- Cole on Monday: Cole testimony, Sept. 17 and 24, 1964, OSC inquiry; Cole testimony, Mar. 26, 1965, Windfall commission.
- "roughed something out": Cole testimony, Mar. 26, 1965, Windfall commission.
- Floor bulletin: exhibit 154, Windfall commission.
- "No further drilling": Cole testimony, Mar. 26, 1965, Windfall commission.
- "Usual criticism" and "talking to a brick wall": Lawson testimony, Oct. 5, 1964, OSC inquiry.
- TSE press release: exhibit 115, Windfall commission.
- "company should do" and "uneasy peace": *Toronto Daily Star*, July 14, 1964.
- Kimber background: *Post*, June 15, 1963.
- Campbell briefs Kimber: John Campbell testimony, Sept. 4 and 9, 1964, OSC inquiry; Kimber testimony, Apr. 13, 1965, Windfall commission.
- "glad to hear it": Ambrose testimony, Mar. 16, 1965, Windfall commission.
- "Let's hope so": Cole testimony, Mar. 26, 1965, Windfall commission.
- Meeting at OSC: Cole testimony, Mar. 26, 1965, Windfall commission; Cole testimony, Sept. 17 and 24, 1964, OSC inquiry; Graham testimony, Mar. 31, 1965, Windfall commission; Graham testimony, Sept. 14, 1964, OSC inquiry; Stearns testimony, Apr. 12, 1965, Windfall commission; Somerville testimony, Apr. 12, 1965, Windfall commission; Froberg testimony, Apr. 12, 1965, Windfall commission; Kimber testimony, Apr. 13, 1965, Windfall commission; McFarland testimony, Apr. 20, 1965, Windfall commission; George MacMillan testimony, Aug. 14, 1964, OSC inquiry; Viola MacMillan testimony, Aug. 21, 1964, OSC inquiry.
- "explosive situation": Cole testimony, Sept. 17 and 24, 1964, OSC inquiry.
- "you don't know that": Stearns testimony, Apr. 21, 1965, Windfall commission.
- "set the camp on fire": McFarland testimony, Apr. 20, 1965, Windfall commission.
- "we hit it": Viola MacMillan testimony, Aug. 21, 1964, OSC inquiry.

Endnotes

- "in the same structure" and "complaining about the wrong people": Kimber testimony, Apr. 13, 1965, Windfall commission.
- "results announced forthwith": exhibit 117, Windfall commission.
- "some allegations made": Stearns testimony, Apr. 12, 1965, Windfall commission.
- "no assays of drill cores" and "all cores will be under guard": exhibit 117, Windfall commission.

CHAPTER SIXTEEN

- Woolverton and MacMillan: Woolverton testimony, Mar. 10, 1965, Windfall commission.
- Bell letter: exhibit 397, Windfall commission.
- MacMillans left at 3 a.m.: Viola MacMillan testimony, Aug. 21, 1964, OSC inquiry.
- George called Cole: Cole testimony, Sept. 17 and 24, 1964, OSC inquiry.
- Reynolds finds MacMillan in restaurant: Reynolds testimony, Mar. 3, 1965, Windfall commission.
- "leave us alone": *Daily Press*, July 16, 1964.
- Woolverton and MacMillan in Empire: Woolverton testimony, Mar. 10, 1965, Windfall commission.
- Mills took core to Timmins: Mills testimony, Sept. 18, 1964, and Oct. 23, 1964, OSC inquiry; George MacMillan testimony, Aug. 13, 1964, OSC inquiry.
- Kimber's request: Cole testimony, Mar. 26, 1965, Windfall commission.
- "day or two" and "People are crazy": Edgar Bradley testimony, Mar. 10, 1965, Windfall commission.
- Texas Gulf hole: Holyk testimony, Mar. 1, 1965, Windfall commission.
- Holyk–MacMillan phone conversation: Holyk testimony, Feb. 22, 1965, OSC inquiry.
- Choppers deliver drill: Viola MacMillan testimony, Aug. 21, 1964, OSC inquiry.
- Editorial decisions: Ackerley testimony, Mar. 29, 1965, Windfall commission; Ackerley testimony, Sept. 10, 1964, OSC inquiry; Brown testimony, Sept. 17, 1965, OSC inquiry; Brown testimony, Mar. 29, 1965, Windfall commission.
- Wardrope–Brown conversation: Brown testimony, Sept. 17, 1965, OSC inquiry.
- *Post* article with debunked rumour: *Post*, July 18, 1964.
- "practically synonymous," "full significance" and front-page article: *Northern Miner*, July 16, 1964.
- Trip to Canadian Jamieson: Ackerley testimony, Mar. 30, 1965, Windfall commission; Ackerley memo, exhibit 134, Windfall commission; Ackerley testimony, Sept. 10, 1964, OSC inquiry; Brown testimony, Sept. 17, 1965, OSC inquiry; Brown testimony, Mar. 29, 1965, Windfall commission; Bragagnolo testimony, Mar. 2, 1965, Windfall commission.
- "saying too much": Ackerley memo, exhibit 134, Windfall commission.
- "bail out": Brown testimony, Mar. 29, 1965, Windfall commission.
- "weirdest conversations": Ackerley testimony, Sept. 10, 1964, OSC inquiry.

- Brown–George MacMillan conversation: Brown testimony, Mar. 29, 1965, Windfall commission.
- MacMillan interested in claims for Golden Arrow: Viola MacMillan testimony, Aug. 20, 1964, OSC inquiry.
- "If—": Kipling, *Rewards and Fairies.*

CHAPTER SEVENTEEN

- MacMillan's plan for short sellers: Reynolds testimony, Mar. 3, 1965, Windfall commission.
- Brown–Bragagnolo conservation: Brown testimony, Mar. 29, 1965, Windfall commission.
- Bragagnolo–Reynolds conversation: Reynolds testimony, Oct. 13, 1964, 44, OSC inquiry.
- Darke left Texas Gulf: Darke testimony, Mar. 1, 1965, Windfall commission.
- Darke wanted to look after his investments: Holyk testimony, Feb. 22, 1965, OSC inquiry.
- Sludge sample results: Hennan testimony, Mar. 11, 1965, Windfall commission.
- Darke's Windfall trading: Darke testimony, Mar. 1, 1965, Windfall commission.
- Lunch: Brown testimony, Sept. 17, 1965, OSC inquiry.
- Doherty, Roadhouse gang: Bragagnolo testimony, Mar. 2, 1965, Windfall commission.
- "same faith": Taylor's testimony, Mar. 30, 1965, Windfall commission.
- Bragagnolo visits Viola: Bragagnolo testimony, Mar. 2, 1965, Windfall commission; Viola MacMillan testimony, Aug. 21, 1964, OSC inquiry.
- "how you figure": Viola MacMillan testimony, Aug. 21, 1964, OSC inquiry.
- Viola called Cole: Cole testimony, Mar. 26, 1965, Windfall commission; Cole testimony, Feb. 18, 1965, OSC inquiry.
- "sheer nonsense": Darke testimony, Mar. 2, 1965, Windfall commission.
- Bragagnolo sells shares: Bragagnolo testimony, Mar. 2, 1965, Windfall commission.
- MacMillan in Schumacher: Reynolds testimony, Oct. 13, 1964, OSC inquiry; Reynolds testimony, Mar. 3, 1965, Windfall commission.
- "Porcupine can have one" and "Babies not yet born": *Daily Press*, July 22, 1964.
- MacMillan visits Drewe: Drewe testimony, Mar. 30, 1967, Windfall commission.
- "large gobs": *Northern Miner*, July 23, 1964.
- "glad to help": exhibit 397, Windfall commission.
- Letters from other companies: Viola MacMillan testimony, Aug. 20, 1964, OSC inquiry.
- "worry more": Cole testimony, Mar. 26, 1965, Windfall commission.
- Viola visits exchange: Viola MacMillan testimony, Aug. 20, 1964, OSC inquiry; Cole testimony, Mar. 26, 1965, Windfall commission.
- "pointers from her" and "everything is 'hot'": Cole letter to Viola MacMillan, MacMillan fonds.
- "take effect upon acceptance" and "With any luck": Cole's memo to Archibald, exhibit 119, Windfall commission.

Endnotes

- Ambrose goes to Timmins: Ambrose testimony, Mar. 16, 1965, Windfall commission.
- Holyk visits Windfall site: Holyk testimony, Feb. 22, 1965, OSC inquiry; Holyk testimony, Mar. 1, 1965, Windfall commission.
- George MacMillan delivers samples: Kerr-Lawson testimony, May 3, 1965, Windfall commission; W.G. Clifford testimony, May 3, 1965, Windfall commission; George MacMillan testimony, Aug. 14, 1964, OSC inquiry.
- Easy voice to imitate: George MacMillan testimony, Mar. 17, 1965, Windfall commission.
- "act dumb": Kerr-Lawson testimony, May 3, 1965, Windfall commission.
- Texas Gulf stops drilling: Holyk testimony, Feb. 22, 1965, OSC inquiry.

CHAPTER EIGHTEEN

- Fake telegrams: telegram to *Financial Post*, exhibit 177, Windfall commission; telegram to Cole: exhibit 411, Windfall commission; N.W.H. Cox testimony, May 25, 1965, Windfall commission; Archibald testimony, May 25, 1965, Windfall commission; Dow testimony, Mar. 30, 1965, Windfall commission; Edgar Bradley testimony, Mar. 10, 1965, Windfall commission.
- "party-blonde": T. Birkett question in McKinnon transcript, Sept. 15, 1964, OSC inquiry.
- Cole's vacation: Cole testimony, Sept. 17 and 24, 1964, OSC inquiry.
- Archibald: Archibald testimony, May 25, 1965, Windfall commission.
- "This is important": Dow testimony, Mar. 30, 1965, Windfall commission.
- "complete hoax": *Toronto Daily Star*, July 28, 1964.
- Bongard: Interview with Strachan Bongard.
- "Stories we hear": Vance testimony, Apr. 9, 1965, Windfall commission.
- Dixon: Dixon testimony, Nov. 20, 1964, OSC inquiry; Dixon testimony, Apr. 29, 1965, Windfall commission.
- Oille's trading: Oille testimony, Nov. 20, 1965, OSC inquiry; Oille testimony, Mar. 10, 1965, Windfall commission; Oille testimony, Apr. 29, 1965, Windfall commission; Applegath testimony, Apr. 26, 1965, Windfall commission.
- Dixon, Oille and drill holes: Dixon testimony, Mar. 8 and 10, 1965, OSC inquiry; Dixon testimony, 1965, Windfall commission; Oille testimony, Nov. 20, 1965, OSC inquiry; Oille testimony, Mar. 10, 1965, Windfall commission; Oille testimony, Apr. 29, 1965, Windfall commission.
- Windfall's drill holes: George MacMillan testimony, May 14, 1965, Windfall commission.
- "no way to drill": Dixon testimony, Nov. 20, 1964, OSC inquiry.
- Oille shared rumours: Croft, *Swindle!*, 93.
- Oille and Dixon bought 10,000 shares each: Windfall commission report.
- Campbell shorts Windfall: John Campbell testimony, Apr. 15, 1965, Windfall commission; John Campbell testimony, Sept. 4 and 9, 1964, OSC inquiry; Harry Richardson testimony, Apr. 20, 1965, Windfall commission.

- MacMillan's excuses: John Campbell testimony, Apr. 15, 1965, Windfall commission.
- MacMillans wanted to wait until Friday: Kimber testimony, Apr. 13, 1965, Windfall commission.
- Ambrose goes to Toronto: Ambrose testimony, Mar. 16, 1965, Windfall commission.
- Directors meeting: Archibald testimony, May 25, 1965, Windfall commission; agenda, exhibit 410, Windfall commission; *Toronto Daily Star*, Nov. 21, 1968.
- Taylor calls MacMillan: Taylor's testimony, Sept. 17, 1964, OSC inquiry.
- Robertson called Oille: Oille testimony, Mar. 10, 1965, Windfall commission; Robertson testimony, Apr. 26, 1965, Windfall commission.
- "top dog": Oille testimony, Mar. 10, 1965, Windfall commission.
- "Does this kill" and "very interesting": *Toronto Daily Star*, Nov. 21, 1968.
- Press release: exhibit 87, Windfall commission.
- "Go on!": *Globe and Mail*, July 31, 1964.
- Scott finds the MacMillans: Scott testimony, Mar. 30, 1965, Windfall commission; Scott testimony, Sept. 16, 1964, OSC inquiry.
- "little bit of Venice": Royal York Hotel ad, *Toronto Daily Star*, Jan. 9, 1961.
- "nothing to get excited": *Globe and Mail*, July 31, 1964.
- "awful lot of money" and "trying to tell a mining company": Scott testimony, Sept. 16, 1964, OSC inquiry.

CHAPTER NINETEEN

- "hope the hole": Cole testimony, Sept. 17 and 24, 1964, OSC inquiry.
- *Globe* story: *Globe and Mail*, Aug. 5, 1964.
- Cole was horrified: Cole testimony, Mar. 26, 1965, Windfall commission.
- "interesting to know": *Globe and Mail*, Aug. 1, 1964.
- Trading volume: Record of Windfall trading, exhibit 79, Windfall commission; Hunter testimony, Apr. 28, 1965, Windfall commission.
- MacMillan transactions at T.A. Richardson: Hunter testimony, Feb. 18 and 22, 1965, OSC inquiry.
- MacMillan trades July 1 to Aug. 10: "Analysis of Dates of Sales and Purchases of Stock of Windfall Oils and Mines Limited," unnumbered exhibit, container 13, Windfall commission; Windfall commission report.
- "get out of there": Bragagnolo testimony, Sept. 15, 1964, OSC inquiry.
- Darke made $300,000 selling claims as part of his partnership: "Windfall Probe Hears of Geologist's Sideline," *Globe and Mail*, Mar. 2, 1965.
- Edwards lost $60,000: Edwards testimony, May 3, 1965, Windfall commission.
- Dixon made $60,000: Dixon testimony, Nov. 20, 1964, OSC inquiry.
- Oille made $20,000: Oille testimony, Mar. 10, 1965, Windfall commission.
- Darke lost $128,000: Darke testimony, Mar. 1, 1965, Windfall commission.
- *Northern Miner* investing rules: Richard Pearce testimony, Mar. 29, 1965, Windfall commission.
- Ackerley lost money: Ackerley testimony, Mar. 29, 1965, Windfall commission.

Endnotes

- Mort Brown made $3,500: Brown testimony, Sept. 17, 1965, OSC inquiry.
- James Scott trading: Scott testimony, Sept. 16, 1964, OSC inquiry.
- Reynolds's mother bought Windfall: Reynolds testimony, Oct. 13, 1964, OSC inquiry.
- "notoriously loose standards," "lamb waiting to be shorn" and "slackness and inefficiency": *Toronto Daily Star*, Aug. 1, 1964.
- "cannot afford another scandal" and "the Windfall fiasco": *Globe and Mail*, Aug. 3, 1964.
- Tom Connors residency: Conners, *Stompin' Tom*, 442–469; Rhindress, *Stompin' Tom Connors*, 74–85; Angus, *Mirrors of Stone*, 123–124.
- "how do you think it went": *Toronto Daily Star*, Oct. 7, 1965.
- brokerage house crowds: *Globe and Mail*, May 21, 1965.
- More than forty: *Globe and Mail*, Mar. 18, 1965.
- "high incidence of amnesia": Windfall commission report.
- "little girl has to take it down": Sedgwick in Viola MacMillan transcript, May 13, 1965, Windfall commission.
- "obviously barren," "not worth a hoot" and "very common": Fenton Scott testimony, Mar. 11, 1965, Windfall commission.
- Allerston at commission: Allerston testimony, Mar. 4, 1965, Windfall commission.
- "criticism has been directed at me": letter, MacMillan fonds.
- Worth $200,000 to the city: Shulman, *Billion Dollar Windfall*, 56.
- "well-spoken prospector": *Globe and Mail*, May 5, 1965.
- "impressive looking!": *Globe and Mail*, Oct. 2, 1965.
- "shocked revulsion": *Toronto Daily Star*, Oct. 8, 1965.
- Kelly's report: Windfall commission report; *Globe and Mail*, Oct. 8, 1965; *Toronto Daily Star*, Oct. 8, 1965; *Gazette*, Oct. 8, 1965.
- All Kelly quotes: Windfall commission report.
- "strongest possible exception": *Globe and Mail*, Oct. 9, 1965.
- "one of the hardest-hitting reports": *Toronto Daily Star*, Oct. 8, 1965.
- "guys sitting around": *Globe and Mail*, Oct. 8, 1965.
- "full commission" and "I know that": Breckenridge testimony, Apr. 27, 1965, Windfall commission.
- "skillfully managed piece of manipulation": Windfall commission report.
- Wash trading charges: *Toronto Daily Star*, Mar. 9, 1966.
- Albert Gould: *Toronto Daily Star*, Dec. 3, 1959; *Globe and Mail*, Apr. 23, 1960.
- Conviction and "up to nine months": *Telegram*, Mar. 10, 1967; *Globe and Mail*, Mar. 11, 1967; *Toronto Daily Star*, Mar. 11, 1967; *Globe and Mail*, Mar. 18, 1967; *Toronto Daily Star*, Mar. 18, 1967; *Telegram*, Mar. 18, 1967.
- Appeal: *Globe and Mail*, Jan. 12, 1968.
- "Wash Trading Was Routine": *Canadian Business*, Dec. 1991.
- "motel-like" and "comfortable rooms": "After 7 Weeks, a Parole-Viola Move," *Telegram*, Feb. 28, 1968.
- Prison letters: MacMillan fonds.
- "everybody should go to jail": Reeves, *Let Me Call You Sweetheart*.
- Headlines: *Toronto Daily Star*, Mar. 18, 1967; *Telegram*, Jan. 12, 1968.

- Parole: *Telegram*, Mar. 5, 1968; *Globe and Mail*, Mar. 16, 1968; *Globe and Mail*, May 30, 1968; *Telegram*, Apr. 24, 1968; *Telegram*, May 30, 1968.
- "preferential treatment": RG 4-2-0-4835—MacMillan, Mrs. Viola; 1968; correspondence with attorney general (names of letter writers redacted).
- "shocked and disturbed": *Globe and Mail*, Oct. 8, 1965.
- Wardrope rumours: *Toronto Daily Star*, Oct. 7, 1965.
- "kept in the dark": Windfall commission report.
- Campbell: *Citizen*, Aug. 26, 1964; *Toronto Daily Star*, Aug. 27, 1964; *Toronto Daily Star*, Sept. 20, 1968.
- "illegal, immoral or unethical": *Toronto Daily Star*, Aug. 27, 1964.
- "wasn't thinking straight": John Campbell testimony, Sept. 4 and 9, 1964, OSC inquiry.
- "most shocking incident": Windfall commission report.
- Angus: *Globe and Mail*, Jan. 13, 1966; *Toronto Daily Star*, Feb. 23, 1967.
- Breckenridge: *Globe and Mail*, Oct. 8, 1968; *Toronto Daily Star*, Mar. 14, 1969.
- Texas Gulf and the SEC: *New York Times*, Feb. 7, 1970; *Globe and Mail*, Dec. 21, 1971.
- "anyone from anywhere": Patrick, *Perpetual Jeopardy*, 181.
- MacMillans turn themselves in: *Telegram*, Oct. 15, 1965; *Globe and Mail*, Oct. 16, 1965.
- Deyman's ruling: *Toronto Daily Star*, Feb. 10, 1969; *Telegram*, Feb. 10, 1969; *Globe and Mail*, Feb. 11, 1969; *Toronto Daily Star*, Feb. 11, 1969.
- "not guilty": *Toronto Daily Star*, Feb. 10, 1969.
- "can't believe it": *Toronto Daily Star*, Feb. 11, 1969.
- "glad it's over": *Telegram*, Feb. 10, 1969.
- Too painful to talk about: Reeves, *Let Me Call You Sweetheart*.
- "old junk": *Toronto Daily Star*, June 29, 1969.
- "five years of hell," "I just love people" and "so many great Canadians": *Telegram*, June 26, 1969.

EPILOGUE

- Eleven holes: Windfall Oils and Mines Progress Report, Nov. 4, 1964, MacMillan fonds.
- "so respected": Cruise and Griffiths, *Fleecing the Lamb*, 175.
- "Scam Capital of the World": *Forbes*, May 19, 1989.
- "undoubtedly the atmosphere": *Northern Miner*, Oct. 5, 1978.
- "they loved her": Reeves, *Let Me Call You Sweetheart*.
- "bucket shops": Prospectors and Developers Association of Canada bio, https://www.pdac.ca/communications/industry-stories/womens-history-month/viola-r-macmillan.
- "full weight came down": Reeves, *Let Me Call You Sweetheart*.
- "worked hard all my life": *Canadian Business*, Dec. 1991.
- Sold claims; Golden Shaft: *Globe and Mail*, Apr. 17, 1993.

INDEX

Note: As a short form, Viola and George MacMillan will be referred to as VM and GM, respectively.

Index

Index

Index

TIM FALCONER spent three summers on mineral exploration crews, worked in two mines and studied mining engineering at McGill for two years before switching into English Literature. His last two books—*Bad Singer: The Surprising Science of Tone Deafness and How We Hear Music* and *Klondikers: Dawson City's Stanley Cup Challenge and How a Nation Fell in Love with Hockey*—made the *Globe and Mail*'s Top 100. He lives with his wife in Toronto.